THE SCHOCKEN BOOK OF
JEWISH MYSTICAL TESTIMONIES

THE SCHOCKEN BOOK OF

Jewish

∾

Mystical

∾

Testimonies

∾

Compiled and with commentary by
LOUIS JACOBS

Foreword by Karen Armstrong

SCHOCKEN BOOKS   NEW YORK

Grateful acknowledgment is made to the following for permission to reprint
previously published material:

The Clarendon Press: Excerpts from *Joseph Karo, Lawyer and Mystic* by R.J.Z.
Werblowsky. Copyright © 1962 by Oxford University Press. Reprinted by permission of The Clarendon Press, Oxford, England. • *Derek Orlans Collections:* Chapter head vignettes from *Or ha-Hammah* by Abraham Azulai,
Prezmysl 1896; *Brit Menuhah* by Abraham of Granada, Warsaw 1880; *Pardes
Rimmonim* by Moses Cordovero, Munkacz 1806(?); *Ez Haim* by Hayyim Vital,
Jerusalem, 1810. Reprinted by permission of Derek Orlans Collection, Jerusalem. • *Schocken Books Inc.:* Excerpts from *Major Trends in Jewish Mysticism*
by Gershom G. Scholem. Copyright © 1941 by Schocken Publishing House,
copyright 1946, 1954 by Schocken Books Inc. Reprinted by permission of
Schocken Books Inc. • *The University of Chicago Press:* Excerpts from *Guide
of the Perplexed* by S. Pines. Copyright © by The University of Chicago Press.
Reprinted by permission of The University of Chicago Press.

Library of Congress Cataloging-in-Publication Data

Jewish mystical testimonies.
The Schocken book of Jewish mystical testimonies / compiled and
with commentary by Louis Jacobs ; [new] foreword by Karen Armstrong.
p.   cm.
Previously published: Jewish mystical testimonies. New York :
Schocken Books, 1977.
Includes bibliographical references.
ISBN 0-8052-4143-4
1. Mysticism—Judaism—History—Sources.   I. Jacobs, Louis.
II. Title.
BM723.J48   1997
296.7′12—dc20   96-24189
CIP

Contents

༄

For my granddaughter
ZIVA

Foreword
by *Karen Armstrong*

Anyone leading a religious life confronts the task of creating a link between mundane experience and the divine which transcends it utterly. This has been a major problem and a central preoccupation for members of all the great faiths. Whenever they have contemplated the tragic, beautiful world in which they live, men and women have discovered a mysterious dimension that they find difficult to describe or conceptualize adequately but which gives significant meaning and substance to their lives. This kind of transcendence has been experienced in many ways: it has filled people with dread, awe, joy, sweetness, and light. As Rudolf Otto explained in his classic book *The Idea of the Holy*, it is felt to be wholly "other" and yet exerts an irresistible attraction. The religious quest has, in all cultures, been an attempt to give this sacred mystery a local habitation and a name while finding ways in which human beings can apprehend it. One of these ways has been the mystical journey.

Precisely because the divine is ineffable and other, it has always, historians of religion tell us, been experienced in something other than itself. We have created symbols that express—however imperfectly—our sense of connection with God. Earthly realities themselves become numinous, redolent of a Reality which, paradoxically, lies essentially beyond them. A symbol can never be the end of the quest. If it is, it becomes an idol. All it can do is introduce us to the divine. Thus God has been experienced in a place, a temple, a sacred text, a law code, or a human being.

Most people are satisfied with the common symbols and observances of their tradition. But in all cultures there are men and women who have the spiritual stamina and talent to discover the divine presence in the depths of their own being. Using techniques that are remarkably similar all the world over, these individuals make an interior journey that is also an ascent to a more exalted dimension of existence. These are the people we know as the mystics and they have surfaced in all cultures and religions, even in the three monotheistic faiths of Judaism, Christianity, and Islam, which are primarily more active than contemplative, more preoccupied, one might think, with the duty of implementing God's will in the external world than with cultivating exotic states of consciousness. But the mystical vocation is irresistible, even if it is not for everybody. The Talmudic tale of the four sages who attempt to enter the orchard (*pardes*) shows this clearly. For those who are not so gifted, mysticism is dangerous to body and spirit. But those who are able to embark on this heroic journey will do so, with or without the blessing of the establishment.

There has often been conflict between the mystics and their more conventional co-religionists. In the Roman Catholic Church, mystics of the stature of the sixteenth-century Spanish Carmelite Teresa of Avila were frequently in trouble with the Inquisition. At a time when the Church was stressing the importance of its authority, the Inquisitors looked askance at men and women who bypassed the hierarchical channels that were supposed to take them to God. In rather the same way, the Sufis, who were often freethinkers, could fall foul of the Muslim clergy. There was tension, too, between Jewish mystics and the rabbinical schools. None of the mystics concerned thought themselves to be heterodox: they were simply exploring the more interior aspects of the Bible and the Koran, reproducing, as it were, the immediacy of the prophetic or Christological experience that lay at the heart of the faith. Mystics would appropriate the symbols of their own tradition, mine their treasures, and prove their vitality by finding a whole new world of significance in the images of Scripture. Their journeys were shaped by the unique symbolism of their own faith and this inevitably affected their course. This would give Jewish mysticism, for example, its special character. Throne mystics and Kabbalists would find their path to the divine through imagery that was different from that encountered by a Christian or a Sufi. And yet they would often have experiences or wrestle with difficulties that are endemic to the mystical way in all traditions. Mystics will very often have more in common with their counterparts in other faiths than with their nonmystical co-religionists.

This fact makes it particularly rewarding and important to look at the mystical testimonies of different traditions, and is one of the reasons why this anthology is so valuable. As Louis Jacobs has pointed out, Jewish mystics are more reticent about their experiences than, for example, Christian or Muslim mystics, so it is helpful to have these writings, which *do* attempt to chart the Jewish ascent to God, made so readily accessible. Besides being an inspiration for Jewish readers, this volume has much to teach people who are versed in the mysticism of other traditions. Where Christian mystics find inspiration in the person of Christ, and

Muslims take as their starting point the ascension of the prophet Muhammad to heaven from the Temple Mount in Jerusalem, Jewish mystics have started their quest by contemplating the Throne Vision of Ezekiel, which itself looks back—as Jacobs points out—to the theophany of Sinai. All these great religious symbols speak eloquently of a dramatic eruption of the divine into our world or of a place where the divine and the human meet. Mystics in all three faiths have attempted to experience these far-off events in their own lives. As Christians try to unite themselves to the person of Jesus, in whom God was mysteriously enshrined, the Jewish mystic "becomes a chariot" like the one which Ezekiel saw bearing the divine presence (p. 21). In much the same way, Sufis hoped to re-create within themselves that perfect *islām,* or "surrender," which made it possible for Muhammad to hear God's word and to pass beyond the limits of human perception through the Seven Heavens to the presence of God. The stories of Muhammad's ascension to the Divine Throne are uncannily similar to the accounts we find in the *Heikhalot* literature.

For Jews, the Temple was the place where God had dwelt with human beings, though they realized that there was an incongruity in the very idea of the divine living in an earthly shrine. "Will God really live with men on earth?" Solomon mused incredulously during the Dedication. "Why, the heavens and their own heavens cannot contain you. How much less this house that I have built!" (I Kings 8:26–27). Solomon's cry expresses the central paradox of the religious experience in all faiths: When one considers the utter holiness of the sacred, any symbol that professes to contain it is bound to be inadequate, whether that symbol is a human being like Jesus or a man-made building such as a temple. The miracle is that God can be experienced and revealed at all. Yet the imagination—surely the chief religious faculty—is able to look beyond the mundane image to the

Reality itself. As this anthology shows so movingly, long after the Temple had been destroyed it still continued to shape Jewish spirituality. We see this in the Throne mystics' gradual progress through the halls of the Heavenly Palace (so reminiscent of the graded holiness of the Temple Courts) and in the Zohar's depiction of the ecstasy of the High Priest. Indeed, the very notion of the ascent *(aliyah)* to God attempted by the Jewish mystics looked back to the *aliyah* of the pilgrims and psalmists when they climbed up the Temple Mount and entered the place where God was. The mystics were aware that any *aliyah* was, as it were, an "ascent inwards." It was, as the Ba'al Shem Tov explained, a return to the Source of being, a state symbolized in the Bible in the imagery of Solomon's Temple and the Garden of Eden.

As Gershom Scholem has pointed out, mystics do not relegate religious events to the past. Certainly they believe in the historicity of Moses, Jesus, or Muhammad. But they also see the inner reality of salvation history as contemporaneous and timeless. It can be appropriated and experienced anew, centuries after the original happening. The Temple might be destroyed, but the kabbalist could still feel what the High Priest experienced when he entered the dark, inaccessible void of the Devir. Even though most Jews regarded the era of prophecy as over, Maimonides and Abraham Abulafia believed that it was possible to attain the rank of prophethood through the mystical disciplines. Sufis, who believe that Muhammad was the Seal of the Prophets, also believe that they can experience his prophetic receptivity to the Divine Word, just as Christians, who regard Christ as God's Last Word to humankind, believe that Christhood is the true destiny of all men and women. By means of their spiritual exercises, therefore, mystics try to become themselves at one with the bridge that originally spanned the gulf between the divine and this mortal world.

Alongside the symbol of the Temple, some Jews (known as the Ḥasidim) cultivated a devotion to leaders, or *zaddikim*, who, in some sense, enshrined the divine mystery and acted as a conduit for divine blessing. They seemed so imbued with heavenly power that their own persons became for their disciples a link with God. Many critics of the Ḥasidim objected that the quasi-divine status of the *zaddikim* was unacceptable. Muslims, who find the Christian doctrine of the incarnation as difficult to accept as Jews do, developed rather similar beliefs, especially in the Shiah. The prophet Muhammad was held to be the Perfect Man and a link with heaven: the Shiite Imams, his descendants, were also thought by their contemporaries to enshrine the divine truth. The Oriental religions also see men and women as avatars of the ultimate mystery. This tendency seems to represent a common yearning to see God as somehow expressed in human form. Clearly it is a devotion that has its dangers. Christians sometimes give the impression that Jesus is God *tout court*, forgetting that he said that he was the Way, not the Terminus of the religious quest. Thus they may well feel that they are in familiar territory when they read of these Jewish mystics' daring attempts to experience anew the biblical doctrine that humanity was created in the image of God.

There are many other comparisons to be made with the various religious traditions throughout this book. Jacobs rightly notes that, unlike Christians or Sufis, Jewish mystics do not claim to have become one with God. Their sense of the divine otherness is too strong for that. But all mysticism does seek to attain a sense of wholeness—the completion of which is felt to have been the proper state of men and women. This longing for a harmony that was believed to be the original condition of humanity is expressed in the near-universal myth of the lost paradise. We recall that when the four sages attempted to enter God's presence, they went into the *pardes*, the orchard or pleasure garden that reminds us of the biblical Eden. The search for the primal harmony is also seen in these pages in the emphasis on the process of "unification," whereby human souls are united to God—a union which reunites the whole spectrum of reality to its Source. This is an aspiration similar to the imperative of *tawhid* ("making one") which is so central to the Muslim vocation.

Closely linked to this idea is the common concern with charity, loving-kindness, and the felt need to overcome that egotism which can destroy human harmony. All the great world faiths insist that the sole test of any spirituality is that it lead to practical compassion. As the Buddha explained: After achieving Enlightenment, a man must come down from the mountaintop, return to the marketplace, and there practice compassion for all beings. Some of the mystics in this volume do not live up to this belief and I have to confess that I have problems with them. I may not be reading him correctly, but Rabbi Joseph Karo (or, rather, his *maggid*) sometimes sounds as though he is more concerned with affirming and exalting Karo's ego than with helping him transcend it. Similarly, I find it difficult to feel wholly enthusiastic about Rabbi Ḥayyim Vital's somewhat complacent account of the stream of visitors who beat a path to his door to tell him how wonderful he was. All the more appealing, then, is the emphasis on healing, harmony, peace, and love in the Bet-El community, the Ba'al Shem Tov's manifest humility, and the selflessness of the Gaon of Vilna that we also encounter in these pages.

Yet, despite many similarities, the various religious and mystical traditions are not identical. Each has its particular genius, its special emphases. Formed as I was in the Christian tradition, I find both the reticence and the stress on the utter holiness or otherness of God to be liberating and challenging. There have been important Christian mystics who have shared this sense of transcendence, of course. One need only mention Denys the Areopagite, Meister Eckhart, or the anonymous English author of *The Cloud of Unknowing*. But more common—at least in Western Christianity—is an emphasis on the symbol of Jesus that can make God seem all too human and accessible. From an early age, Christians are taught to talk freely and spontaneously to him and, helpful as this can be, it can also diminish the sense of silence, awe, and mystery which is an important part of the numinous experience. It is too easy to make Jesus or God into a reflection of our own selves, making them fit our needs and neuroses. This has often been the case with women mystics. The seventeenth-century contemplative Margaret Mary Alacoque, for example, made Jesus into a rather puling, self-pitying creature—very different from the bracing figure in the Gospels. Others took the bridal imagery, so often used by mystics in all faiths, too literally and transformed Jesus into a lover in a most unhealthy manner. Some women fell into so-called ecstatic states that have more in common with hysteria than with genuine mysticism. Catherine of Siena, a fourteenth-century Dominican saint, once fell into the fire when she succumbed to an ecstatic trance while cooking the dinner. Such "freaking out" has nothing in common with the ecstatic states described by the great spiritual masters. Mysticism, practiced correctly, should make one more alert and aware. Indeed, one great test of a valid mystical experience is that it be healthily integrated with normal, waking life.

It has not, of course, escaped my notice that there are no women mystics in this volume. One of the peculiarities of Jewish mysticism is that it has long been closed to women. This is not simply because women were debarred from the study of Torah and Talmud; Christian women were also denied the opportunity to study. It seems that from the outset kabbalistic symbolism associated woman not with tender-

ness but with the demonic realm—this, in spite of the fact
that the image of the *Shekhinah*, the divine presence on
earth, suggested that there was a female element in God.
Jewish women today, at least in Reform Judaism, are now
permitted to engage in the study of the Torah and are admitted to the Rabbinate. Like Christian and Muslim
women, they are gradually throwing off the aura of inferiority imposed upon them over the centuries. Christian
women were also associated with the demonic; they were
regarded as more easily prone to sin than men and blamed
for the fall of humanity. Had not Eve been the first to pluck
the forbidden fruit? The negative view of womankind in the
Kabbalah meant that Jewish mysticism remained exclusively male. Perhaps Jewish women will soon persuade their
menfolk that their demonization in Kabbalah was an unhealthy accretion and that they too are as well equipped as
men for the mystical quest. The moving mythology of the
Shekhinah, which we encounter in these pages, provides us
with a much more positive image of the female and would
be an excellent place to begin this process of reclamation.
Jewish women should not be deterred from the mystical
path by the failings of the Christian women mystics I have
mentioned. As the great Teresa of Avila was well aware,
women got into difficulties not because of an essential flaw
in the female psyche but because they were deprived of education and often lacked adequate spiritual direction. There
is no reason for any woman to labor under such difficulties
today.

Mysticism is not a "do-it-yourself" discipline. It can be
successfully undertaken only with expert guidance. This
was well understood by the Jewish mystics. Kabbalah is an
esoteric tradition, a closed book to the uninitiated. Nor is
mysticism suitable for everybody. Some people—male as
well as female—are just not capable of this type of spirituality. The apparent accessibility of Christ sometimes encour-

ages people to think that anybody can embark on the mystical journey and that any Christian worthy of the name is capable of experiencing divine rapture. This can lead to feelings of inadequacy. For years as a child and, later, as a young nun, I felt a constant failure because I never came within shouting distance of the mystical heights achieved with such apparent lack of effort by the saints. I was convinced that there must be something wrong with me. It would have been a great relief if some kind person had read me the story of the four sages who entered the *pardes*, explained that I was not mystical material, and should try to find a form of spirituality more suited to my temperament.

The fearful and unimaginable vision of Ezekiel is a valuable reminder that the reality we call God is never easily attainable or fitted snugly into our human frames of reference. So, too, are the dizzy distances imagined by the Riders of the Chariot. Yet Jewish mystics never forgot that the transcendent God of monotheism is, in some sense, a God who speaks and who has, as it were, come to meet us. The wonder, awe, and insight experienced by those who have—however tenuously—sensed this Presence are memorably expressed in this book.

JULY 1996

THE SCHOCKEN BOOK OF
JEWISH MYSTICAL TESTIMONIES

Introduction

⌇⌇

The difficulties encountered in attempting to define mysticism are notorious. David Knowles (*What Is Mysticism?*,
London, 1967, p. 9) rightly states at the beginning of his ex-
ploration: "Everyone in our day who proposes to speak or
write of mysticism must begin by deploring both the ambi-
guity of the word itself and the difficulty of defining it in any
of its meanings." The type of mysticism described in the following pages is that problematic subcategory known by
scholars as mysticism in theistic religion. Dean Inge (*Mysticism in Religion*, London, 1969, pp. 31–37) refers to his Bamp-
ton Lectures in which he quoted no fewer than twenty-six
definitions of mysticism and to which he adds others. All of
these refer to religious experience, more specifically, to
communion with God, of an intense and direct nature. For
our purpose, then, Jewish mysticism can be defined as that
aspect of the Jewish religious experience in which man's
mind is in direct encounter with God. It is necessary to
speak of the mind in this context since it is undoubtedly

true that in most varieties of Jewish mystical experience there is a strong intellectual content.

Jewish mysticism is sometimes equated with Kabbalah—that great manifestation of religious energy that came to the foreground in the 12th and 13th centuries and remained a major factor for centuries, but this identification is neither accurate nor particularly helpful. The Kabbalah was indeed produced by mystics, and it contains both the fruit of profound religious meditation and the instruments used by later mystics to attain their aim of encountering God. However, there were many mystics who flourished before the kabbalistic era and the Kabbalah deals with many matters that are not mystical.

Jewish mystics tended to be reticent about their own mystical experiences. The Kabbalah, as a theosophical system, has had numerous devotees but some of these, at least, engaged in its study as a purely intellectual exercise; of a religious nature, to be sure, as part of the supreme ideal of Torah study. The Torah was thought of as having two elements—the exoteric (*nigleh*, "revealed"), consisting of the Bible, Talmud, religious philosophy and the legal Codes; and the esoteric (*nistar*, "hidden"), consisting of the Zohar and the other kabbalistic works. The usual name for the Kabbalah is, in fact, *ḥokhmah nistarah*, "the hidden science." Even kabbalistic ideas that are mystical are presented as part of an objective scheme from which the personal elements have been rigorously excluded. At all events, direct, mystical testimonies on the part of Jewish mystics, of the order, say, of St. John of the Cross and St. Theresa among Christians and Rumi among Muslims, are exceedingly hard to find.

Professor Gershom Scholem has called attention to this phenomenon in his monumental *Major Trends in Jewish Mysticism*, a work to which every student of the subject is enormously indebted. Scholem writes:

If you compare the writings of Jewish mystics with the mystical literature of other religions you will notice a considerable difference, a difference which has, to some extent, made difficult and even prevented the understanding of the deeper meaning of Kabbalism. Nothing could be further from the truth than the assumption that the religious experience of the Kabbalists is barren of that which, as we have seen, forms the essence of mystical experience, everywhere and at all times. The ecstatic experience, the encounter with the absolute Being in the depths of one's own soul, or whatever description one may prefer to give to the goal of the mystical nostalgia, has been shared by the heirs of rabbinical Judaism. How could it be otherwise with one of the original and fundamental impulses of man? At the same time, such differences as there are, are explained by the existence of an overwhelmingly strong disinclination to treat in express terms of these strictly mystical experiences. Not only is the form different in which these experiences are expressed, but the *will* to express them and to impart the knowledge of them is lacking, or is counteracted by other considerations.

It is well known that the autobiographies of great mystics, who have tried to give an account of their inner experiences in a direct and personal manner, are the glory of mystical literature. These mystical confessions, for all their abounding contradictions, not only provide some of the most important material for the understanding of mysticism, but many of them are also veritable pearls of literature. The Kabbalists, however, are no friends of mystical autobiography. They aim at describing the realm of Divinity and the other objects of the contemplation in an impersonal way, by burning, as it were, their ships behind them. They glory in an objective description and are deeply averse to letting their own personalities intrude into the picture. The wealth of expression at their disposal is not inferior to that of their autobiographical confreres. It is as though they were hampered by a sense of shame. Documents of an intimate and personal nature are not entirely lacking, but it is characteristic that they are to be found almost wholly in manuscripts which the Kabbalists themselves would hardly have allowed to be printed. There has even been a kind of voluntary censorship which the Kabbalists themselves exercised by deleting certain passages of a too intimate nature from the manuscripts, or at least seeing to it that they were not printed. . . . On the whole, I am inclined to believe that this dislike of a too personal indulgence in self-expression may have been caused by the fact among others that the Jews retained a particularly vivid sense of the incongruity between mystical experience and that idea of God which stresses the aspects of Creator, King and Law-giver. It is obvious that the absence of the autobiographical element is a serious obstacle to the psychological understanding of Jewish mysticism as the psychology of mysticism has to rely primarily on the study of such autobiographical material (pp. 15–16).

Scholem here suggests as one of the reasons for the lack of personal mystical testimonies in Jewish literature, that the Jews retained a sense of the incongruity between mystical experience and the idea of God as Creator, King and Law-giver. But in addition to different concepts of the Deity, another factor seems to have operated. In rabbinical Judaism the concept of the *mitzvah*, the precept ordained by God, is a basic idea. The study of the Torah is the highest *mitzvah*, and there are the many practical *mitzvot*, on all of which tomes without number have been composed. But mystical experience is rarely thought of as a *mitzvah*. One does not have to have had such experiences in order to qualify as a good Jew or even in order to attain to the highest ranks in Jewish worship. When mystical experience did eventually come to be seen by some teachers as a *mitzvah*, even as the chief aim of the whole Torah, then, indeed, was the experience recorded and guidance given for its attainment. Very revealing is the passage quoted in this book about the Gaon of Vilna, the great exponent of traditional rabbinism who was himself a mystic. The Gaon declares that mystical experiences are in the nature of "rewards" and that the aim of man in his life is not to desire to enjoy such "rewards" but to carry out the *mitzvot*. Significant, too, in this connection is the attempt, especially by the 18th-century Ḥasidim, to interpret the references to the esoteric side of Judaism as meaning not the knowledge of a science but the achievement of personal, mystical experience. Once such a step is taken, mystical experience is equated with the "study" of the Torah, i.e., in its esoteric aspect, and thus becomes in its turn part of the highest *mitzvah*.

A statement of Menahem Mendel of Peremyshlany (b. 1728), a disciple of the Ba'al Shem Tov, the founder of the hasidic movement, is germane to the issue:

> *Nistar* refers to something it is impossible to communicate to another, the taste of food, for example, which cannot be conveyed to someone who has never tasted that particular food . . . So it is with regard to the love and fear of the Creator, blessed be He. It is impossible to convey to another how this love is in the heart. This is called *nistar*. But how can it be correct to call the kabbalistic science *nistar*? Whoever wishes to study "the Kabbalah" has the book open for him. If he cannot understand the book he is simply an ignoramus for whom the Talmud and the Tosafists would also be *nistar*. But the meaning of *nistarot* ("the secret things") in the whole of the Zohar and the writings of the Ari of blessed memory, is that these are all constructed on the idea of attachment (*devekut*) to the Creator, for whosoever is privileged to become attached

to the Chariot on High and to gaze at it, like the Ari of blessed memory for whom the Heavenly Paths were clearly illumined so that he was able to walk constantly in them guided by the eyes of his intellect . . .

(This passage is from *Yosher Divrei Emet* by Meshullam Phoebus of Zbarazh, *Kunteros* I, no. 22, Munkacz, 1905.)

Whatever the reason, the extreme rarity of personal mystical testimonies is a fact of Jewish literature. Yet here and there, such testimonies are found and they provide a fascinating glimpse into an aspect of Judaism that is frequently ignored completely. This book is an anthology of personal mystical testimonies, peak religious experiences, examples of ecstatic prayer and the like and the reports of these which have been culled from a literature extending from biblical times down to the present. These texts have not been chosen haphazardly but as the main examples we have of this *genre*.

The first chapter of Ezekiel is included because it is the most vivid and elaborate illustration of a prophetic vision and because it is the basis for much subsequent mystical speculation known as Merkabah mysticism. The "riders of the Chariot," for over a period of a thousand years, took their journey on the route provided by the ancient prophet. The talmudic passage about the four who entered the king's orchard (chapter 2) and the midrashic text in chapter 3 are basically reports about the experiences of others but belong nonetheless in this anthology since these accounts are obviously based on the actual techniques of the Merkabah mystics.

The passage from Maimonides' *Guide for the Perplexed* is in a category of its own. Although Maimonides' statement is in the form of an objective presentation, it is clear that he is not only drawing on his personal experience but is offering guidance for his pupil to follow in his footsteps. Seen in this way, as it should be, the statement is a kind of manual for the attainment of the lower degrees of prophecy. This theme, though with a different approach, is taken up by Abraham Abulafia and his pupil in the passages quoted from their works. Abulafia wrote a commentary to Maimonides' *Guide*, which greatly influenced his own ideas regarding prophetic mysticism. The passage from Eleazar of Worms is an illustration of the mystical approach of a contemporary of Maimonides.

Jacob of Marvège's *Responsa from Heaven* is relevant to our theme in that the author engaged in various techniques in order to receive his replies and believed, moreover, that he was the recipient of heavenly communications.

The two passages from the Zohar on the high priest's ecstasy on the Day of Atonement, though not a direct personal account, and while the idea of ecstasy in the mystical life is not found elsewhere in the Zohar, do serve as reflecting actual mystical experiences and so demand inclusion. The comparison with the visions of Abraham of Granada is instructive. It would seem that the theme of the high priest in the Holy of Holies became a paradigm of the ecstatic experiences of the mystics.

The accounts of Joseph Karo's *maggid* provide insights into a rather different type of mystical experience. They have the advantage of being intensely personal, having been recorded by Karo himself, except for the statement by Solomon Alkabetz who claims to have heard the *maggid* speaking out of Karo's mouth. The visions of Ḥayyim Vital are chiefly in the nature of dreams, but there are, too, experiences he claims to have had while in the waking state or in a trance. The *maggid* of Moses Ḥayyim Luzzatto is basically the same kind of experience as that of Karo. Indeed, it is fairly clear that Karo's *maggid* is the source of Luzzatto's particular inspiration and the two follow more or less the same pattern, even to the extent that some of the terms used by Karo are also used by the later mystic.

The eighteenth century was a great age for Jewish mysticism. Scholem has rightly disagreed with Dubnow's description of the famous epistle of the Ba'al Shem Tov (see chapter 13) as the "hasidic manifesto." It is certainly not that, but it is a mystical testimony of much importance. The Ba'al Shem Tov's contemporary in Jerusalem, Shalom Sharabi, was developing his own system of mystical meditation while the Vilna Gaon, in the stronghold of opposition to Hasidism, believed, like the Ba'al Shem Tov, that ascents of the soul were possible and that he had experienced these. The two epistles by the son and disciple of Elimelech of Lyzhansk are important for the light they throw on how the Hasidim themselves thought of the experiences of the *zaddikim*. In more systematic form the same theme is found in the writings of Kalonymus Kalman Epstein of Cracow, the favorite disciple of Elimelech. Alexander Susskind of Grodno is in a category of his own but chronologically he belongs together with the Gaon of Vilna.

Dov Baer of Lubavich's *Tract on Ecstasy* has as its purpose the offering of guidance to mystical adepts and, more than any of the other texts presented in this volume, describes in detail the problems of the mystical life and its varied mental and emotional states and conflicts. Dov Baer is speaking from personal experience and is addressing those who have advanced in the mystical way.

The diary of Isaac Eizik of Komarno owes much, it is obvious, to Vital's reports of his visions. Here, too, the actual terms used by Vital are used by the hasidic master, and the book as a whole clearly has Vital's book for its model. The meditations of Aaron Roth are those of an equally unconventional hasidic master and are of special interest in that they convey the thoughts of a contemporary Jewish mystic.

Certain common features are present in all these accounts. Light as the symbol of the Object apprehended is used by the mystics of all religions to describe haltingly the Reality they claim to have encountered. Speaking of this symbol, Edwyn Bevan (*Symbolism and Belief*, London, 1962, pp. 132–133) remarks:

> We can apply the metaphor to that which God reveals of Himself within the range of our earthly experiences. There are moments, which come no doubt to poets and mystics oftener than to us ordinary men, when the natural world round us is seen clothed in a glory, analogous, in the feeling it arouses, to bright concentrated light. Still more, as the highest expressions of the spirit of man, may the great utterances and heroic deeds be regarded as manifestations of the glory of God. All these things are within the range of our experience, and we know what the reality is which we describe as glorious. But when we speak of the glory of God, as the mode in which Christians believe that He manifests Himself to beings on a higher plane than ours, to those human spirits who attain, beyond their earthly experienece, to the Beatific Vision, we use the symbol to indicate something which in our present plane of being we cannot even imagine. If our idea of God, as a whole, is an act of faith, our attribution of glory to God will necessarily be part of such an act, not a matter of demonstration. What we mean is that we believe that, if we could have a more perfect apprehension of God's being than we can have under earthly conditions, that apprehension would involve something analogous to the feeling now aroused in us by bright concentrated light, something which cannot possibly be described in human language, except by our pointing to that feeling. Thus the light metaphor would not here be the use of a figure for mere poetical or imaginative embellishment, in order to say something which we could say more precisely in other terms: it would be the most precise way in which the Reality can be expressed in human language.

And yet, while we use it, we have to recognize that it is only a figure, not a literal description.

Bevan is writing as a Christian thinker. The mystics discussed in this book make the same point in their own language and from the standpoint of their own religion.

The symbol of light is found in practically all the texts quoted but is especially prominent among the "riders of the Chariot," in Abulafia, the Zohar, Abraham of Granada, Dov Baer of Lubavich, Isaac Eizik of Komarno and Aaron Roth.

The converse is the mystical "dark night of the soul." Although this term is not found among the Jewish mystics, a similar image—*katnut de-mohin*, "smallness of mind"—is found frequently. The "dark night" has been described by an authority on Catholic mysticism as follows (David Knowles, *What Is Mysticism?* London, 1967, pp. 68–69):

> The element of darkness is seen most strikingly in the phases in the mystical life which have been given the names of desolations and nights, and in the descriptions of those nights in the works of St. John of the Cross, in whose classic presentation are summed up the less accurate sketches of medieval writers. The clarity of the mind's judgment seems to fade, and the life runs for a time, and perhaps for a long time, in a maze of doubt and uncertainty which to an observer and to a reader bear a strong superficial resemblance to the phases of psychological illness. It is one of the most notable of St. John's achievements as a mystical theologican that he was able to explain what others had only described. The two nights, very different in their intensity, are not primarily evidences of physiological or psychological weakness, though they may contain an element of one of these; they are in essence the reaction of the powers of the soul, as yet weak and impure, to the superior light and love that is being poured into it, and that is experienced as darkness

and aridity by the senses and by the mind. St. John, in a vivid simile, compares this sense of instability and moral impurity to the blackening and exudates of a burning log under the influence of the flame that will in time render it incandescent.

Some of our authors speak of the same experience. It is especially prominent in Karo, Vital, Kalonymus Kalman Epstein, Dov Baer of Lubavich, Isaac Eizik of Komarno and Aaron Roth. Jewish mystical texts frequently use the terms *katnut*, *gadlut* and *devekut* and an explanatory word or two regarding their precise meaning is in order. *Devekut* ("attachment" to God) means having God in mind at all times; every thought and action being for the sake of God. But the practitioners of this extremely difficult, not to say, superhuman, art are keenly aware that there is an ebb and flow in the mystical life. The state in which God's presence is acutely felt, when, as it were, the soul is expanded to its limits, when there is rapture and ecstasy, is known as that of *gadlut* ("greatness"). The opposite state, the above-mentioned "dark night of the soul" is known as *katnut* ("smallness"). It must, however, be appreciated that these terms are taken from the Kabbalah and have a meaning based on the kabbalistic system. Here the terms in full are respectively: *gadlut de-moḥin* ("greatness of the brains") and *katnut de-moḥin* ("smallness of the brains"). The reference is to the kabbalistic doctrine of the *Sefirot* and their configurations (to be described later in this book). According to this doctrine there is a dynamic life in the Godhead. At times harmony reigns supreme in the supernal realm and then the divine grace can flow freely. At other times there is disharmony on high and then the divine flow is arrested. The harmony and disharmony are described in terms of the higher *Sefirot* or divine potencies (the "brains" or "intellects") controlling the lower *Sefirot* (the *middot*, "qualities" or "emotions"). When the "brains" are much in evidence, as it were, among the lower *Sefirot* there is *gadlut de-mohin*. When they are far less in evidence there is *katnut de-mohin*. Now since man, created in the image of God, mirrors in his own being these divine processes, these two states are present in his mystical experience. There are times when all is well, when *devekut* is easily attained. And there are other times when man seems to be rejected by God. The mystical writers urge the adept not to be disturbed when he finds himself in the state of *katnut*. On the contrary, this state is to be seen as an essential element in the mystical dialectic. Without the occasional "dryness" or "fall" there can be no freshness or elevation to ever greater heights. The "descent" is for the purpose of the "ascent."

The awareness on the part of the writers of these testimonies, that they are trying to give expression to that which is really unutterable and even incomprehensible, emerges not only from their explicit statements that this is the case, but also from the generally elusive tone of their observations. Terms are simply not available, so that expressions, such as "in the category of" and "as it were" abound, and they seek to convey their meaning by hint and at one stage removed. Dov Baer, the most precise of the writers considered, feels obliged to burst into Yiddish from time to time in his realization that the Hebrew he knows is inadequate to convey the more subtle nuances. Illustrations from daily life, both for the intense forms of rapture and for the failure to attain these, are used by some of the writers; the delight in seeing a king in his majesty, for instance, is used by Ezekiel and the "riders of the Chariot." Sexual raptures are used by Maimonides, oddly enough, in view of his somewhat negative attitude to sex, as they are by Eleazar of Worms, the Zohar, the Ba'al Shem Tov and Isaac Eizik of Komarno. Dov Baer's unique illustrations from the business world are not surprising since his epistle is addressed to followers mainly engaged in business. On the other hand, the idea that the spiritual life in its highest form is only possible to the man ready to relinquish worldly pleasures is behind all the writings. The ascetic tendency is especially to be observed in Maimonides, Eleazar of Worms, Abulafia, Karo, the Gaon of Vilna, Alexander Susskind, Elimelech of Lyzhansk and Aaron Roth. Isaac Eizik's vision of the *Shekhinah*, in the form he gives it, is extremely unconventional, though Karo's *maggid* is also a personification of the *Shekhinah* and Alexander Susskind, following the Lurianic Kabbalah, similarly personalizes the *Shekhinah* to an astonishing degree.

The selections provide some material for the study of the relationship between intellectual ability and mystical experience. Maimonides and Karo were the authors of gigantic and authoritative works of Jewish law and the Gaon of Vilna was a complete master of the whole range of Jewish literature. In these three, in any event, there can be no suggestion of any incompatibility between legal acumen and spiritual flights. The picture of the sober legalist who has no room in his soul for mysticism is fictitious. Indeed, so far as Karo is concerned, a good case can be made out for the view that this legal genius required the psychological relief provided by his *maggid* in order to bring his work to a successful conclusion. Legalism and mysticism are uniquely combined in *Responsa from Heaven*. Eleazar of Worms was the author of the legal compendium *Rokeaḥ*. Moses Ḥayyim Luzzatto, though a very young man, was a master of the talmudic literature, was familiar with Latin and other languages besides Hebrew, was a poet and dramatist of talent, and wrote works in a lucid style on ethics, logic and rhetoric, to say nothing of his remarkably acute systematic presentation of the Lurianic Kabbalah. Isaac Eizik was a prolific writer both as an outstanding talmudist and kabbalist.

The techniques used by our authors are varied. The "riders of the Chariot" evidently relied on fasting and, though this has not been definitely established, such means as gazing into a highly polished mirror (self-hypnosis?). Maimonides relies on a prior severe engagement in metaphysical thought, scientific and philosophical discipline, and a perpetual being-with-God in the mind. Eleazar of Worms stresses sound ethical and pious conduct as the preliminaries. Abraham Abulafia and his pupil use the technique of combining various divine names. A similar method is adopted by Abraham of Granada. So far as we can tell, Jacob of Marvège sought to obtain his replies from Heaven through fasting, the theurgic use of the divine names, and prayer for the result to be achieved. There are no indications of how Karo and Luzzatto set about obtaining their mentors or whether there was any conscious attempt to obtain them at all. Ḥayyim Vital relies on *yihudim*, "unifications" of the divine names, as does the Ba'al Shem Tov. Dov Baer believes that the profoundest mystical experiences come without awareness or contrivance, yet his scheme is based on the conviction that such experiences are bound to result if contemplation on the divine is authentic and in depth. The Vilna Gaon appears to hold that mystical experiences are entirely involuntary; they are a divine gift for those who study the Torah. For Shalom Sharabi and Alexander Susskind, the mystical state seems to be conditioned by the kind of *kavvanot*, mystical intentions, they both enjoin. In Alexander Susskind, indeed, the appeal sometimes seems to be to the reader to induce the state of rapture by working himself up to it, in what at times appears to be a purely artificial way. For the disciples of Elimelech of Lyzhansk, for Isaac Eizik of Komarno and for Aaron Roth, God reveals Himself to the Ḥasid who lives a life of purity and is assisted in his quest by the Guru-type master.

On this question of techniques, it is important to realize that the mystical adepts were extremely circumspect in conveying these to any but chosen disciples and then only under conditions of the utmost secrecy. Our knowledge of them is consequently limited, and we can only guess at them from the oblique references in the few manuscripts and printed works in which the matter is discussed. On Abulafia's techniques, in addition to the material presented here, we have an interesting description from his *Sefer ha-Nikkud* quoted by Moses Cordovero (1522–1570) in Cordovero's *Pardes Rimmonim* (chapter 21, ed. Jerusalem, 1962, p. 97). Reflection on the letters of the divine name in their various combinations and their vowel-pointings should be attended by breathings and by movements of the head. Each letter has its own form of breathing, some very short, to suggest simple unity, others longer to suggest the unity attained through diversity, and so forth. The head should be moved to east, west, north and south, and above and below, in accord with the particular vowel-point of the letter. For instance the letter *he* with the vowel *ḥolam* (*ho* with long *o*) should be pronounced with a long breath and with the head inclined high to the right. Scholem (*Major Trends*, p. 139) compares these techniques to the Yoga discipline.

The *yiḥudim* techniques involve sustained reflection on various combinations of the divine names. Ḥayyim Vital devotes a special book, *Shaar ha-Yiḥudim* ("Gate of Unifications"), to this subject. For instance, there is the mysterious "*Yiḥud* of the Beard" in which the mystical adept allows his thoughts to dwell at length on the flow of the thirteen paths of grace from the thirteen "hairs of the beard of the Ancient One," all described in the richest detail. This *yiḥud* is said to be especially appropriate during the days from the beginning of the month of Elul until Yom Kippur and especially effective if performed at the graves of the saints. Or, to give another example, before performing *yiḥudim*, a special *yiḥud* is performed to drive away the demonic forces which seek to intervene. The letters of the Tetragrammaton and the names "Ehyeh" and "Adonai" are combined and read in the mind backwards and forward: "Reflect on them well and then you can proceed in safety to perform whatever *yihud* you require." There were special times, places and opportunities for each *yihud* and the performace of a *yihud* in an inopportune moment was fraught with danger. Buber's novel, *For the Sake of Heaven* (New York, 1958, pp. 285–86), captures this sense of danger in his account of the eighteenth-century hasidic masters who tried by magical means, including the use of *yihudim*, to bring on the advent of the Messiah: "Kalman said: 'I am worried about the life of the Yehudi. There is a secret Unification which may be accomplished on this day. But none can accomplish it and live, save in the land of Israel. And it seems to me as though the Yehudi were daring to accomplish it.' 'Well,' said Shmuel, 'it may be that this is the day of the approach of which he had knowledge quite a long time ago. And assuredly he has sought to accomplish a matter which cannot be accomplished, save in the land of Israel, without the occurrence of death. But when will one accomplish it in the land of Israel?' They did not continue this conversation but proceeded on their respective journeys." A more detailed account of *yihudim* during prayer is to be found in the section in this book on Shalom Sharabi (chapter 14).

Is the experience described by these mystics a union with God—the so-called *unio mystica*? To quote Scholem (*Major Trends*, p. 5) again:

> To the general history of religion, this fundamental experience is known under the name of *unio mystica*, or mystical union with God. The term, however, has no particular significance. Numerous mystics, Jews as well as non-Jews, have by no means represented the essence of their ecstatic experience, the tremendous uprush and soaring of the soul to its highest plane, as a union with God. To take an

instance, the earliest Jewish mystics who formed an orga-
nized fraternity in Talmudic times and later, describe their
experience in terms derived from the diction characteristic of their age. They speak of the ascent of the soul to the
Celestial Throne where it obtains an ecstatic view of the
majesty of God and the secrets of His realm.

What Scholem says of the "riders of the Chariot," the group
to which he refers, is true of the majority of the mystics considered in this book. Most of them certainly do not interpret their experience as being a union with God. The
closest approximation to the concept is found in the Zoharic description of the *Sefirot* taking over, as it were, the
personality of the high priest so as to speak the words of
pardon through his mouth. Something similar is found in
Kalonymus Kalman Epstein's account. Dov Baer of Lubavich speaks of the "divine soul" as a portion of the Deity, as
it were, revealed in mystical rapture through the "garments"
of the natural soul.

I.

Ezekiel's Vision of
the Heavenly Throne

ᗡᘉ

Introduction

According to the superscription to the first chapter of the
biblical book of Ezekiel, the prophet saw his vision of the
Throne in Babylon, where he was in exile, during the fifth
year of King Jehoiachin's captivity, which corresponds with
July 28th in the year 593 B.C.E. The first Book of Chronicles
(28:18), speaking of the cherubim covering the ark in the
Temple, refers to the "chariot" (*merkavah*) and the Apoc-
ryphal book of Ecclesiasticus (49:8) refers to Ezekiel seeing
the "chariot": "Ezekiel had a vision of the Glory, which was
revealed enthroned on the chariot of the cherubin." The
Mishnah (*Megillah* 4:10; *Ḥagigah* 2:1) refers to Ezekiel's vision as of the "chariot" (*merkavah*) and the exposition of
this chapter in rabbinic literature is generally called "the account of the chariot" (*ma'aseh merkavah*). Visions of the
Throne of God are found in other parts of the Bible (I Kings
22:19; Isaiah 6:1–8; Daniel 7:9–10) but that of Ezekiel is the
most detailed and comprehensive.

Whether the first chapter of Ezekiel was composed by the prophet himself depends on the more general question of the authorship of the book as a whole. The verdict of modern scholarship is that while a good deal of the book may well go back to the prophet himself there is much evidence of a later editing of the book. It is consequently precarious to conclude that this chapter contains the *ipsissima verba* of the prophet. However, even if the detailed account is not from the prophet himself, there is no reason for doubting that the account is based on his actual experience. There is a further account of the chariot in chapter 10 of the book of Ezekiel.

A noteworthy feature of the vision is the frequent use of the word "likeness" (*demut*). The prophet seems bent on qualifying his experience. He makes no claim to have seen things as they are but as they appear to be. All through the account, there is the suggestion of mystery, of elusiveness, of attempting to describe the indescribable. When describing the One who sits on the Throne the suggestion of ineffability becomes even more pronounced:

> And above the firmament that was over their heads was
> the likeness of a throne, as the appearance of a sapphire
> stone; and upon the likeness of the throne was a likeness
> as the appearance of a man upon it above (verse 26).

Ezekiel sees in his vision a great cloud with brightness all around it. In the midst of this cloud there is something resembling the flash of *hashmal* (of doubtful meaning, perhaps "electrum" or "amber"). From this there emerges the appearance of four living creatures. These resembled men in form but each had four faces—of a man, a lion, an ox, and an eagle. Each of these also had four wings. There were wheels (*ofanim*) full of eyes and there were "wheels within wheels." Over above the living creatures was a firmament (*raki'a*), a kind of platform upon which the throne rested. On this platform was set the great throne and on the throne there rested "the appearance of the likeness of the glory of the Lord." When the prophet saw this, he fell on his face in awe and dread and he heard a voice proclaiming a message to him.

There has been a good deal of speculation on the psychological background of Ezekiel's vision. Images such as that of the thick cloud, the storm and the bright light are found elsewhere in the Bible. The theophany at Sinai (Exodus 19:16–20) is described in not dissimilar terms. Jewish tradition has it, in fact, that on Shavuot, the festival on which the revelation at Sinai is celebrated, the prophetic reading (the *haftarah*) is this very chapter of Ezekiel, as if to draw the analogy between the revelation to the people as a whole and that vouchsafed to the individual prophet. Other features of the vision such as the four-headed creatures and the wheels are peculiar to Ezekiel. It has been conjectured that the prophet's subconscious mind had absorbed the images of the bull-like figures guarding the entrance to the Babylonian temples. This certainly cannot be discounted but it remains no more than theory. Even though the term "chariot" is not used in the account of the vision, the term is not inappropriate. It is possible that the significance of the vision of a throne carried on wheels is that the prophet sees his vision outside the holy land so that he sees God as transporting His throne in order to speak to His servant.

The translation of chapter one of Ezekiel is taken from the Jewish Publication Society of America edition of the Holy Scriptures, Philadelphia, 1917.

Text

¹Now it came to pass in the thirtieth year, in the fourth month, in the fifth day of the month, as I was among the captives by the river Chebar, that the heavens were opened,

and I saw visions of God. [2]In the fifth day of the month, which was the fifth year of King Jehoiachin's captivity, [3]the word of the Lord came expressly unto Ezekiel the priest, the son of Buzi, in the land of the Chaldeans by the river Chebar; and the hand of the Lord was there upon him.

[4]And I looked, and, behold, a stormy wind came out of the north, a great cloud, with a fire flashing up, so that a brightness was round about it; and out of the midst thereof as the color of electrum, out of the midst of the fire. [5]And out of the midst thereof came the likeness of four living creatures. And this was their appearance: they had the likeness of a man. [6]And every one had four faces, and every one of them had four wings. [7]And their feet were straight feet; and the sole of their feet was like the sole of a calf's foot; and they sparkled like the color of burnished brass. [8]And they had the hands of a man under their wings on their four sides; and as for the faces and wings of them four, [9]their wings were joined one to another; they turned not when they went; they went every one straight forward. [10]As for the likeness of their faces, they had the face of a man; and they four had the face of a lion on the right side; and they four had the face of an ox on the left side; they four had also the face of an eagle. [11]Thus were their faces; and their wings were stretched upward; two wings of every one were joined one to another, and two covered their bodies. [12]And they went every one straight forward whither the spirit was to go, they went; they turned not when they went. [13]As for the likeness of the living creatures, their appearance was like coals of fire, burning like the appearance of torches; it flashed up and down among the living creatures; and there was brightness to the fire, and out of the fire went forth lightning. [14]And the living creatures ran and returned as the appearance of a flash of lightning.

[15]Now as I beheld the living creatures, behold one wheel at the bottom hard by the living creatures, at the four faces

thereof. [16]The appearance of the wheels and their work was like unto the color of a beryl; and they four had one likeness; and their appearance and their work was as it were a wheel within a wheel. [17]When they went, they went toward their four sides; they turned not when they went. [18]As for their rings, they were high and they were dreadful, and they four had their rings full of eyes round about. [19]And when the living creatures went, the wheels went hard by them; and when the living creatures were lifted up from the bottom, the wheels were lifted up. [20]Whithersoever the spirit was to go, as the spirit was to go thither, so they went; and the wheels were lifted up beside them; for the spirit of the living creatures was in the wheels. [21]When those went, these went, and when those stood, these stood; and when those were lifted up from the earth, the wheels were lifted up beside them; for the spirit of the living creature was in the wheels.

[22]And over the heads of the living creatures there was the likeness of a firmament, like the color of the terrible ice, stretched forth over their heads above. [23]And under the firmament were their wings conformable the one to the other; this one of them had two which covered, and that one of them had two which covered, their bodies. [24]And when they went, I heard the noise of their wings like the noise of great waters, like the voice of the Almighty, a noise of tumult like the noise of a host; when they stood, they let down their wings. [25]For, when there was a voice above the firmament that was over their heads, as they stood, they let down their wings.

[26]And above the firmament that was over their heads was the likeness of a throne, as the appearance of a sapphire stone; and upon the likeness of the throne was a likeness as the appearance of a man upon it above. [27]And I saw as the color of electrum, as the appearance of fire round about enclosing it, from the appearance of the loins and upward;

and from the appearance of the loins and downward I saw as it were the appearance of fire, and there was brightness round about him. ²⁸As the appearance of the bow that is in the cloud in the day of rain, so was the appearance of the brightness round about. This was the appearance of the likeness of the glory of the Lord. ²⁹And when I saw it, I fell upon my face, and I heard a voice of one that spoke.

Comments

1. *in the thirtieth year:* The meaning is unclear. The medieval commentator David Kimhi understands it to mean the 30th year of the Jubilee cycle of 50 years. Some modern scholars understand it to refer to Ezekiel's age at the time.
river Chebar: Probably at Nippur in Babylonia; the New English Bible translates: "on the Kebar canal."
visions of God: The Septuagint reads this in the singular: "a vision of God."

2, 3. *In the fifth day . . . the word of the Lord came:* The medieval Jewish Bible commentator Rashi and most moderns understand verses in the third person as an editorial gloss.

4. *electrum:* or "amber": The meaning of the Hebrew *hashmal* is uncertain. This word, incidentally, is used in modern Hebrew for "electricity" on the basis of the usual translation of the word here.

5. *living creatures:* Hebrew *hayyot*, a word that can also mean "beasts." In Ezekiel, chapter 10, these four are called "cherubim."
the likeness of a man: Although three of their four faces were not human, their general appearance was human-like.

9. *they turned not when they went:* When they wished to change direction, they had no need to turn around since each had a face in all four directions.

10. *As for the likeness of their faces:* These four faces—man, lion, ox, and eagle—represent the four most majestic of creatures.

12. *the spirit:* The Hebrew word *ru'ah* can mean either "spirit" or "wind." Here the meaning seems to be the vital force which propelled the living creatures.

14. *ran and returned:* The later Jewish mystics interpreted this verse to mean that whenever the living creatures approached too near to the Throne, they recoiled immediately in dread.

15. *one wheel:* The wheels were later identified as superior angels, hence the reference in the Jewish liturgy to the *Ofanim:* "And the *Ofanim* and the holy *Hayyot* with a noise of great rushing, upraising themselves towards the Seraphim, those over against them offer praise and say: 'Blessed be the glory of the Lord from His place.'"

18. *As for their rings:* The new English Bible translates, "hubs."
they were dreadful: Hebrew *yirah,* the same word that is generally used for the fear of God; they had a numinous quality. "We find the power of the numinous—in its phase of the mysterious—to excite and intensify the imagination displayed with particular vividness in Ezekiel" (L. R. Otto). The New English Bible reading "and they had the power of sight" (from Hebrew *ra'ah,* "to see") is jejune.

21. *When those went, these went:* The wheels were not attached to the living creatures but were under the indirect control of the living creatures, so that when the latter moved the wheels moved.

22. *terrible ice:* Hebrew *ha-kerah ha-nora,* again the suggestion of the numinous. The New English Bible translates, "glittering like a sheet of ice, awe-inspiring."

23. *conformable:* Hebrew *yesharot,* "straight," i.e., reaching the same level under the firmament.

25. *For, when there was a voice:* The tumult caused by the wings ceased whenever the voice was heard so that just before the voice was to be heard the wings stopped moving. New English Bible: "A sound was heard above the vault over their heads, as they halted with drooping wings."

26. *the appearance of a sapphire stone:* This verse had a direct parallel in Exodus 24:10: "And they saw the God of Israel; and there

was under His feet the like of a paved work of sapphire stone, and the like of the very heaven for clearness."

27. *And I saw:* Rashi comments: "No permission has been given to reflect on this verse."

28. *As the appearance of the bow:* The many-colored rainbow is symbolic of God's glory.

29. *I fell upon my face:* In awe and dread.

2

The Four Who Entered
the King's Orchard

ન્ટર

Introduction

This famous passage in the Babylonian Talmud, *Hagigah* 14b
(with parallels and variants in the Tosefta, *Hagigah* 2:3–4
and the Jerusalem Talmud, *Hagigah* 2:1, 77a), has been discussed at length through the centuries as the main statement in rabbinic literature of mystical experience. The
passage is introduced with the formula: *teno rabbanan*, "Our
Rabbis taught," a formula which is used in the Babylonian
Talmud to introduce a *baraita*, i.e., a teaching from the age
of the *tannaim* and therefore not later than the end of the
second century C.E. The four sages mentioned all flourished
in the first half of the second century. The word *pardes* (literally "orchard," occurring once in the Bible in Song of
Songs 4:13) is a Persian word, from which the word "paradise" for "heaven" is derived. The word is frequently translated here, too, as "paradise," hence: "Four entered Paradise
while still alive." But while the meaning of the passage may

well be that the four sages went to heaven (Rashi's comment to the passage is: "They ascended to heaven by means of a divine name"), it is extremely doubtful whether this translation is correct. Nowhere in the whole of the rabbinic literature do we find the term "paradise" used for "heaven." (Nor, for that matter, do we find the name *shamayyim*, "heaven," for this. The usual term is *Gan Eden*, "The Garden of Eden.") It is true that J. T. Milik has published two fragments found at Qumran of an Aramaic text of the Book of Enoch in which the "paradise of the righteous" appears as *pardes kushta* (Scholem, p. 16) but Urbach (p. 13) rightly says that this usage is never found in the rabbinic literature and that the meaning of *pardes* in our passage is that the mystical ascent of the sages is compared to men who enter the orchard (*pardes*) of a king. These must be circumspect, not entering the more private quarters and not cutting down any shoots. Thus "entering the orchard" is no more than an illustration meaning that those who engaged in the mystical ascent of the soul are to be compared to those who enter a king's orchard. (The Tosefta, in the parallel passage, uses, in fact, the expression: "To what can this be compared? To the orchard of a king. . . .") As to the object of this mystical contemplation, it is in all probability the Chariot of Ezekiel (see Hai Gaon's comment quoted below and Scholem and Urbach).

Text

Our Rabbis taught: Four entered an orchard and these are they: Ben Azzai, Ben Zoma, Aḥer and Rabbi Akiva. Rabbi Akiva said to them: "When you reach the stones of pure marble, do not say: 'Water, water!' For it is said: 'He that speaketh falsehood shall not be established before Mine eyes.'" Ben Azzai gazed and died. Of him Scripture says: "Precious in the sight of the Lord is the death of His saints."

Ps. *101:7*

Ps. *116:15*

Ben Zoma gazed and was stricken. Of him Scripture says: "Hast thou found honey? Eat as much as is sufficient for thee, lest thou be filled therewith, and vomit it." Aḥer cut down the shoots. Rabbi Akiva departed in peace.

Prov. 25:16

Comments

Ben Azzai and Ben Zoma were both named Simeon. They were never ordained as rabbis and it has been suggested that this is why they are not referred to as "Simeon ben Azzai" and "Simeon ben Zoma," it being considered insulting to them to refer to them by their full name without the title. Aḥer is Elisha ben Avuyah. "Aḥer" means "the other one," a name given to him when he became an apostate, according to the implications of our passage, as a result of his vision. Based on this passage the term "cutting down the shoots" is used in later Jewish literature as a synonym for "heresy." In the passage, it is implied that the mystical ascent of the soul is fraught with danger both to body and soul. Only Rabbi Akiva emerges unscathed. Rashi's comment to the passage deserves to be quoted in full as evidence of how this matter was viewed in the traditions of 11th-century France. Rashi comments as follows:

> *Pure marble:* shining like clear water. *Do not say: Water, water!* is here, how can we go on further? *Gazed:* towards the *Shekhinah.* *Precious in the sight of the Lord is the death of His saints:* His death was hard for God since he was still a young man, yet he had to die because it is said: "For man shall not see Me and live" (Exodus 33:20). *Was stricken:* He became demented.

Relevant to the understanding of this passage are the traditions preserved by the Babylonian *geonim,* although the latter lived centuries after the four heroes of the narrative. Hai Gaon (939–1038) was asked regarding the meaning of this mysterious account (Lewin, pp. 13–15): What is the orchard? At what did Ben Zoma gaze that he became stricken and what is the meaning of "stricken"? What is the meaning of "cutting down the shoots" and what are the "shoots"? Where did Rabbi Akiva go that it is said of him that he departed in peace? And why was it that Rabbi Akiva alone emerged unscathed? It cannot be that Rabbi Akiva alone was a righteous man, for all four were righteous men.

In his reply, Hai refers to the mystic circles of those who gaze at the heavenly chariot, the *merkavah*, seen by Ezekiel. These circles produced the *Heikhalot* ("Heavenly Halls") literature. Hai gives an interesting description, based on contemporary practices, of this kind of activity:

> You may perhaps know that many of the Sages hold that when a man is worthy and blessed with certain qualities and he wishes to gaze at the heavenly chariot and the halls of the angels on high, he must follow certain exercises. He must fast for a specified number of days, he must place his head between his knees whispering softly to himself the while certain praises of God with his face towards the ground. As a result he will gaze in the innermost recesses of his heart and it will seem as if he saw the seven halls with his own eyes, moving from hall to hall to observe that which is therein to be found.

It is to this mystical ascent of the soul, says Hai, that our passage refers, describing it figuratively as "entering an orchard." Two considerations, Hai argues, demonstrate that this is the proper meaning of the passage. First, the passage is appended in the Talmud to the Mishnah (Ḥagigah 2:1) which speaks of the *merkavah*. Secondly, it is stated in the *Heikhalot* literature that at the entrance of the sixth hall, there is an appearance of myriads of dancing waves though, in reality, there is not a drop of water there, only the sparkling atmosphere given off by pure shining marble. Ben Azzai gazed and died, for his time had come. Hai implies that his death was not due to a punishment for having gazed or because, as Rashi has it, "no man can see Me and live." According to Hai, Ben Azzai would have died in any event at that time but God first allowed him the tremendous privilege of gazing at the *merkavah*. When it is said that Ben Zoma gazed and was stricken, the meaning, according to Hai, is that the terrifying visions he had seen drove him out of his mind. Aḥer, as a result of his vision, became a dualist, believing, like the Zoroastrians who believe in Ormuzd and Ahriman, that there are two divine powers, one the source of good the other of evil, one all light and the other all dark. Since the experience is described in our passage in terms of entering an orchard, the abuses to which it led in the case of Aḥer are described as cutting down the shoots which grow in the orchard, as having insufficient regard for the property of the owner of the orchard. Rabbi Akiva alone was sufficiently mature to undergo the experience without coming to harm. He had perfected the art of seeing visions, without these either frightening him out of his mind or causing him to entertain heretical ideas.

It is well known, continues Hai, that God vouchsafes visions to the saints of every age just as He granted visions to the prophets. The opinion of Samuel ben Hophni (Hai's father-in law, the rationalist among the *geonim*), that only prophets can have visions, must be rejected. Samuel ben Hophni and those who think like him have been unduly influenced by the gentile literature they are over-fond of reading. This leads them to reject narratives such as this even though they are in the Talmud, which they regard are binding only in its legal portions and not in matters such as this. Hai concludes: "We hold that the Holy One, blessed be He, performs miracles and great wonders for the saints and it is not impossible to maintain that He shows to them in their innermost heart the vision of His halls and the place where stand the angels."

Hai's recognition that our passage belongs to the mystical texts of the *Heikhalot* literature is furthered by Scholem's analysis. Scholem quotes this from a manuscript of the *Heikhalot Zutrati* in the Jewish Theological Seminary of America:

> Ben Azzai beheld the sixth palace and saw the ethereal splendor of the marble plates with which the palace was tessellated and his body could not bear it. He opened his mouth and asked them: "What kind of waters are there?" Whereupon he died. Of him it is said: "Precious in the sight of the Lord is the death of His saints." Ben Zoma beheld the splendor of the marble plates and he took them for water and his body could not bear it not to ask them but his mind could not bear it and he went out of his mind . . . Rabbi Akiva ascended in peace and descended in peace.

Scholem has further demonstrated that ecstatic journeys of this kind into the heavenly halls are well known in Jewish literature from the days of the earliest apocalypticists (see introduction to the next chapter), to those of the *Heikhalot*. The heroes change but the basic idea remains: under the guidance of angels, man beholds those mysterious realms which God permits him to see. Scholem quotes in this connection the saying of Paul in II Corinthians 12:2–4: "I know a man belonging to the Messiah, who fourteen years ago, was caught up to the third heaven—whether in the body or out of the body, I do not know, God knows. And I know that this man was caught up into Paradise—whether in the body or out of the body, I do not know, God knows—and he heard things that cannot be told, that man cannot utter."

In the continuation of this passage in the Babylonian Talmud there are a number of speculations on the heavenly halls and the angels who inhabit them, and much of this material, too, is paralleled in the *Heikhalot* literature.

3

The Riders of the Chariot
and Those Who Entered
the Heavenly Halls

༄

Introduction

It has been noted in the previous chapter that there were circles of mystics engaged in ascents of the soul in order to gaze at the *merkavah* and the heavenly halls, the *heikhalot*. It has been noted that Hai Gaon refers to those circles which existed in his day, and yet the literature concerning these ascents dates back to the period of the apocalypticists—visionaries living at the beginning of the Present Era, who, by gazing into the future, sought to describe the events that would transpire at the end of time. At approximately the same time there arose the movement later known among Christians as the Gnostic ("Knowledge") movement. The Gnostics tended to hold dualistic theories regarding creation and claimed to be in possession of esoteric wisdom, especially on the subject of God's nature and His relationship to the universe. Scholem observes that the period in which these Gnostic speculations and ascents took place extended over almost a thousand years, from the first century B.C.E. to the tenth century C.E. The term generally used for the "chariot gazers" is *yoredei ha-merkavah*, literally "those who go down in the chariot" or "riders of the chariot." The *Heikhalot* literature has been preserved in various midrashic collections. The text quoted in this chapter is, according to Scholem, probably the earliest example of *merkavah* literature. This text, found in the Cairo *Genizah*, dates from the fourth, or, at the latest, the fifth, century C.E. It is in the form of a *midrash* to the first verse of the book of Ezekiel and in this resembles rabbinic *midrashim*, but it contains, too, important hints of the actual techniques of mystical contemplation in the period.

Fragments of this text were published by A. Marmorstein in *Jewish Quarterly Review* (New Series), 8 (1917–18), 367–78 and by J. Mann in *Ha-Ẓofeh le-Ḥokhmat Yisrael*, 5, 256–64. A full, critical edition with notes has recently been published by I. Gruenwald, under the title, *"Re'iyyot Yehezkiel,"* in *Temirin*, 1 (1972), 101–39.

Text

The Vision of Ezekiel.

Ez. 1:1   *Now it came to pass in the thirtieth year:* What is the significance of these? These thirty years correspond to the thirty kings who arose in Israel. For thus did they (the people) say to Ezekiel: Our fathers were smitten for forty years in the

Num.
14:33–34   wilderness, "for every day a year," and we, too, have been smitten for the number of years corresponding to the number of kings who have arisen among us.

Ez. 1:1   *In the fourth month, in the fifth day of the month:* Why did
Ta'an. 4:6   Ezekiel see his vision of the Power in the month of Tammuz? Is this not a month of evil omen for Israel, since the sages teach in the Mishnah that on the seventeenth day of Tam-

muz the tablets of stone were broken? But Rabbi Levi said: It is to tell you of the power and praise of the Holy One, blessed be He, that in the month of Tammuz, the very month in which they were smitten, there extended to them the mercies of the Holy One, blessed be He.

Of Hosea it is written: "The word of the Lord that came unto Hosea" and so you might ask, why does Ezekiel have to say: *and I was among the captives*? Rabbi (Judah Ha-Nasi) said: Ezekiel began to complain to the Holy One, blessed be He, saying: Sovereign of the universe! Am I not a priest and a prophet? Why did Isaiah prophesy in Jerusalem yet I have to prophesy among the captives? Why did Hosea prophesy in Jerusalem yet I have to prophesy among the captives? Of Isaiah it is written: "The vision of Isaiah." If it is because their prophecies brought good tidings and mine evil, it is not so, but mine are good and theirs were evil. A parable was told. To what can this be compared? To a king of flesh and blood with many servants to whom he allotted tasks to perform. He made the cleverest among them a shepherd, whereupon that clever man protested: My colleagues stay in an inhabited place, why should I have to be in the wilderness? So, too, Ezekiel protested: All my colleagues were in Jerusalem, why should I have to be among the captives? No sooner did Ezekiel speak thus than the Holy One, blessed be He, opened seven compartments down below. Ezekiel gazed into these in order to see all that is on high. These are the seven compartments down below: *Adamah* ("ground"); *Erez* ("Earth"); *Heled* ("World"); *Neshiyyah* ("Forgetfulness") *Dumah* ("Silence"); *She'ol* ("Pit"); and *Tit ha-Yaven* ("Miry Clay"). Where is *Adamah* mentioned? In the verse: "The ground did cleave." Where is *Erez* mentioned? In the verse: "And the earth opened her mouth." Where is *Heled* mentioned? In the verse: "Give ear, all ye inhabitants of the world." Where is *Neshiyyah* mentioned? In the verse: "And Thy righteousness in the land of forgetfulness." Where is

Hos. 1:1

Ez. 1:1

Isa. 1:1

Num. 16:31
Num. 16:32
Ps. 49:2
Ps. 88:13

Ps. 115:17
Num. 16:33
Dumah mentioned? In the verse: "Neither any that go down into silence." Where is *She'ol* mentioned? In the verse: "So they, and all that appertained to them, went down alive into the pit." Where is *Tit ha-Yaven* mentioned? In the Ps. 40:3 verse: "He brought me up also out of the tumultuous pit, and out of the miry clay."

Rabbi Isaac said: The Holy One, blessed be He, showed Ezekiel where the primordial waters are situated in the Job 38:16 Great Sea and in its terraces, as it is said: "Hast thou entered into the springs of the sea?" He showed him a mountain beneath the sea from whence the sacred vessels of the Temple will be restored in the future.

As Ezekiel gazed, the Holy One, blessed be He, opened to him the seven heavens and he saw the Power. A parable was told. To what can this be compared? To a man who visited his barber. After the barber had cut his hair he gave him a mirror in which to look. As he was looking into the mirror the king passed by and he saw the king and his armies passing by the door (reflected in the mirror). The barber said to him: Look behind you and you will see the king. The man replied: I have already seen. Thus Ezekiel stood beside the river Chebar gazing into the water and the seven heavens were opened to him so that he saw the Glory of the Holy One, blessed be He, the *hayyot*, the ministering angels, the angelic hosts, the seraphim, those of sparkling wings, all attached to the *merkavah*. They passed by in heaven while Ezekiel saw them (reflected) in the water. Ez. 1:1 Hence the verse says: "by the river Chebar."

It should have said: "Heaven was opened." Why does it Ez. 1:1 say: "The heavens were opened?" This teaches that seven heavens were opened to Ezekiel: *Shamayyim*; *Shemei ha-Shamayyim*; *Zevul*; *Araphel*; *Shehakim*; *Aravot*; and the Throne of Glory. Rabbi Levi said in the name of Rabbi Yose of Ma'on: Rabbi Meir said: The Holy One, blessed be He, created seven heavens and in these there are seven chariots. It is impossible to say that the Holy One, blessed be He, declared to Ezekiel: I show you My *merkavah* on condition that you explain it to Israel, as it is said: "Declare all that thou seest to the house of Israel," and it is said: "Moreover, He said unto me: Son of man, all My words that I shall speak unto thee receive in thy heart, and hear with thine ears. And go, get thee to them of the captivity, unto the children of thy people, and speak unto them, and tell them." But it was in order to expound to man the extent to which the eye can see and the ear hear.

Ez. 3:4

Ez. 3:10–11

Rabbi Isaac said: It is a five-hundred-year journey from the earth to the firmament (*raki'a*), as it is said: "That your days may be multiplied, and the days of your children . . . as the days of the heaven upon the earth." The thickness of the firmament is a five-hundred-year journey. The firmament contains only the sun, moon and stars but there is one *merkavah* therein. What is the name of this *merkavah*? It is *Rekhesh*, as it is said: "Bind the chariot [*ha-merkavah*] to the swift steed [*rekhesh*]." The waters above the firmament are a five-hundred-year journey, as it is said "And God called the firmament Heaven [*Shamayyim*]." Read not: *Shamayyim* but *Sham Mayyim* ("water is there"). How is it fashioned? It is like a tent, as it is said: "It is He that sitteth above the circle of the earth . . . And spreadeth them out as a tent to dwell in." It is fashioned in no other way than as a dome. It is thicker than the earth and its edges reach to the sea and the wind enters in at the sides in order to divide the upper waters from the lower waters. From the sea to the Heaven of Heavens [*Shemei ha-Shamayyim*] is a five-hundred-year journey. There are to be found the angels who say the *Kedushah*. They are not there permanently but, as Rabbi Levi said: "They are new every morning." Rabbi said: And from where are they created? From *nehar di-nur* ("River of Fire"). No sooner have they been created than they stretch out their hands to take of the fire of *nehar di-nur* with which they

Deut. 11:21

Micah 1:13

Gen. 1:8

Isa. 40:22

Lam. 3:23

wash their lips and tongues before reciting the *Kedushah*. Their voices continue unceasingly from sunrise to sunset, as it is said: "From the rising of the sun unto the going down thereof the Lord's name is praised." Then they are hidden away and others are created to take their place. Therein is a *merkavah*. What is the name of this *merkavah*? It is *Susim* ("Horses"), as it is said: "I saw in the night, and behold a man riding upon a red horse [*sus*]."

Ps. 113:3

Zech. 1:3

It is a five-hundred-year journey from *Shemei ha-Shamayyim* to *Zevul*. What is there in *Zevul*? Rabbi Levi said in the name of Rabbi Ḥama bar Ukba in the name of Rabbi Johanan: The Prince is in no other place than in *Zevul* and he is the very fullness of *Zevul* and before him there are thousands of thousands and myriads of myriads who minister before him. Of them Daniel says: "I beheld till thrones were placed . . . A fiery stream . . . Thousand thousands ministered unto him. . . ." What is his name? It is *Kimos*. Rabbi Isaac said: *Me'attah* is his name. Rabbi Inyanei bar Sisson said: *Bi-Zevul* ("In *Zevul*") is his name. Rabbi Tanḥum the Elder said: *Atatiya* is his name. Eleazar Nadva-daya said: *Metatron*, like the name of the Power. And those who make the theurgical use of the divine name say: *Sanas* is his name; *Kas, Bas, Bas, Kevas* is his name, like the name of the Creator of the world. And what is the name of the *merkavah* that is in *Zevul*? *Halvayah* is its name, concerning which David said: "To Him that rideth upon the heaven of heavens."

Dan. 7:9–10

Ps. 68:34

From *Zevul* to *Araphel* is a five-hundred-year journey and the thickness thereof is a five-hundred-year journey. Therein is the Canopy of the Torah, as it is said: "But Moses drew near unto the thick darkness [*araphel*] where God was." There is the *merkavah* upon which the Holy One, blessed be He, descended upon Mount Sinai. What is its name? It is *Chariot of Kings*, concerning which David said: "The chariots of God are myriads, even thousands upon thousands; the Lord is among them, as in Sinai, in holiness."

Ex. 20:18

Ps. 68:18

From *Araphel* to *Shehakim* is a five-hundred-year journey and the thickness thereof is a five-hundred-year journey. What is therein? The rebuilt Jerusalem, the Temple and the Sanctuary, the Testimony, the Ark, the *Menorah*, the Table, the sacred vessels and all the adornments of the Temple together with the Manna that was eaten by the Israelites. How do we know that all the sacred vessels are there? For it is said: "Ascribe ye strength unto God . . . and His strength is in the skies [*shehakim*]." Therein is a *merkavah*. What is the name of this *merkavah*? It is *Cherubim*, upon which He rode when He went down to the sea, as it is said: "And He rode upon a cherub, and did fly." *Ps. 68:35*

Ps. 18:11

From *Shehakim* to *Makhon* is a five-hundred-year journey. What is therein? The storehouses of snow and the storehouses of hail, the dreadful punishments reserved for the wicked and the rewards for the righteous.

From *Makhon* to *Aravot* is a five-hundred-year journey and the thickness thereof is a five-hundred-year journey. What is therein? The treasurehouses of blessing, the storehouses of snow, the storehouses of peace, the souls of the righteous and the souls yet to be born, the dreadful punishments reserved for the wicked and the rewards for the righteous. What is the name of the *merkavah* that is there? *Av* ("cloud") is its name, as it is said: "The burden of Egypt. Behold, the Lord rideth upon a swift cloud [*av*]." *Isa. 19:1*

From *Aravot* to the Throne of Glory is a five-hundred-year journey and the thickness thereof is a five-hundred-year journey. What is therein? The hooves of the *hayyot* and part of the wings of the *hayyot*, as it is said: "And under the firmament were their wings conformable." Therein is a great chariot upon which the Holy One, blessed be He, will descend in the future to judge all the nations, concerning which Isaiah said: "For, behold, the Lord will come in fire, And His chariots shall be like the whirlwind." What is its name? It is: Chariots of Fire and Whirlwind. *Ez. 1:23*

Isa. 66:15

Above are the wings of the *hayyot*, corresponding in size

to the total length of the seven heavens and the seven thicknesses between them. Above them is the Holy One, blessed be He. May the name of the King of the kings of kings, blessed be He, be blessed, praised, glorified, aggrandized, magnified, adored, raised up, exalted and sanctified. He endures for ever. Amen. Amen *Nezah*. Selah. Forever.

This concludes the vision of Ezekiel the son of Buzi the Priest.

Comments

The material in this passage is typical of the general speculations of the *merkavah* mystics. This kind of material—descriptions of the seven heavens and the angelic hosts—is found in abundance in the *Heikhalot* literature and in rabbinic sources. The best-known passage in the latter is in tractate *Hagigah* 12b–13a. Here it is said that there are seven heavens, their names being: *Vilon, Raki'a, Shehakim, Zevul, Ma'on, Makhon, Aravot*. The sun, moon and stars are in *Raki'a*. In *Shehakim* are the millstones that grind manna for the righteous. In *Zevul* is the heavenly Jerusalem and the Altar, and there Michael, "the great Prince," stands and offers thereon an offering. In *Ma'on* are the ministering angels. In *Makhon* are the storehouses of snow and hail. In *Aravot* are the treasures of life, of peace, of blessing, the souls of the righteous and the souls yet to be born. There, too, are the *Ofanim* and the seraphim and the *hayyot*, and the Throne of God and the King, the Living God, high and exalted, dwells over them in *Aravot*. Rabbi Aha ben Jacob adds that there is still another heaven above the heads of the *hayyot* but of this it is not permitted to speak. The passage concludes with the following account of the seven heavens:

> The distance from the earth to the firmament is a journey of five hundred years, and the thickness of the firmament is a journey of five hundred years, and likewise the distance between one firmament and the other. Above them are the holy *hayyot*. The feet of the holy *hayyot* are equal to all of them together. The an-

kles of the *hayyot* are equal to all of them. The legs of the *hayyot* are equal to all of them. The knees of the *hayyot* are equal to all of them. The thighs of the *hayyot* are equal to all of them. The bodies of the *hayyot* are equal to all of them. The necks of the *hayyot* are equal to all of them. The heads of the *hayyot* are equal to all of them. The horns of the *hayyot* are equal to all of them. Above them is the Throne of Glory. The feet of the Throne are equal to all of them. The Throne of Glory is equal to all of them. The King, the Living and Eternal God, High and Exalted, dwells above them.

It can be seen that in our passage we have the same framework as that preserved in the Babylonian Talmud but with notable differences. Evidently, the *merkavah* mystics had various traditions and engaged in their speculations according to their particular traditions. Of course, the possibility has also to be considered that in some of these texts different traditions have been combined. This certainly seems to have happened with regard to *Makhon* in our text. This seems to come from a different source.

The following brief notes on each paragraph are intended only to point to matters requiring further elucidation. For a complete account of the text readers are referred to Gruenwald's very comprehensive critical edition with notes.

The reference to the thirty kings is not clear, although the general meaning is: Ezekiel had to wait thirty years before he had his vision and this corresponds to the reign of the thirty kings.

Power, *Gevurah*, is a frequent name in the rabbinic literature for God—the Dynamis.

On the divisions of the netherworld, Gruenwald points out that while the actual divisions are found in other texts the idea that Ezekiel saw his vision of the world on high through the seven compartments of the netherworld is peculiar to our text.

The reference to the sacred vessels in the mountain beneath the sea contradicts the statement later on in the text that the sacred vessels are in the Heaven known as *Shehakim*. Probably here, too, we have a combination of two different traditions.

The parable of the mirror is noteworthy. As Gruenwald remarks, this probably means that the *merkavah* mystics used the technique of gazing into a mirror or into clear water before they began their ascents. Gruenwald suggests that these techniques were used from the earliest period and suggests that this helps to explain the rabbinic references to prophets seeing their vision "in a glass darkly" (see the references quoted by Gruenwald). One must be cautious, however, in drawing too hasty conclusions. There is no definite reference to the procedure elsewhere and it is not mentioned in Hai Gaon's account quoted in the previous chapter.

The idea that there is a *merkavah* in each of the seven heavens is peculiar to our text. The passage about God advising Ezekiel is not too clear. Possibly the meaning is that we might have supposed that, as with other visions of Ezekiel, he was instructed to impart his information to everyone but this is "impossible" since these esoteric matters must be kept secret.

The *Kedushah* is the Trisagion, the "Holy [*kadosh*], Holy, Holy" of Isaiah 6:3. *Nahar di-nur*, the "River of Fire," is from Daniel 7:10.

There is a vast literature on *Metatron*, see especially Odeberg, *III Enoch*, 79–146; Scholem, *Gnosticism*, 44–45, and Scholem's article in *Encyclopaedia Judaica*, vol. 11, 1443–46. Scholem points to the parallel passage in *Hagigah* 12b where, in *Zevul*, Michael "the Great Prince" offers up sacrifices. Scholem concludes that, in fact, the figures of Michael, the guardian angel of Israel, and Metatron, were consolidated and that Metatron was a secret name of Michael, just like the other mysterious names mentioned in this passage. In the Babylonian Talmud, *Sanhedrin* 38b, it is said that the name of Metatron is "like the name of his Master." The same idea is found here.

The remainder of the text presents no particular difficulties. No doubt, texts of this kind circulated among the *merkavah* mystics and were both a spur to their ascents of soul and at the same time a record of those ascents.

4.

Maimonides on Being
with God

∽∾

Introduction

Moses Maimonides (1135–1204), who is almost universally regarded as the greatest Jew of the Middle Ages, compiled his major philosophical work, the *Guide of the Perplexed*, in Arabic. The conventional understanding of Maimonides as the supreme rationalist and philosopher requires considerable qualifications. This chapter is a remarkable illustration of the mystical tendencies in Maimonides' thought but, as Heschel has shown, a careful reading between the lines demonstrates even more, that, in fact, what Maimonides is offering his pupil—for whom he wrote this book—is a method for attaining to the gift of prophecy, which Maimonides believed he himself had attained, at least in its lower stages. It might be remarked that the emphasis in 18th-century Ḥasidism on the ideal of *devekut*, perpetually being with God, owes much to this chapter in Maimonides (section 3, chapter 51) and the indebtedness was not infrequently acknowledged.

Text

This chapter that we bring now does not include additional matter over and above what is comprised in the other chapters of this treatise. It is only a kind of conclusion, at the same time explaining the worship as practiced by one who has apprehended the true realities peculiar only to Him after he has obtained an apprehension of what He is; and it also guides him toward achieving this worship, which is the end of man, and makes known to him how providence watches over him in this habitation until he is brought over to the "bundle of life."

I shall begin the discourse in this chapter with a parable that I shall compose for you. I say then: The ruler is in his palace, and all his subjects are partly within the city and partly outside the city. Of those who are within the city, some have turned their backs upon the ruler's habitation, their faces being turned another way. Others seek to reach the ruler's habitation, turn toward it, and desire to enter it and to stand before him, but up to now they have not yet seen the wall of the habitation. Some of those who seek to reach it have come up to the habitation and walk around it searching for its gate. Some of them have entered the gate and walk about in the antechambers. Some of them have entered the inner court of the habitation and have come to be with the king, in one and the same place with him, namely in the ruler's habitation. But their having come into the inner part of the habitation does not mean that they see the ruler or speak to him. For after their coming into the inner part of the habitation, it is indispensable that they should make another effort; then they will be in the presence of the ruler, see him from afar or from nearby, or hear the ruler's speech or speak to him.

Now I shall interpret to you this parable that I have invented. I say then: Those who are outside the city are all human individuals who have no doctrinal belief, neither one based on speculation nor one that accepts the authority of tradition; such individuals as the furthermost Turks found in the remote North, the Negroes found in the remote South, and those who resemble them from among them that are with us in these climes. The status of these is like that of irrational animals. To my mind they do not have the rank of men, but have among the beings a rank lower than the rank of men but higher than the rank of the apes. For they have the external lineaments of a man and a faculty of discernment that is superior to that of the apes.

Those who are within the city, but have turned their backs upon the ruler's habitation, are people who have opinions and are engaged in speculation, but who have adopted incorrect opinions either because of some great error that befell them in the course of their speculation or because of their following the traditional authority of one who had fallen into error. Accordingly because of these opinions, the more these people walk, the greater is their distance from the ruler's habitation. And they are far worse than the first. They are those concerning whom necessity at certain times impels killing them and blotting out the traces of their opinions lest they should lead astray the ways of others.

Those who seek to reach the ruler's habitation and to enter it, but never see the ruler's habitation, are the multitude of the adherents of the Law, I refer to the ignoramuses who observe the commandments.

Those who have come up to the habitation and walk around it are the jurists who believe true opinions on the basis of traditional authority and study the law concerning the practices of divine service, but do not engage in speculation concerning the fundamental principles of religion and make no inquiry regarding the rectification of belief.

Those who have plunged into speculation concerning

the fundamental principles of religion, have entered the antechambers. People there indubitably have different ranks. He, however, who has achieved demonstration, to the extent that that is possible, of everything that may be demonstrated; and who has ascertained in divine matters, to the extent that that is possible, everything that may be ascertained; and who has come close to certainty in those matters in which one can only come close to it—has come to be with the ruler in the inner part of the habitation.

Know, my son, that as long as you are engaged in studying the mathematical sciences and the art of logic, you are one of those who walk around the house searching for its gate, as the Sages, may their memory be blessed, have said resorting to a parable: "Ben Zoma is still outside." If, however, you have understood the natural things, you have entered the habitation and are walking in the antechambers. If, however, you have achieved perfection in the natural things, have understood divine science, you have entered in the ruler's place into the inner court and are with him in one habitation. This is the rank of the men of science; they, however, are of different grades of perfection.

There are those who set their thought to work after having attained perfection in the divine science, turn wholly toward God, may He be cherished and held sublime, renounce what is other than He, and direct all the acts of their intellect toward an examination of the beings with a view to drawing from them proof with regard to Him, so as to know His governance of them in whatever way it is possible. These people are those who are present in the ruler's council. This is the rank of the prophets. Among them is he who because of the greatness of his apprehension and his renouncing everything that is other than God, may He be exalted, has attained such a degree that it is said of him, Ex. 34:28 "And he was there with the Lord," putting questions and receiving answers, speaking and being spoken to, in that holy

place. And because of his great joy in that which he apprehended, "he did neither eat bread nor drink water." For his
intellect attained such strength that all the gross faculties
in the body ceased to function. I refer to the various kinds
of the sense of touch. Some prophets could only see, some of
them from close by and some from afar, as a prophet says:
"From afar the Lord appeared unto me." The various degrees of prophecy have already been discussed by us. Let us
now return to the subject of this chapter, which is to con-
firm men in the intention to set their thought to work on
God alone after they have achieved knowledge of Him, as
we have explained. This is the worship peculiar to those
who have apprehended the true realities; the more they
think of Him and of being with Him, the more their worship
increases.

As for someone who thinks and frequently mentions
God, without knowledge, following a mere imagining or following a belief adopted because of his reliance on the authority of somebody else, he is to my mind outside the
habitation and far away from it and does not in true reality
mention or think about God. For that thing which is in his
imagination and which he mentions in his speech does not
correspond to any being at all and has merely been invented
by his imagination, as we have explained in our discourse
concerning the attributes. This kind of worship ought only
to be engaged in after intellectual conception has been
achieved. If, however, you have apprehended God and His
acts in accordance with what is required by the intellect,
you should afterwards engage in totally devoting yourself to
Him, endeavor to come closer to Him, and strengthen the
bond between you and Him—that is, the intellect. Thus it
says: "Unto thee it was shown, that thou mightest know
that the Lord, and so on"; and it says: "Know this day, and
lay it to thy heart, and so on"; and it says: "Know ye that the
Lord He is God." The Torah has made it clear that this last

Ex. 34:28

Jer. 31:3

Deut. 4:35
Deut. 4:39
Ps. 100:3

worship to which we have drawn attention in this chapter can only be engaged in after apprehension has been achieved; it says: "To love the Lord your God, and to serve Him with all your heart and with all your soul." Now we have made it clear several times that love is proportionate to apprehension. After love comes this worship to which attention has also been drawn by the Sages, may their memory be blessed, who said: "This is the worship of the heart." In my opinion it consists in setting thought to work on the first intelligible and in devoting oneself exclusively to this as far as this is within one's capacity. Therefore you find that David exhorted Solomon and fortified him in these two things, I mean his endeavor to apprehend Him and his endeavor to worship Him after apprehension has been achieved. He said: "And thou, Solomon my son, know thou the God of thy father and serve Him, and so on. If thou seek Him, He will be found of thee, and so on." The exhortation always refers to intellectual apprehensions, not to imagination; for thought concerning imaginings is not called knowledge but "that which cometh into your mind." Thus it is clear that after apprehension, total devotion to Him and the employment of intellectual thought in constantly loving Him should be aimed at. Mostly this is achieved in solitude and isolation. Hence every excellent man stays frequently in solitude and does not meet anyone unless it is necessary.

A call to attention. We have already made it clear to you that that intellect which overflowed from Him, may He be exalted, towards us is the bond between us and Him. You have the choice: if you wish to strengthen and to fortify this bond, you can do so; if, however, you wish gradually to make it weaker and feebler until you cut it, you can also do that. You can only strengthen this bond by employing it in loving Him and in progressing toward this, just as we have explained. And it is made weaker and feebler if you busy

Deut. 11:13

1 Chron. 28:9

Ez. 20:32

your thought with what is other than He. Know that even if
you were the man who knew most the true reality of the divine science, you would cut that bond existing between you
and God if you would empty your thought of God and busy
yourself totally in eating the necessary or in occupying yourself with the necessary. You would not be with Him then,
nor He with you. For that relation between you and Him is
actually broken off at that time. It is for this reason that excellent men begrudge the times in which they are turned
away from Him by other occupations and warn against this,
saying: "Do not let God be absent from your thought." And
David says: "I have set the Lord always before me; because   *Ps. 16:8*
He is at my right hand, I shall not bend down"; he means
to say: I do not empty my thought of Him, and it is as if
He were my right hand from which, because of the rapidity
of its motion, my attention is not distracted even for an
instant, and therefore I do not bend down—that is, I do
not fall.

Know that all the practices of the worship, such as reading the Torah, prayer, and the performance of the other
commandments, have only the end of training you to occupy yourself with His commandments, may He be exalted,
rather than with matters pertaining to this world; you
should act as if you were occupied with Him, may He be exalted, and not with that which is other than He. If, however, you pray merely by moving your lips while facing a
wall, and at the same time think about your buying and sell-
ing; or if you read the Torah with your tongue while your
heart is set upon the building of your habitation and does
not consider what you read; and similarly in all cases in
which you perform a commandment merely with your
limbs—as if you were digging a hole in the ground or hew-
ing wood in the forest—without reflecting either upon the
meaning of that action or upon Him from whom the commandment proceeds or upon the end of the action, you

should not think that you have achieved the end. Rather
Jer. 12:2 you will then be similar to those of whom it is said: "Thou
art near in their mouth, and far from their reins."

From here on I shall begin to give you guidance with regard to the form of this training so that you should achieve
this great end. The first thing that you should cause your
soul to hold fast onto is that, while reciting the Shema
prayer, you should empty your mind of everything and pray
thus. You should not content yourself with being intent
while reciting the first verse of Shema and saying the first
benediction. When this has been carried out correctly and
has been practiced consistently for years, cause your soul,
whenever you read or listen to the Torah, to be constantly
directed—the whole of you and your thought—toward reflection on what you are listening to or reading. When this
too has been practiced consistently for a certain time, cause
your soul to be in such a way that your thought is always
quite free of distraction and gives heed to all that you are
reading of the other discourses of the prophets and even
when you read all the benedictions, so that you aim at me-
diating on what you are uttering and at considering its
meaning. If, however, while performing these acts of worship, you are free from distraction and not engaged in
thinking upon any of the things pertaining to this world,
cause your soul—after this has been achieved—to occupy
your thought with things necessary for you or superfluous in
your life, and in general with worldly things, while you eat
or drink or bathe or talk with your wife and your small children, or while you talk with the common run of people.
Thus I have provided you with many and long stretches of
time in which you can think all that needs thinking regarding property, the governance of the household, and the wel-
fare of the body. On the other hand, while performing the
actions imposed by the Law, you should occupy your
thought only with what you are doing, just as we have ex-

plained. When, however, you are alone with yourself and no one else is there and while you lie awake upon your bed, you should take care during these precious times not to set your thought to work on anything other than that intellectual worship consisting in nearness to God and being in His presence in that true reality that I have made known to you and not by way of affections of the imagination. In my opinion this end can be achieved by those of the men of knowledge who have rendered their souls worthy of it by training of this kind.

And there may be a human individual who, through his apprehension of the true realities and his joy in what he has apprehended, achieves a state in which he talks with people and is occupied with his bodily necessities while his intellect is wholly turned toward Him, may He be exalted, so that in his heart he is always in His presence, may He be exalted, while outwardly he is with people, in the sort of way described by the poetical parables that have been invented for those notions: "I sleep, but my heart waketh; it is the voice of my beloved that knocketh," and so on. I do not say that this rank is that of all the prophets; but I do say that this is the rank of Moses our Master, of whom it is said: "And Moses alone shall come near unto the Lord, but they shall not come near"; and of whom it is said: "And he was there with the Lord"; and to whom it was said: "But as for thee, stand thou here by Me." All this according to what we have explained regarding the meaning of these verses. This was also the rank of the Patriarchs, the result of whose nearness to Him, may He be exalted, was that His name became known to the world through them: "The God of Abraham, the God of Isaac, and the God of Jacob . . . this is My name for ever." Because of the union of their intellects through apprehension of Him, it came about that He made a lasting convenant with each of them: "Then I will remember My covenant with Jacob," and so on. For in these four, I

Song 5:2

Ex. 24:2
Ex. 34:28
Deut. 5:28

Ex. 3:15

Lev. 26:42

mean the Patriarchs and Moses our Master, union with God—I mean apprehension of Him and love of Him—became manifest, as the texts testify. Also the providence of God watching over them and their prosperity was great. Withal they were occupied with governing people, increasing their fortune and endeavoring to acquire property. Now this is to my mind a proof that they performed these actions with their limbs only, while their intellects were constantly in His presence, may He be exalted. It also seems to me that the fact that these four were in a permanent state of extreme perfection in the eyes of God, and that His providence watched over them continually even while they were engaged in increasing their fortune—I mean while they tended their cattle, did agricultural work, and governed their household—was necessarily brought about by the circumstance that in all these actions their end was to come near to Him, may He be exalted; and how near! For the end of their efforts during their life was to bring into being a religious community that would know and worship God. "For I have known him, to the end that he may command," and so on. Thus it has become clear to you that the end of all their efforts was to spread the doctrine of the unity of the Name in the world and to guide people to love Him, may He be exalted. Therefore this rank befitted them, for these actions were pure worship of great import. This rank is not a rank that, with the view to the attainment of which, someone like myself may aspire for guidance. But one may aspire to attain that rank which was mentioned before this one through the training that we described. One must beseech God that He remove the obstructions that separate us from Him, even though most of them come from us, as we have explained in certain chapters of this Treatise: "Your iniquities have separated between you and your God."

Gen. 18:19

Isa. 59:2

A most extraordinary speculation has occurred to me

just now through which doubts may be dispelled and divine secrets revealed. We have already explained in the chapters concerning providence that providence watches over everyone endowed with intellect proportionately to the measure of his intellect. Thus providence always watches over an individual endowed with perfect apprehension, whose intellect never ceases from being occupied with God. On the other hand, an individual endowed with perfect apprehension, whose thought sometimes for a certain time is emptied of God, is watched over by providence only during the time when he thinks of God; providence withdraws from him during the time when he is occupied with something else. However, its withdrawal then is not like its withdrawal from those who have never had intellectual cognition. But in his case that providence merely decreases because that man of perfect apprehension has, while being occupied, no intellect in *actu*; but that perfect man is at such times only apprehending potentially, though close to actuality. At such times he is like a skillful scribe at the time when he is not writing. On the other hand, he who has no intellectual cognition of all of God is like one who is in darkness and has never seen light, just as we explained with regard to its dictum: "The wicked shall be put to silence in darkness." He who apprehends and advances with his whole being toward the object of his apprehension, is like one who is in the pure light of the sun. He who has had apprehension, but is occupied, is while he is occupied in this state like one who has a cloudy day in which the sun does not shine because of the clouds that separate it and him. Hence it seems to me that all prophets or excellent and perfect men whom one of the evils of this world befall, had this evil happen to them during such a time of distraction, the greatness of the calamity being proportionate to the duration of the period of distraction or to the vileness of the matter with which he was occupied. If this is so, the great

1 Sam. 2:9

doubt that induced the philosophers to deny that divine providence watches over human individuals and to assert equality between them and the individuals of other kinds of animals is dispelled. For their proof for this opinion was the fact that excellent and good men experienced great misfortunes. Thus the secret with regard to this has been explained even according to the requirements of their opinions: The providence of God, may He be exalted, is constantly watching over those who have obtained this overflow, which is permitted to everyone who makes efforts with a view to obtaining it. If a man's thought is free from distraction, if He apprehends Him, may He be exalted, in the right way and rejoices in what he apprehends, that individual can never be afflicted with evil of any kind. For he is with God and God is with him. When, however, he abandons Him, may He be exalted, and is thus separated from God and God separated from him, he becomes in consequence of this a target for every evil that may happen to befall him. For the thing that necessarily brings about providence and deliverance from the sea of chance consists in that intellectual overflow. Yet an impediment may prevent for some time its reaching the excellent and good man in question, or again it was not obtained at all by such and such imperfect and wicked men, and therefore the chance occurrences that befell them happened. To my mind this belief is shown as true by a text of the Torah; He, may He be exalted, says: "And I will hide My face from them, and they shall be devoured, and many evils and troubles shall come upon them: so they will say in that day: Are not these evils come upon us because our God is not among us?" It is clear that we are the cause of this "hiding of the face," and we are the agents who produce this separation. This is the meaning of His saying: "And I will surely hide My face in that day for all the evil which they have wrought." There is no doubt that what is true of one is true of a community. Thus it has

Deut. 31:17

Deut. 31:18

become clear to you the reason for a human individual's being abandoned to chance so that he is permitted to be devoured like the beasts is his being separated from God. If, however, his God is within him, no evil at all will befall him. For He, may He be exalted, says: "Fear thou not, for I am with thee; be not dismayed for I am thy God," and so on. *Isa. 41:10*

He says: "When thou passeth through the waters, I will be with thee, and through the rivers, they shall not overflow thee," and so on. The determination that "when thou passeth through the waters and I will be with thee, and rivers shall overflow thee," is accounted for by the fact that everyone who has rendered himself so worthy that the intellect in question overflows toward him, has providence attached to him, while all evils are prevented from befalling him. It says: "The Lord is for me, I will not fear; what can man do unto me?" And it says, "Acquaint now thyself with Him, and be at peace," meaning to say: turn toward Him and you will be safe from all ill. *Isa. 43:2*

Ps. 118:6
Job 22:21

Consider the Song on Mishaps. You will find that it describes this great providence and the safeguard and the protection from all bodily ills, both the general ones and those that concern one individual rather than another, so that neither those that are consequent on the nature of being nor those that are due to the plotting of man would occur. It says: "That He will deliver thee from the snare of the fowler, and from the noisome pestilence. He shall cover thee with His pinions, and under His wings shalt thou take refuge; His truth is a shield and a buckler. Thou shalt not be afraid of the terror by night, nor of the arrow that flieth by day; of the pestilence that walketh in darkness, nor of the destruction that wasteth at noonday." He then goes on to describe the protection against the plotting of men, saying: If you should happen to pass on your way a widely extended field of battle and even if one thousand were killed to your left and ten thousand to your right, no evil at all would be- *Ps. 91:3–6* fall you. Do you not perceive and see with your eye God's judgment and retribution directed against the wicked that Ps. 91:7–8 are killed while you are safe? These are its words: "A thousand may fall at thy side, and ten thousand at thy right hand; it shall not come nigh thee. Only with thine eyes shalt thou behold, and see the recompense of the wicked." This is followed by what is said about divine safeguard; then it gives the reason for this great protection, saying that the reason for this great providence being effective with regard Ps. 91:14 to the individual in question is this: "Because he hath set his passionate love upon Me, therefore I will deliver him; I will set him on high, because he hath known My name." We have already explained in preceding chapters that the meaning of "knowledge of the Name" is: apprehension of Him. It is as if the Psalm said that this individual is protected because he hath known Me and passionately loved Me. You know the difference between the terms "one who loves" (*ohev*) and "one who loves passionately" (*hoshek*); an excess of love (*mahabbah*, so that no thought remains that is directed toward a thing other than the Beloved, is passionate love (*'ishk*).

The philosophers have already explained that the bodily faculties impede in youth the attainment of most of the moral virtues, and all the more that of pure thought, which is achieved through the perfection of the intelligibles that lead to passionate love of Him, may He be exalted. For it is impossible that it should be achieved while the bodily humors are in effervescence. Yet in the measure in which the faculties of the body are weakened and the fire of the desires is quenched, the intellect is strengthened, its lights achieve a wider extension, its apprehension is purified, and it rejoices in what it apprehends. The result is that when a perfect man is stricken with years and approaches death, this apprehension increases very powerfully, joy over this apprehension and a great love for the object of apprehension becomes stronger, until the soul is separated from the body at that moment in this state of pleasure. Because of this the Sages have indicated with reference to the deaths of Moses, Aaron and Miriam that the three of them "died" by a kiss." They said that the dictum, "And Moses the ser- *Deut. 34:5* vant of the Lord died there in the land of Moab by the mouth of the Lord" indicates that he died by a kiss. Simi- larly, it is said of Aaron: "By the mouth of the Lord, and *Num. 33:38* died there." And they said of Miriam in the same way: "She also died by a kiss." But with regard to her it is not said, "by the mouth of the Lord"; because she was a woman, the use of the figurative expression was not suitable with regard to her. Their purpose was to indicate that the three of them died in the pleasure of this apprehension due to the inten- sity of passionate love. In this dictum the Sages, may their memory be blessed, followed the generally accepted poeti- cal way of expression that calls the apprehension that is achieved in a state of intense and passionate love for Him, may He be exalted, a kiss, in accordance with the dictum: "Let him kiss me with the kisses of his mouth," and so on. *Song 1:2* The Sages, may their memory be blessed, mention the oc- currence of this kind of death, which in true reality is salva- tion from death, only with regard to Moses, Aaron, and Miriam. The other prophets and excellent men are beneath this degree; but it holds good for all of them that the appre- hension of their intellects becomes stronger at the separa- tion, just as it is said: "And thy righteousness shall go before *Isa. 58:8* thee; the glory of the Lord shall be at thy rear." After having reached this condition of enduring permanence, that intel- lect remains in one and the same state, the impediment that sometimes screened him off having been removed. And he will remain permanently in that state of intense pleasure, which does not belong to the genus of bodily plea- sure, as we have explained in our complications and as oth- ers have explained before us.

Bring your soul to understand this chapter, and direct your efforts to the multiplying of these times in which you are with God or endeavoring to approach Him and to decreasing those times in which you are with other than He and in which you make no efforts to approach Him. This guidance is sufficient in view of the purpose of this treatise.

Comments

This chapter is largely self-explanatory. "Ben Zoma is still outside" (page 48) is in the Babylonian Talmud, Hagigah 15a (see Text of chapter 2). "This is the worship of the heart" (page 50) is in Ta'anit 2a. "Do not let God be absent from your thought" is in Sabbath 149a. The passage about the death of the three by a kiss (page 59) is in Bava Batra 17a.

It should be especially noted that while Maimonides expressly denies that what he has to say applies to the rank attained by Moses and the Patriarchs, he goes on to state explicitly that through the training he has mentioned it is possible for men to attain "that rank which was mentioned before this one," i.e., the rank of the prophets. It appears that Maimonides was convinced that if his method of constantly reflecting on God, after adequate intellectual preparation for the purpose of refining one's ideas about God, is followed, the result will be that man becomes close to God and therefore immune from all bodily mishap, at least during the time he is actually in a state of meditation.

5

The Mystical Piety of Rabbi Eleazar of Worms

∽

Introduction

Eleazar ben Judah of Worms (c. 1165–c. 1230) belonged to the circle of mystics known as the Ḥasidei Ashkenaz ("The Saints of Germany"), the circle which produced the famous moralistic and religious work *Sefer Ḥasidim* ("Book of the Saints"), and the leader of which, Judah ben Samuel he-Ḥasid, was Eleazar's teacher.

Eleazar is best known for his halakhic compendium, entitled *Sefer ha-Roke'ah*, but his mystical views are presented in his *Sodei Razayya* ("Secrets of Secrets"). A part of this work found its way into the strange mystical collection known as *Sefer Raziel* ("The Book of Raziel"), which purports to be a communication to Adam by the angel Raziel. Although this book was published in Amsterdam as late as 1701 and does not appear to be earlier, in its present form, than the 17th century, it is generally acknowledged that a section of Eleazar's work has been incorporated into the book.

The following selection contains Eleazar's description of the fear and love of God as a prelude to his account of the *merkavah*, the heavenly chariot. The passage is, then, more than an appeal to the life of piety. It was evidently intended as a kind of mystical exercise to be engaged in by the adept before he began to study the mysteries of the *merkavah*. Scholem thus describes the kind of approach among the Ḥasidei Ashkenaz, an approach exemplified in this passage from Eleazar's work: "It is characteristic of this stage that the fulfillment of the divine will becomes purely an act of love. As in the contemporaneous Christian mystical love-poetry, the relation of the mystic to God is described in terms of erotic passion, not infrequently in a way which shocks our modern sensibilities."

The selection from *Sefer Raziel* is from the edition printed in Medzibezh in 1818, pages 9b–10a.

Text

Now I shall instruct you how to love God, blessed be He, and then I shall write out for you the secret of the *merkavah*.

Bet. 17a

"Let a man always be subtle in the fear of God." This means that he should reflect on the subtleties and glories of the world, how, for example, a mortal king orders his soldiers to go out to do battle. Even though they know that they may be killed in battle, yet they are afraid of him and they obey him, even though they know that the fear of him is not everlasting, since one day he will die and perish, and they can run away to another country. How much more so, then, should man fear the King of the kings of kings, the Holy One, blessed be He, and walk in His ways, for He is everywhere and He gazes at the wicked and the good. Whenever a man sees groups of the righteous he should attach himself to them so that he should have a portion among them. He should do it for the sake of heaven and walk in the ways He has created. Whenever he recites a benediction he should concentrate on the meaning, as it is written: "I have set the Lord always before me." That is why the Rabbis ordained that we should say in the benediction: "Blessed art Thou," as if a man were conversing with his neighbor. He should also consider that whenever a man sins, when, for example, he steals or fornicates with his neighbor's wife, how much subtlety does he display in order to prevent others knowing of it so that he should not be put to shame. How much more so should a man worship his Creator. And he should be subtle in doing good deeds, just as Jehu did it in subtlety when he said: "Ahab served Baal a little: but Jehu will serve him much," only his mouth caused him to stumble. A man should further develop this *a fortiori* argument so as never to be guilty of forgetting the will of the Creator. Suppose men are brought for trial to a ruler. If a man knows that the ruler is a magician or has control over the demons or knows the stars so that he knows exactly what happened, that man would not dare to deny his crime, since he knows that the ruler knows of it and, furthermore, he is ever afraid to do any harm to another lest he be summoned before that ruler. The living should take it to heart, *a fortiori*, that the Holy One, blessed be He, sees all his ways, knowing all his thoughts and understanding all his deeds, so how can I contend with Him, who knows, and is both the witness and the complainant? Therefore, I shall never utter vain things or words of falsehood and iniquity but only words that are true, as it is written: "The remnant of Israel shall not do iniquity." And he should think to himself: If I sin and people get to hear of it, I shall be, in my embarrassment in being found out, compelled to lie about it, saying that I am not guilty and then I shall have committed falsehood, and it is said: "He that speaketh falsehood shall not be established before Mine eyes." So at all times and in

Ps. 16:8

2 Kings 10:18–19 Yal., Kings, par. 23

Zeph. 3:13

Ps. 101:7

every moment a man should dwell on the love of God who searches out the heart and the reins and let him cleave to His commandments and let the fear of God always be upon his face.

THE ROOT of saintliness (*hasidut*) is for man to go beyond the letter of the law, as it is written: "And gracious (*ve-hasid*) in all His works."

Ps. 145:17

THE ROOT of fear is when it is hard for a man to do the thing, as it is said: "For now I know that thou art a God-fearing man."

Gen. 22:12

THE ROOT of prayer is that the heart rejoices in the love of the Holy One, blessed be He, as it is written: "Let the heart of them rejoice that seek the Lord," which is why David used to play on the harp.

1 Chron. 16:10

THE ROOT of the Torah is to study with profundity so as to know how to carry out all God's commands, as it is written: "A good understanding have all they *that do*."

Ps. 111:10

THE ROOT of the precepts consists of eight things corresponding to the eight threads of the *zizit*, as it is written: "And remember all the commandments of the Lord." The first thread represents the eyes, that they should not see any sin; that man should not be haughty; that he should not go after his eyes; that he should not wink with his eyes. These are the negative precepts having to do with the eyes. The positive precepts are: "Only take heed to thyself, and keep thy soul diligently, lest thou forget the things which thine eyes saw"; "He will save him that is lowly of eyes"; "and for a memorial between thine eyes." The second thread represents the ears: "Thou shalt not hear a false report"; not to listen to vain words. This is the negative precept. The positive precept is: "And now, O Israel, hearken unto the statutes." The third thread represents the throat: "Thou shalt not eat any abominable thing." This is the negative precept. The positive precept is to eat unleavened bread on Passover and so forth. The fourth thread represents the or-

Num. 15:39

Deut. 4:9

Job 22:29

Ex. 13:9

Ex. 23:1

Deut. 4:1

Deut. 14:3

gans of speech, the mouth and the tongue, that these should not utter vain words, for if a man does this he transgresses a negative precept, as it is written: "All things toil to weariness; man cannot utter it"; "Thou shalt not take the name of the Lord thy God in vain"; "And ye shall not swear by My name falsely"; "Nor lie to one another"; "Thou shalt not bear false witness." These are the negative precepts. The positive precepts are: "And thou shalt teach them diligently unto thy children"; "And my tongue shall speak of Thy righteousness." The fifth thread represents the hands: "Put not thy hand with the wicked"; "Thou shalt not rob." These are the negative precepts. The positive precepts are: "Thou shalt surely open thy hand" "And thou shall bind them for a sign upon thy hand." The sixth thread represents the feet: "Thou shalt not go up and down as a talebearer"; "And go not after other gods"; "And he that hasteth with his feet sinneth." These are the negative precepts. The positive precepts are: "After the Lord your God shall ye walk"; "Ye shall walk in all the way which the Lord your God hath commanded you"; "Guard thy foot when thou goest to the house of God." The seventh thread corresponds to the sexual organ: "Thou shalt not commit adultery." This is the negative precept. The positive precepts are: "And you, be ye fruitful, and multiply"; and circumcision. The eighth thread corresponds to the nose: anger and stubbornness and smelling the perfumes of idols, as it is written: "And there shall cleave nought of the devoted thing to thy hand." These are the negative precepts. The positive precept is to smell myrtle branches on the Sabbath and so forth.

Let a man remember these eight things. Let them always be in his heart. One, the eyes; two, the ears; three, the tongue; four, the throat; five, the hands; six, the feet; seven, the sexual organ; eight, the nose. He should not sin with any of these and his heart should be on each to plan how to keep these things. A *midrash* on the verse: "The small and

Eccles. 1:8

Ex. 20:7

Lev. 19:12

Lev. 19:11

Ex. 20:13

Deut. 6:7

Ps. 35:28

Ex. 23:1

Lev. 19:13

Deut. 15:8

Deut. 6:8

Lev. 19:16

Jer. 25:6

Prov. 19:2

Deut. 13:5

Deut. 5:30

Eccles. 4:17

Ex. 20:13

Gen. 9: 7

Deut. 13:18

Job 3:19

great are there alike" remarks: If here one is great and the other small, there they are alike. It can be compared to two soldiers who went out to war. One returns with crowns on his shield while the other returns with arrows in his body. Which of the two is greater? Surely it is the one who returns with crowns on his shield. When the wicked man dies his nose decays because he enjoyed the smell of idolatry. His eyes become blind because he went after idols. His head is turned into Hell because the fringes of his hair were grown long so that he could take pride in his long hair, as it is said: *Ez. 32:27* "and they that are inferior to the uncircumcised shall not lie with the mighty." But the righteous is full of good deeds. One, the *tefillin* are on his head; two, his teeth utter words of Torah; three, his mouth studies the *halakhot*; four, his nose smells the *mitzvot*; five, his hands give charity; six, his innards are full of Torah, and he prays to the Holy One, blessed be He; seven, his body is circumcised; eight, his feet lead him to synagogues and houses of learning and so all his body is whole.

THE ROOT of the fear of the Lord is when a man desires something and yet he gives up the pleasure for which his evil inclination craves because he fears the Lord. It is not that he fears punishment in this world or the next but he is afraid that he may not be perfect before God whom he loves. When a good deed presents itself to him and he finds it very difficult to perform, he still performs it, as did Abraham when he bound his son on the altar, as it is written: *Gen. 22:12* "For now I know that thou art a God-fearing man." "*Now* I know?" Surely, He knew it before the world was created, as *Jer. 1:5* it is said: "Before I formed thee in the belly I knew thee." But the meaning is: I shall not test you any further, for since you have done this thing it is known by it that your heart is whole in all that I command you. I do not have to test you any further since if you were ready to do this, all else is included. This has to be understood on the basis of the verse:

"Now I know that the Lord is greater than all gods," i.e., there is no longer any need to try any other gods. And Joseph said: "For I fear God." It is hard for me to send you away since you are spies but I fear God who does not want your children to go hungry. And Obadiah "feared the Lord greatly" because he found it a very difficult thing to do for if Jezebel heard of it she would have had him killed. But when it says: "Thou shalt fear thy God," it refers to something in the heart. And when it says: "Thou shalt fear the Lord thy God" and: "O fear the Lord, ye His holy ones") it refers to things very hard for the heart to bear and they present a challenge to the fear of God. If Abraham had feared God because he imagined that if he did not take Isaac, God would kill him (that would have been a hard thing to do) but here Abraham is prepared to kill himself. This was the most difficult thing of all and yet he overcame his reluctance because he feared God.

THE ROOT of love is to love the Lord. The soul is full of love, bound with the bonds of love in great joy. This joy chases away from his heart all bodily pleasure and worldly delight. The powerful joy of love seizes his heart so that at all times he thinks: How can I do the will of God? The pleasures of his children and the company of his wife are as nothing in comparison with the love of God. Imagine a young man who has not been with a woman for a very long time. He longs for her, his heart burns for her. Imagine his great love and desire when he cohabits with her and how when his sperm shoots like an arrow he has so much pleasure. All this is as nothing compared with his desire to do the will of God, to bring merit to others, to sanctify himself, to sacrifice his life in his love just as Phinehas sacrificed himself to slay Zimri, and like Abraham who said: "I have lifted up my hand unto the Lord, God Most High, Maker of heaven and earth, that I will not take a thread nor a shoe-latchet," like Elisha who refused to take anything from Naa-

Ex. 18:11

Gen. 42:18

1 Kings 18:3

Lev. 19:14
Deut. 10:20
Ps. 34:10

Num. 25:1–9
Gen. 14:22–23

man. The love of Heaven in his heart is like the flame attached to the coal. He does not gaze at women, he does not engage in frivolous talk, but he concerns himself only to toil to do the will of God and he sings songs in order to become filled with joy in the love of God.

THE ROOT of humility is that man keeps himself far from the honor paid to noblemen. If he sits at the feet of his teacher and he knows of a certain problem and appreciates that his teacher or his companion knows of it too, let him allow them to ask and he should remain silent. If they do not ask it, he should say: So-and-so asks this and he gave this reply and he should pay honor to his companion and not take any credit for himself, as it is said: "Choose *us* out men," and it is written: "Whom shall I send, and who will go *for us*?" The reason it says "Whom shall I send?" and not "Whom shall *we* send?" is because of the heretics who would then say that there is more than one divine power. A further mark of humility is that a man should always give precedence to his neighbor's name before his own, as the School of Hillel did for the School of Shammai, and he should always state his neighbor's reasoning before his own. To sum it all up, he should decrease as far as he possibly can his own honor and should increase the honor of those who fear the Lord, as it is written: "But he honoreth them that fear the Lord" and it is written: "In whose eyes a vile person is despised." If he sees modest persons who are greater than he but who in their humility do not wish to walk in front of him, he should walk in front of them even though he is embarrassed by it. For this is true humility in that he is prepared to suffer embarrassment by honoring them in that they allow him to go in front. If a man is called "teacher" he should not call him "Rabbi" because this causes him to be embarrassed. A man should not praise one of his teachers in the presence of another of his teachers and he should not say: "Your teacher said thus," as we find in the first chapter

2 Kings 5:16

Ex. 17:9
Isa. 6:8

Ps. 15:4

of *Yevamot*, page 19, that the disciples of Rabbi Eliezer, when referring to Rabban Johanan ben Zakkai, said: "Your colleagues permitted it."[1] And a man should never be pleased with himself when others praise him and he should never praise himself, as it is written: "Let another man praise thee, and not thine own mouth," except that a man may praise himself to colleagues and disciples if his intention is for them to learn from his ways, as it is said: "And I was single-hearted with Him"; "For I have kept the way of the Lord"; "And the saying of the man raised on high." And the same applies to the rabbinic statements about longevity, where the disciples ask their master to what he attributes his long life and he tells them in order that they should do likewise.

Prov. 27:2

Ps. 18:24
Ps. 18:22
2 Sam 23:1

Meg. 27b–28a

Carry out all your good deeds in secret and walk humbly with thy God. But if you do it in order that they might learn from you, then do it in the presence of all; for example, *tefillin* and *ẓiẓit* and studying the Torah, for the envy of the scribes increases wisdom and good deeds. Whenever you are about to perform a good deed, do it for the sake of heaven, as it is said: "If thou be righteous thou doest for Him." Any good deed that others overlook, you do it and let the love of your Creator be in your heart and the fear of your Maker upon your countenance. Be energetic in performing good deeds and never speak vain things.

BB 21a

Job 35:7

In all places, and especially in the synagogue where the *Shekhina* is in front of you, sit in His presence in dread and set your heart to give thanks unto Him. It is not sufficient that you refrain from committing the sins for which a man suffers embarrassment when he is found out; even if you refrain when no one knows, do not do so because you are afraid that they might find out. But even the sins which everyone commits, your reward is double if you refuse to commit them. For all men gaze at the face of a king and the face of a woman. To be sure it is a *mitzvah* to gaze at the countenance of the king, for "thine eyes shall see the king

Isa. 33:17

in his beauty." But it is forbidden to gaze at women, as it is said in the first chapter of tractate *Avodah Zarah* [20b] that it is even forbidden to gaze at a single girl, how much more so at a married woman. So if you control yourself and refuse to gaze at women your reward will be doubled and doubled again. And know that the more one speaks the greater the likelihood of sinning. Consider the loss caused by a good deed in relation to the gain thereof and let all your deeds be for the sake of heaven. It is good that you take greater care in this matter than others do. If you will so do, then happy are you in this world and it shall be well with you in the next. My help is from the Lord, Maker of heaven and earth.

Comments

1. The quotation from "the first chapter of tractate *Yevamot*, page 19," is a printer's error. It is not clear exactly to which passage the reference is.

6.

The Prophetic
Mysticism of
Abraham Abulafia

Introduction

Abraham ben Samuel Abulafia, who was born in Saragossa, Spain, in 1240, developed the theory of prophetic mysticism. He believed that his technique of combining the letters of the various divine names would result, if undertaken with a spirit of purity and dedication, in an outpouring of the holy spirit, so that the adept would become a prophet. He claimed that he himself had reached such a status and implied that he was the Messiah, for which he was severely criticized by the official representatives of Judaism, especially the famous Rabbi Solomon Ibn Adret of Barcelona (*Responsa Rashba*, no. 548). Abulafia wandered from place to place attracting disciples. In the first passage from his writings here translated, there is a reference to the imprisonment of a disciple, and this probably refers to the persecutions Abulafia's own disciples were obliged to endure. This passage was published by A. Jellinek from a manuscript source together with Abulafia's *Sefer ha-Ot*, under the title "Apokalypse des Pseudo-Propheten und Pseudo-Messias Abraham Abulafia," in *Graetz-Jubelschrift* (1887), 65–88. The second passage is from Abulafia's *Sefer Ḥayyei ha-Olam ha-Ba*, and was translated by G. Scholem from manuscript and included in his *Major Trends in Jewish Mysticism* (1955³), 136–37. The lengthy third selection by a disciple of Abraham Abulafia is from a book written in 1295 called *Sha'arei Ẓedek*. The translation, also by G. Scholem, appears in *Major Trends in Jewish Mysticism*, 147–55.

Text

I. ON PROPHECY

Prophecy is a mode of the Intellect (*inyan silkhli*).[1] It is the expression of the love of the Lord our God, the Lord is One. It is well known that those who love prophecy love God and they are beloved of God. Undoubtedly these are called sages and prophets. Observe and realize that the numerical value of the word "lovers" (*'ohavim*) is the same as that of the word "prophecy" (*nevu'ah*) and by "lovers" I mean "beloved prophets." This stage of prophecy is itself the worship of God in love. Appreciate that whoever knows the name of God has the spirit of God, the holy spirit, within him. That holy influence, descending by virtue of divine grace, will bestir, move and incline a man to strive to attain the knowledge of God so as to sanctify Him and declare His name to all the earth. Know and realize that those who prophesy by virtue of their knowledge of God are beloved of God. Now, my son, you may have misgivings, saying to yourself: When will I ever reach this lofty stage since there are so many hindrances, as I am only too well aware, caused by my weak constitution, for instance, and there seems to be no way of changing it so as to be able to reach this stage? There is also the hindrance caused by poverty, which demands the pursuit of food, clothing and economic satisfaction, essential if man is to remain in a state of stability. There is also the hindrance caused by exile in which a man is like a slave sold to those who force him to toil in order to make bricks and mortar. And there are many similar hindrances. But, my son, I swear to you that all these are excuses made by that harsh evil inclination which engages in battle in order to seduce you to die without wisdom, understanding and the knowledge of God, soiling you with bricks and mortar so that no portion in the World to Come can be given you.

If, however, God is with you, it is right for you to consider that wisdom is the food of the soul, so that if wisdom, I mean the true wisdom, is lacking, the soul will expire through death by torture; that soul shall be utterly cut off with its sin upon it. But if you do not lack the true wisdom then you will live, for of it Scripture says: "For it is your life *Deut. 30:20* and the length of your days." Reflect upon this: Just as the body dies without food so the soul needs this science. Appreciate how improper it is for the hungry man to say that he refuses to eat all but the most delicious food. Rather he should be happy, for the time being, to eat whatever food comes his way to satisfy his hunger, otherwise he will die, and when he is able to eat better food he can then eat as much as he requires. So must you do, my son, with regard to the true science. If you hunger and thirst for it, it is only right for you to satisfy your hunger and slake your thirst from whatever is to hand in order to save your soul from the pit. For it matters not whether one achieves much or little provided the intention is for the sake of heaven. But this applies only to one who strives unceasingly to allow his heart to reach out to acquire wisdom. Then will he be able to comprehend, by studying daily and to the best of his ability, at the feet of sages and by reading the holy books. But let him not say: "My heart is directed towards heaven and all my deeds are for the sake of heaven" if he has little interest in the deeds that can bring him the wisdom God loves and if he is unaware that while study inevitably leads to practice it does not follow that practice inevitably leads to study. He should be aware that practice is easy even for youths, to say nothing of intellectuals, whereas study, which is the science of God, is hard even for the venerable, to say nothing of those afflicted by vain delusions, imagining that deeds are acceptable merely because there has been an utterance of the mouth or because a deluded impression has been made on the heart. For no deed is good at all unless it be based on the practice of this science. Then, and not as commands learned by rote, is it acceptable to God.

Hul. 13b   Observe and appreciate how our Sages of blessed memory hinted at this when they said that the Gentiles are not idolators and yet we see that all their efforts and all their deeds are based on idolatry. But the meaning is that since there is no understanding of the basic idea, it is as if it has no significance. So, you see, an act without knowledge is nothing at all. Observe that the Sages continue: "For they [the Gentiles] simply follow the habits of their ancestors," namely, as commands learned by rote.[2]

Know, my son, that whoever fails to strive to acquire this science, to know the deeds required by God and carry them out adequately, if not in totality at least partially, the reason for it is because of the evil inclinations which kills the living, and God will judge such a one for failing to choose life. If you will reflect on this no hindrance whatsoever will prevent you from seeking wisdom. For you will know that if these hindrances sought to prevent you from eating the food your body requires, you would not stand for it but would cry out to God and to His creatures to sustain you and you would be prepared to run from city to city. You would even fly in the air, were you able to do it, all for the sake of obtaining the sustenance you need in any way possible. And all this is for keeping the body, drawn to the evil inclination, alive. If God will help you keep this picture in your mind, to have confidence in it and to follow it with all the strength you can muster, know that no hindrance—whether it be of poverty or exile or even of imprisonment—will prevent you from seeking wisdom, understanding and knowledge, ruler in all of the six directions. Who is so stupid, coarse and insensitive not to flee from death when he knows what death is, a descent into the abyss? And yet the majority of men cannot distinguish between life and death but in their ignorance try to turn life itself into death, fleeing from eternal life in order to prefer temporal existence. They engage in much activity and kill themselves before their time in their efforts to leave their wealth to others, it may be their enemies or their sons, in order that these, too, might enjoy that inferior order of life over which time has dominion and they fail to realize that they and all that is theirs are His. And know, my son, that as a result of this they forget eternal life completely until they return to the darkness they have preferred. It is in this connection that the prophet cries out: "Woe unto them who declare evil *Isa. 5:20* good and good evil, who turn darkness into light and light into darkness, who make the bitter sweet and the sweet bitter."

But you, my son, if you are wise and love God with all your heart, reflect on the root from which you were hewn. Know that you have been taken from the Throne of Glory and have been endowed with the light of reason and have been created in God's image and have been brought into existence by the grace of His Being and your coming here has not been purposeless. Return therefore, for the Holy One of Israel has redeemed you and His holy name is your glory. Hearken, therefore, my son to these words of mine. Bind them upon your neck, write them upon the tablets of your heart. They will be a diadem of grace upon your head and a necklace around your throat. Trust in God, not in man, for cursed is he who trusts in man.

Strive day and night to meditate on the Torah of the Lord, the Torah of Moses the man of God, the divine wisdom. Read the prophetic books with understanding. Şing the words of the Hagiographa. Study the sayings of the Sages of blessed memory with a clear and alert mind. Gaze with divine intelligence into the works of the kabbalists. Here you will discover that which you seek and you will see that they all cry out in protest against the absence of wisdom, against unworthy deeds, and against limited understanding. For not a single word contains neither wisdom nor understanding nor knowledge nor word nor deeds, in the Torah, the Prophets, the Hagiographa and all the words of the Rabbis.

After you have done this set your heart to know the glorious and tremendous name of God, blessed be He. Engrave it upon your heart never to be erased. For in this connection the Rabbis say that the sacred names are not to be erased. Since they point to a picture of God, how then can that which depicts be erased since He who is depicted can never be erased? Never utter the names without concentration but sanctify them, know them, and reflect that they are the angels of all being and the angels of God sent to you in order to raise you higher and higher and elevate you over all the nations upon earth. All the people on earth will see that the name of the Lord is called upon you and they will fear you.

Here is the strong foundation which I deliver to you that you should know it and engrave it upon your heart: The Holy Name. The whole of the Torah, the sacred Scriptures and all the prophetic books, are all full of divine names and tremendous things. Join one to the other. Depict them to yourself. Test them, try them, combine them. Consider that they are the writtings of the King who has sent them to you that it may be well with you and that you may live long. Occupy yourself with them, with a refined, pure and clear activity, and keep yourself far from all sin and transgression and clean from all guilt, iniquity and wickedness.

Now the time has come to elevate you in the stages of love so that you become beloved on high and delightful here on earth. First, begin by combining the letters of the name YHWH. Gaze at all its combinations. Elevate it. Turn it over like a wheel which goes round and round, backwards and forward like a scroll. Do not leave it aside except when you observe that it is becoming too much for you because of the confused movements in your imagination. Leave it for a while and you will be able to return to it later. You can then make your request of it and when you attain to wisdom do not forsake it. For the initial letters and the final letters, the numerical values, the *notarikons*, the combination of letters and their permutations, their accents and the forms they assume, the knowledge of their names and the grasping of their ideas, the changing of many words into one and one into many, all these belong to the authentic tradition of the prophets. By means of these God will answer when you call upon Him, for you belong to His family. And now, my son, the secret of the Lord is with them that fear Him and to them will He make His covenant known. He will make known His covenant to the man who fears Heaven and whose covenant is perfect. Otherwise, He will hide it, for honor is not fitting for the fool.

We know by a prophetic divine tradition of the Torah that when the sage who is an adept combines (the letters of the divine name) one with the other, the holy spirit flows into him. This is the sign. When you look at these holy letters in truth and reliance and when you combine them—

placing that which is at the beginning at the end and that which is at the end at the beginning, that which is the middle at the beginning and that which is at the beginning in the middle, that which is at the end in the middle and that which is in the middle at the end and so forth in like manner—these letters will all roll backwards and forward with many melodies. Let him begin gently and then make haste. Let him train himself to be thoroughly familiar with the changes as they are combined and it is essential, too, for him to be thoroughly familiar with the secrets of the Torah and the wisdom thereof in order to know that which he brings about through these combinations. Let him awaken his heart to reflect on the spiritual, divine, prophetic picture. At first, when he engages in the task of combination in solitude, a feeling of terror and trembling will result so that his hair will stand on end and his limbs will tremble. Afterwards, if he is worthy, the spirit of the living God will pass over him and the spirit of the Lord will rest upon him, the spirit of wisdom and understanding, the spirit of counsel and might, the spirit of knowledge and the fear of the Lord. It will seem to him then as if his body had been anointed, from head to foot, with anointing oil. He will become the anointed of the Lord and His agent. He will be called an angel of God and his name will be that of his Master, *Shaddai*, as Metatron, the Prince of the Presence, is called. The numerical value of Metatron and *Shaddai* is the same.[3]

II. ABULAFIA'S TECHNIQUE

Be prepared for thy God, O Israelite! Make thyself ready to direct thy heart to God alone. Cleanse thy body and choose a lonely house where none shall hear thy voice. Sit there in thy closet and do not reveal thy secret to any man. If thou canst, do it by day in the house, but it is best if thou completest it during the night. In the hour when thou preparest thyself to speak with the Creator and thou wishest Him to reveal His might to thee, then be careful to abstract all thy thought from the vanities of this world. Cover thyself with thy prayer shawl and put *tefillin* on thy head and hands that thou mayest be filled with awe of the *Shekhina* which is near thee. Cleanse thy clothes, and, if possible, let all thy garments be white, for all this is helpful in leading the heart towards the fear of God and the love of God. If it be night, kindle many lights, until all be bright. Then take ink, pen and a table to thy hand and remember that thou art about to serve God in joy of the gladness of heart. Now begin to combine a few or many letters, to permute and to combine them until thy heart be warm. Then be mindful of their movements and of what thou canst bring forth by moving them. And when thou feelest that thy heart is already warm and when thou seest that by combinations of letters thou canst grasp new things which by human tradition or by thyself thou wouldst not be able to know and when thou art thus prepared to receive the influx of divine power which flows into thee, then turn all thy true thought to imagine His name and His exalted angels in thy heart as if they were human beings sitting or standing about thee. And feel thyself like an envoy whom the king and his ministers are to send on a mission, and he is waiting to hear something about his mission from their lips, be it from the king himself, be it from his servants. Having imagined this very vividly turn thy whole mind to understand with thy thoughts the many things which will come into thy heart through the letters imagined. Ponder on them as a whole and in all their detail, like one to whom a parable or a dream is being related, or who meditates on a deep problem in a scientific book, and try thus to interpret what thou shalt hear that it may as far as possible accord with thy reason, . . . And all this will happen to thee after having flung away tablet and quill or after they have dropped from thee because of the intensity of thy thought. And know, the stronger the intellectual influx within thee, the weaker will become thy outer and thy inner parts. Thy whole body will be seized by an extremely strong trembling, so that thou wilt think that surely thou art about to die, because thy soul, overjoyed with its knowledge, will leave thy body. And be thou ready at this moment consciously to choose death, and then thou shalt know that thou hast come far enough to receive the influx. And then wishing to honor the glorious Name by serving it with the life of body and soul, veil thy face and be afraid to look at God. Then return to the matters of the body, rise and eat and drink a little, or refresh thyself with a pleasant odor, and restore thy spirit to its sheath until another time, and rejoice at thy lot and know that God loveth thee!

III. THE TESTIMONY OF
ABULAFIA'S DISCIPLE

I, so and so, one of the lowliest, have probed my heart for ways of grace to bring about spiritual expansion, and I have found three ways of progress towards spiritualization: the vulgar, the philosophic, and the kabbalistic way. The vulgar way is that which, so I learned, is practiced by Muslim ascetics. They employ all manner of devices to shut out from their souls all "natural forms," every image of the familiar, natural world. Then, they say, when a spiritual form, an image from the spiritual world, enters their soul, it is isolated in their imagination and intensifies the imagination to such a degree that they can determine beforehand that which is to happen to us. Upon inquiry, I learned that they summon the Name, ALLAH, as it is in the language of Ishmael. I investigated further and I found that, when they pronounce these letters, they direct their thought completely away from every possible "natural form," and the very letters ALLAH and their diverse powers work upon them. They are carried off into a trance without realizing how, since no *kabbalah* has been transmitted to them. The removal of all natural forms and images from the soul is called *Effacement*.

The second way is the philosophic, and the student will experience extreme difficulty in attempting to drive it from his soul because of the great sweetness it holds for the human reason and the completeness with which that reason knows to embrace it. It consists in this: That the student forms a notion of some science, mathematics for instance, and then proceeds by analogy to some natural science and then goes on to theology. He then continues further to circle round this center of his, because of the sweetness of that which arises in him as he progresses in these studies. The sweetness of this so delights him that he finds neither gate nor door to enable him to pass beyond the notions which have already been established in him. At best, he can perhaps enjoy a (contemplative) spinning out of his thoughts and to this he will abandon himself, retiring into seclusion in order that no one may disturb his thought until it proceeds a little beyond the purely philosophic and turns as the flaming sword which turned every way. The true cause of all this is to be found in his contemplation of the letters through which, as intermediaries, he ascertains things. The subject which impressed itself on his human reason dominates him and his power seems to him great in all the sciences, seeing that this is natural to him. He contends that given things are revealed to him by way of prophecy, although he does not realize the true cause, but rather thinks that this occurred to him merely because of the extension and enlargement of his human reason. . . . But in reality it is the letters ascertained through thought and imagination, which influence him through their motion and which concentrate his thought on difficult themes, although he is not aware of this.

But if you put the difficult question to me: "Why do we nowadays pronounce letters and move them and try to produce effects with them without however noticing any effect being produced by them?"—the answer lies, as I am going to demonstrate with the help of *Shaddai*, in the third way of inducing spiritualization. And I, the humble so and so, am going to tell you what I experienced in this matter.

Know, friends, that from the beginning I felt a desire to study Torah and learned a little of it and of the rest of Scripture. But I found no one to guide me in the study of the Talmud, not so much because of the lack of teachers, but rather because of my longing for my home, and my love for father and mother. At last, however, God gave me strength to search for the Torah; I went out and sought and found, and for several years I stayed abroad studying Talmud. But the flame of the Torah kept glowing within me, though without my realizing it.

I returned to my native land and God brought me together with a Jewish philosopher with whom I studied some of Maimonides' *Guide of the Perplexed* and this only added to my desire. I acquired a little of the science of logic and a little of natural science, and this was very sweet to me for, as you know, "nature attracts nature." And God is my witness: If I had not previously acquired strength of faith by what little I had learned of the Torah and the Talmud, the impulse to keep many of the religious commands would have left me although the fire of pure intention was ablaze in my heart. But what this teacher communicated to me in the way of philosophy (on the meaning of the commandments), did not suffice me, until the Lord had me meet a godly man, a kabbalist who taught me the general outlines of the Kabbalah. Nevertheless, in consequence of my smattering of natural science, the way of Kabbalah seemed all but impossible to me. It was then that my teacher said to me: "My son, why do you deny something you have not tried? Much, rather, would it befit you to make a trial of it. If you then should find that it is nothing to you—and if you are not perfect enough to find the fault with yourself—then you may say that there is nothing to it." But in order to make things sweet to me until my reason might accept them and I might penetrate into them with eagerness, he used always to make me grasp in a natural way everything in which he instructed me. I reasoned thus within myself: There can only be gain here and no loss. I shall see; if I find something in all of this, that is sheer gain; and if not, that which I have already had will still be mine. So I gave in and he taught me the method of the permutations and combinations of letters and the mysticism of numbers and the other "Paths of the book *Yezirah*." In each path he had me wander for two weeks until each form had been engraven in my heart, and so he led on for four months or so and then ordered me to "efface" everything.

He used to tell me: "My son, it is not the intention that you come to a stop with some finite or given form, even though it be of the highest order. Much rather is this the 'Path of the Names.' The less understandable they are, the higher their order, until you arrive at the activity of a force which is no longer under your control, but rather your reason and your thought is in its control." I replied: "If that be so [that all mental and sense images must be effaced], why then do you, Sir, compose books in which the methods of the natural scientists are coupled with instruction in the holy Names?" He answered: "For you and the likes of you among the followers of philosophy, to allure your human intellect through natural means, so that perhaps this attraction may cause you to arrive at the knowledge of the Holy Name." And he produced books for me made up (of combinations of) letters and names and mystic numbers, of which nobody will ever be able to understand anything, for they are not composed in a way meant to be understood. He said to me: "This is the 'Path of the Names.'" And indeed, I would see none of it, for my reason did accept it. He said: "It was very stupid of me to have shown them to you."

In short, after two months had elapsed and my thought had disengaged itself (from everything material) and I had become aware of strange phenomena occurring within me, I set myself the task at night of combining letters with one another and of pondering over them in philosophical meditation, a little different from the way I do now, and so I continued for three nights without telling him. The third night, after midnight, I nodded off a little, quill in my hands and paper on my knees. Then I noticed that the candle was about to go out. I rose to put it right, as oftentimes happens to a person awake. Then I saw that the light continued. I was greatly astonished, as though, after close examination, I saw that it issued from myself. I said: "I do not believe it." I walked to and fro all through the house and, behold, the light is with me; I lay on a couch and covered myself up, and behold, the light is with me all the while. I said: "This is truly a great sign and a new phenomenon which I have perceived."

The next morning I communicated it to my teacher and I brought him the sheets which I had covered with combinations of letters. He congratulated me and said: "My son, if you would devote yourself to combining holy Names, still greater things would happen to you. And now, my son, admit that you are unable to bear not combining. Give half to this and half to that, that is, do combinations half of the night, and permutations half of the night." I practiced this method for about a week. During the second week the power of meditation became so strong in me that I could not manage to write down the combinations of letters (which automatically spurted out of my pen), and if there had been ten people present they would not have been able to write down so many combinations as came to me during the influx. When I came to the night in which this power was conferred on me, and midnight—when this power especially expands and gains strength whereas the body weakens—had passed, I set out to take up the Great Name of God, consisting of seventy-two names,[4] permuting and combining it. But when I had done this for a little while, behold, the letters took on in my eyes the shape of great mountains, strong trembling seized me and I could summon no strength, my hair stood on end, and it was as if I were not in this world. At once I fell down, for I no longer felt the least strength in any of my limbs. And behold, something resembling speech emerged from my heart and came to my lips and forced them to move. I thought—perhaps this is, God forbid, a spirit of madness that has entered into me? But behold, I saw it uttering wisdom. I said: "This is indeed the spirit of wisdom." After a little while my natural strength returned to me, I rose very much impaired and I still did not believe myself. Once more I took up the Name to do with it as before and, behold, it had exactly the same effect on me. Nevertheless I did not believe until I had tried it four or five times.

When I got up in the morning I told my teacher about it. He said to me: "And who was it that allowed you to touch the Name? Did I not tell you to permute only letters?" He spoke on: "What happened to you represents indeed a high stage among prophetic degrees." He wanted to free me of it for he saw that my face had changed. But I said to him: "In heaven's name, can you perhaps impart to me some power to enable me to bear this force emerging from my heart and to receive influx from it?" For I wanted to draw this force towards me and receive influx from it, for it much resembles a spring filling a great basin with water. If a man (not being properly prepared for it) should open the dam, he would be drowned in its waters and his soul would desert him. He said to me: "My son, it is the Lord who must bestow such power upon you, for such power is not within man's control."

That Sabbath night also the power was active in me in the same way. When after two sleepless nights, I had passed day and night in meditating on the permutations or on the principles essential to a recognition of the true reality and to the annihilations of all extraneous thought—then I had two signs by which I knew that I was in the right receptive mood. The one sign was the intensification of natural thought on very profound objects of knowledge, a debility of the body and strengthening of the soul until I sat there, my self all soul. The second sign was that imagination grew strong within me and it seemed as though my forehead was going to burst. Then I knew that I was ready to receive the Name. I also, that Sabbath night, ventured at the great ineffable Name of God (the name YHWH). But immediately that I touched it, it weakened me and a voice issued from me saying: "Thou shalt surely die and not live! Who brought thee to touch the Great Name?" And behold, immediately I fell prone and implored the Lord God saying: *1 Chron. 28:9* "Lord of the universe! I entered into this place only for the sake of heaven, as Thy glory knoweth. What is my sin and what my transgression? I entered only to know Thee, for has not David already commanded Solomon: "Know the God of thy father and serve Him"; and has not our master Moses, peace be upon him, revealed this to us in the Torah *Ex. 33:13* saying: "Show me now Thy way, that I may know Thee, that I may there find grace in Thy sight?" And behold, I was still speaking and oil like the oil of the anointment anointed me from head to foot and very great joy seized me which for its spirituality and the sweetness of its rapture I cannot describe.

All this happened to your servant in his beginnings. And

I do not, God forbid, relate this account from boastfulness in order to be thought great in the eyes of the mob, for I know full well that greatness with the mob is deficiency and inferiority with those searching for the true rank which differs from it in genus and in species as light from darkness.

Now, if some of our own philosophizers, sons of our people who feel themselves attracted towards the naturalistic way of knowledge and whose intellectual power in regard to the mysteries of the Torah is very weak, read this, they will laugh at me and say: See how he tries to attract our reason with windy talk and tales, with fanciful imaginations which have muddled his mind and which he takes at their face value because of his weak mental hold on natural science. Should however kabbalists see this, such as have some grasp of this subject or even better such as have had things divulged to them in experiences of their own, they will rejoice and my words will win their favor. But their difficulty will be that I have disclosed all of this in detail. Nevertheless, God is my witness that my intention is *in majorem dei gloriam*, and I would wish that every single one of our holy nation were even more excellent herein and purer than I. Perhaps it would then be possible to reveal things of which I do not as yet know. . . . As for me, I cannot bear not to give generously to others what God has bestowed upon me. But since for this science there is no naturalistic evidence, its premises being as spiritual as are its inferences, I was forced to tell this story of the experience that befell me. Indeed, there is no proof in this science except experience itself. . . . That is why I say, to the man who contests this path, that I can give him an experimental proof, namely my own evidence of the spiritual results of my own experiences in the science of letters according to the book *Yezirah*. I did not, to be sure, experience the corporeal (magic) effects (of such practices); and even granting the possibility of such a form of experience, I for my part want none of it, for it is an inferior form, especially when measured by the perfection which the soul can attain spiritually. Indeed, it seems to me that he who attempts to secure these (magic) effects desecrates God's name, and it is this that our teachers hint at when they say: Since license prevailed, the name of God has been taught only by the most reticent priests.

Kid. 71a

The third is the kabbalistic way. It consists of an amalgamation in the soul of man of the principles of mathematical and of natural science, after he has first studied the literal meanings of the Torah and of the faith, in order thus through keen dialectics to train his mind and not in the manner of a simpleton to believe in everything. Of all this he stands in need only because he is held captive by the world of nature. For it is not seemly that a rational being held captive in prison should not search out every means, a hole or a small fissure, of escape. If today we had a prophet who showed us a mechanism for sharpening the natural reason and for discovering there subtle forms by which to divest ourselves of corporeality, we should not need all these natural sciences in addition to our Kabbalah which is derived from the basic principles or heads of chapters of the book *Yeẓirah* concerning the letters (and their combinations). . . . All this he would convey to us directly whereas now we are forced to take circuitous routes and to move about restrainedly and go out and come in on the chance that God may confront us. For as a matter of fact every attainment in this science of Kabbalah looked at from its point of view is only a chance, even though, for us, it is the very essence of our being.

This kabbalistic way, or method, consists, first of all, in the cleansing of the body itself, for the body is symbolic of the spiritual. Next in the order of ascent is the cleansing of your bodily disposition and your spiritual propensities, especially that of anger, or your concern for anything whatsoever except the Name itself, be it even the care for your

only beloved son; and this is the secret of the Scripture that
"God tried Abraham." A further step in the order of ascent   *Gen. 22:1*
is the cleansing of one's soul from all other sciences which
one has studied. The reason for this is that being naturalistic and limited, they contaminate the soul, and obstruct the
passage through it of the divine forms. These forms are extremely subtle; and though even a minor form is something
innately great in comparison with the naturalistic and the
rational, it is nevertheless an unclean, thick veil in comparison with the subtlety of the spirit. On this account seclusion in a separate house is prescribed, and if this be a house
in which no noise can be heard, the better. At the beginning it is advisable to decorate the house with fresh greens
in order to cheer the vegetable soul which a man possesses
side by side with the animal soul. Next, one should pray and
sing Psalms in a pleasant, melodious voice, and (read) the
Torah with fervor, in order to cheer the animal soul which a
man possesses side by side with his rational soul. Next one
directs his imagination to intelligible things and to understanding how one thing proceeds from another. Next, one
proceeds to the moving of letters which (in their combinations) are unintelligible, this to detach the soul (from the
senses) and to cleanse it of all the forms within it. In the
same way, one proceeds with the improvement of his (bodily) matter by meat and drink and improves it (the body) by
degrees. As to the moving of letters, we shall deal with
some methods in the chapter "Letters." Next, one reaches
the stage of "skipping," as Scripture says: "and his banner   *Song 2:4*
over me was love."[5] It consists of meditating, after all opera-
tions with the letters are over, on the essence of one's
thought, and of abstracting from it every word, be it connected with a notion or not. In the performance of this
"skipping" one must put the consonants which one is combining into a swift motion. This motion heats the thinking
and so increases joy and desire that craving for food and

sleep or anything else is annihilated. In abstracting words
from thought during contemplation, you force yourself so
that you pass beyond the control of your natural mind, and
if you desire *not* to think, you cannot carry out your desire.
You then guide your thinking step by step, first by means of
script and language and then by means of imagination.
When, however, you pass beyond the control of your thinking, another exercise becomes necessary which consists in
drawing thought gradually forth—during contemplation—
from its source until through sheer force that stage is
reached where you do not speak nor can you speak. And if
sufficient strength remains to force oneself even further and
draw it out still farther, then that which is within will manifest itself without, and through the power of sheer imagination will take on the form of a polished mirror. And this is
Gen. 3:24 "the flame of the circling sword," the rear revolving and becoming the fore. Whereupon one sees that his inmost being
is something outside of himself. Such was the way of the
Urim and *Thummim*, the priest's oracle of the Torah, in
which, too, at first the letters shine from inside and the
message they convey is not an immediate one nor arranged
in order, but results only from the combination of the letters. For a form, detached from its essence, is defective until
it clothe itself in a form which can be conceived by imagination, and in this imaginable form the letters enter into a
complete, orderly and understandable combination. And it
seems to me that it is this form which the kabbalists call
"clothing," *malbush.*

Comments

I

1. "Intellect" here is a concept much used in medieval philosophy. Seen both as an incorporeal, universal heavenly sub-

stance and as a personal psychic faculty, it is both within man and without.

2. The saying of the Sages about the Gentiles is in the Babylonian Talmud, tractate Ḥullin 13b. Abulafia's argument is that if idolatry is not called such where there is no real understanding of its meaning, it must follow *a fortiori* that the bare practice of the precepts is meaningless without an understanding of their (mystical) significance.

3. On Metatron see comments to chapter 3.

III

Although Abulafia's name is not mentioned explicitly in this passage he is obviously the sage referred to, as Scholem has demonstrated and as becomes perfectly clear when this passage is compared with I and II.

4. The Great Name of 72 names is derived from the letters of verses 19 to 21 of the Book of Exodus.

5. The reference to "skipping" is in *Midrash Song of Songs* 2:4 where the word *ve-diglo*, "his banner," is read as *dillugo*, "his skipping." In the context the meaning is that even if a man skips certain words of the prayers God still hears them. Here the meaning is that an aspect of the technique is to skip certain letters and combine the others.

7

Responsa from Heaven

∾

Introduction

The following text consists of extracts from one of the most remarkable books in Jewish literature: *She'elot u-Teshuvot min ha-Shamayyim* ("Responsa from Heaven") by Jacob of Marvège (12th–13th century). The translation is based on the edition of Reuben Margaliot (1957³), a critical edition based on the first printed edition together with supplementary questions from manuscript. The numbers are those of Margaliot.

Responsa literature in general contains the questions put to distinguished legal authorities and their replies. Doubts arose from time to time, especially when the authorities disagreed, as to what the actual ruling was in a given case. The usual procedure was for the great respondents to work out the decision on the basis of the Talmud and the codes of law by means of their own reasoning. *She'elot u-Teshuvot min ha-Shamayyim* is unique in that the questions are addressed *by* a great master of the law, not *to* one, and the replies are given "from heaven," i.e., in a dream. There is a considerable discussion among the later codifiers whether Jacob of Marvège's procedure was legitimate. Is a sage allowed to appeal to heaven instead of working out the matter for himself? The Talmud seems to frown on any appeal to the supernatural in matters where the law has to be decided, but the later defenders of *She'elot u-Teshuvot min ha-Shamayyim* made the distinction between an appeal to heaven to decide a law that was in doubt, which was illegitimate, and an appeal to decide among conflicting opinions, which was quite legitimate (see the lengthy discussion in Azulai and in greater detail in Margaliot, Introduction).

It is clear from the following that Jacob of Marvège did not simply wait for a dream to come to him but "submitted" the questions to heaven before he went to sleep. A few details of his technique are given and it is likely that in addition he fasted beforehand and used various combinations of divine names in order to achieve the desired result. In any event (as Margaliot has shown) techniques of this kind were used by other practitioners of the art.

Text

1. I ASKED: When women recite the benediction over the *lulav* or when someone recites the benediction over blowing the *shofar* on behalf of women is it or is it not wrong and is the benediction in such cases a vain benediction?

THEY REPLIED: Have the generations improved? "In all that Sarah saith unto thee, hearken unto her voice"; "Go say to them: Return ye to your tents"; "And bless the Lord your God." The proof is from *Megillah* and Ḥanukkah. This they explained as follows: Just as we find that women are obliged to keep the precepts of *Megillah* and Ḥanukkah, and

Gen. 21:12
Deut. 5:27
Neh. 9:5

they recite the benediction over them, because they, too, were involved in the miracle, so, too, with regard to *lulav* there is support for women keeping this precept, since the *lulav* has only one heart and that is directed to its Father in Heaven. And in connection with the *shofar*, too, we say that the Holy One, blessed be He, says: "Recite *Malkhuyyot* before Me so as to make Me King over you; recite *Zikhronot* so that the remembrance of your ancestors should come before Me for good; and how should you do this? by means of the *shofar*." Women also require to be remembered for good. Consequently, if they wish to recite the benedictions over the *lulav* and the *shofar*, they are allowed to do so.

3. I ASKED ANOTHER QUESTION: This is how I asked it: O Great, Mighty and Awesome King, Wise in secrets, Revealing mysteries, Telling hidden things, Keeping the Covenant of Mercy, let Thy Mercy be great this day and command Thy holy angels to impart information to me concerning the doubts we have in connection with the correct order of the sections of the *tefillin*. For some authorities say that the sections beginning with: "And it shall come to pass" have to be in the middle, otherwise the *tefillin* are unfit for use, while other authorities say that the sections have to be placed in the order in which they occur in Scripture, otherwise the *tefillin* are unfit for use. Now, O King of kings, command Thy holy angels to inform me of the correct ruling and which opinion is preferred by Thee.

THEY REPLIED: Both opinions are the words of the living God. Just as there is a debate on earth so is there a debate on high. The Holy One, blessed be He, holds that these sections have to be in the middle but all the Heavenly Family holds that the sections have to follow the order in which *Lev. 10:3* they appear in Scripture. "This is it that the Lord spoke, saying: Through them that are nigh unto Me I will be sanctified, and before all the people I will glorified." This is His glory that the section containing the "yoke of the Kingdom of Heaven" should be placed first.

5. We had further doubt regarding the need for those who have had a seminal emission to undergo immersion. For we say that this immersion has been nullified following the opinion of Rabbi Judah ben Bathyra. But the *geonim* write that this ruling only applies to the reading of the *Shema* and to the study of the Torah. Before prayers immersion is required or, the pouring of nine *kav* of water over the body. Others, however, argue that the nullification applies to prayers as well. These rely on the Jerusalem Talmud, Chapter *Yom ha-Kippurim*. The Mishnah states that it is forbidden to bathe and to have marital relations on the Day of Atonement. The Jerusalem Talmud asks: Since it is stated that to bathe on the Day of Atonement is forbidden, why should it be necessary to state that marital relations are forbidden? They would be forbidden, in any event, since the prayers on that day could not be recited without immersion, which is forbidden. The answer given is that the Mishnah speaks of a place in which it is not customary to have immersion or that the Mishnah was taught at a time prior to the enactment of immersion. THIS WAS MY QUESTION: Can one rely on the Jerusalem Talmud that the enactment of Ezra was not accepted everywhere, so that where it is in operation it is in operation, but elsewhere it is permitted to say the prayers without undergoing immersion or having nine *kav* poured over the body, or is the ruling according to the *geonim* who are strict in the matter, holding that immersion or nine *kav* is required?

THEY REPLIED: "And ye shall serve the Lord your God," Ex. 23:25 which refers to prayer and how can one who is unclean offer a sacrifice? If you argue that it only applies to other forms of impurity, on the contrary, impurity which comes inadvertently cannot be compared in severity to impurity which comes as a result of intention, and impurity which comes from elsewhere cannot be compared in severity to impurity which proceeds from man's own body. And when Ezra ordained it he did so in accordance with his vision by means of the holy spirit. As for the Jerusalem Talmud, if Ezra had been present when they discussed this question in the House of Learning they would not have had a leg to stand on. Furthermore, the Jerusalem Talmud itself changes its mind and goes on to say that the Mishnah was recorded before Ezra's enactment. This thing causes the exile to be prolonged. For if the prayers of Israel had been offered correctly the prayers of Israel would have been accepted long ago. However, the burden of exile and the Torah they study and the good deeds they perform, these stand on Israel's side.

AFTERWARDS THEY REPLIED: We have heard from behind the curtain that it is impossible for all Israel to be pure. But if the leaders of the prayers everywhere will purify themselves it will hasten the advent of the Redeemer. "And in every place where a pure offering is brought to Me I shall come there to bless you."

Ex. 20:21

After I had seen all this I ASKED, on the night of the third day, the nineteenth day of Kislev, if this had come to me from the Lord or if not. THIS IS HOW I ASKED IT: O Supernal King, the Great, Mighty and Awesome God, Who keeps His covenant of mercy to those who love Him, keep Thy covenant of mercy with us. Command Thy holy angels appointed to give replies to questions put in dreams to reply to me that which I ask from before Thy glorious Throne. Let it be a true and correct reply, each thing in its place, clearly defined, whether in connection with Scripture or with legal rulings, so that no further doubt will be possible, Behold, I ASK: All those things that came into my mouth as a result of the question I asked concern the immersion of those who have had a seminal emission, did these things come to me by the holy spirit? Is it advantageous and correct to reveal them to my son-in-law, Rabbi Joseph, and to instruct him to inform the sages of the land of them, or did they come to me by another spirit so that they have no advantage and it is better for me to conceal and hide them?

THEY REPLIED: They were truly the word of the Lord and the words are ancient, the Ancient of Days said them. Today is a day of good tidings. They waited until morning and then they replied: "And the man that doeth presumptuously, in not hearkening unto the priest that standeth to minister there . . . even that man shall die"; "Behold, I am with thee, and will keep thee, whithersoever thou goest."

Deut. 17:12

Gen. 28:15

9. I ASKED ANOTHER QUESTION: Is it permitted to make theurgic use of the Holy Name of forty-two letters, to conjure the holy angels appointed over the Torah to make a man wise in all that he studies and never forget his learning? And is it permitted to conjure by means of the name the angels appointed over wealth and victory over enemies and in order to find grace in the eyes of princes? Or is it forbidden to make theurgic use of the name for any of these purposes?

THEY REPLIED: "Holy, holy, holy, is the name of Lord of hosts." He alone will satisfy all your needs.

Isa. 6:3

26. I ASKED ANOTHER QUESTION: Do those who fail to don the *tefillin* daily commit a great sin and will they be heavily punished? Can it be compared to the case of those who say to a man: "Make a *sukkah*" and he fails to do so, or: "Take the *lulav*" and he fails to do so? There the rule is that he is to be flogged until he expires or until he fulfills his obligation, or is the case of *tefillin* different since it can be argued: The *tefillin* require a clean body so that no one is allowed to sleep in them or to break wind while wearing them and that is why we do not wear them daily?

THEY REPLIED: We do not compare one precept to the other. There are light precepts such as *sukkah* and *lulav* and the like where one who fails to perform them is severely punished because his failure suggests that he denies them. But one who fails to carry out part of a precept cannot be compared to one who nullifies the whole of a precept. And the Torah was not given to the ministering angels. All this is the answer they truly gave to me. So it appears that the punishment is not as great as is that of one who fails to carry out the precept of the *sukkah*. For all that, it is sinful if we do not wear the *tefillin* out of fear that we might sleep in them or break wind while wearing them. For it is better to nullify a part than the whole.

Comments

1. Strictly speaking women have no obligation to take the palm branch (*lulav*) on the festival of Tabernacles (Sukkot) or to hear the blowing of the ram's horn (*shofar*) on the festival of the New Year since women are exempt from carrying out all precepts which depend for their performance on a given time. Yet it was the custom not alone for women to carry out the precepts of *lulav* and *shofar* but even to recite a benediction before carrying them out and it was about this practice that the question was asked. The reply given is: the Talmud states explicitly that women are obliged to carry out the duty of hearing the *Megillah*, the Scroll of Esther, read on the festival of Purim and to light the Ḥanukkah lights, even though these depend on time. The reason given is that the miracles wrought for our ancestors, which the festivals of Purim and Ḥanukkah commemorate, were performed not alone for the men but also for the women. From this it follows that women can recite the benediction over the *lulav* and the *shofar* since the aims these precepts are to inculcate apply to women as well as to men. The rabbinic *midrash* says that the *lulav* has a single heart or stem to suggest that man's heart be directed to the One God and this applies to women as well as to

men. The Rabbis state further that the *Malkhuyyot* ("Kingship"), *Zikhronot* ("Remembrance") and *Shofarot* texts recited on the New Year festival are intended to imply that God is King and He remembers. This applies to women as well as to men.

3. This concerns a well-known debate between Rashi and his grandson Rabbenu Tam regarding the order of the *tefillin*. The four sections of the *tefillin* are: "Sanctify unto Me." (Exodus 13:1–10); "And it shall come to pass . . ." (Exodus 13:11–16); "Hear, O Israel" (Deuteronomy 6:4–9); "And it shall come to pass . . ." (Deuteronomy 11:13–21). If the two sections beginning with: "And it shall come to pass" are in the middle, then the *Shema*, "Hear O Israel," will be at the end. God in the debate on high, does not mind this but the Heavenly Family prefer to have the *Shema*, the "yoke of the Kingdom of Heaven," as it is called in the rabbinic literature, first.

5. The Talmud, in the third chapter of the tractate *Berakhot*, discusses at length the enactment, attributed to Ezra, that after a seminal emission immersion is required before prayers can be recited or before the Torah can be studied. But the conclusion is that eventually this was set aside following Rabbi Judah ben Bathyra who held that "words of Torah cannot suffer contamination." The *geonim*, however, said that the duty of immersion was still binding before prayer and that the Talmud does not refer to it; but others argued that, from the Jerusalem Talmud, which deals with prayers on the Day of Atonement, it is clear that it applies to prayer as well. In fact, in the Middle Ages opinions were divided on the matter and so Rabbi Jacob asks his heavenly mentors to decide. The identity of Rabbi Joseph, Rabbi Jacob's son-in-law, is uncertain.

9. The holy name of forty-two letters is referred to in the Babylonian Talmud, *Kiddushin* 71a.

26. In medieval France and Germany there were many who only carried out the duty of wearing *tefillin* occasionally, on the grounds that the Talmud is very strict about not wearing the *tefillin* when the body is not perfectly clean.

8.

The Zohar on the
High Priest's Ecstasy

∾

Introduction

The most famous book of Jewish mystical literature, the
Zohar ("Illumination"), contains a record of the revelations
regarding the divine mysteries alleged to have been vouchsafed to the second-century Palestinian teacher, Rabbi
Simeon bar Yoḥai, and his circle of saints. It was through
the efforts of the 13th-century Spanish kabbalist, Moses de
Leon, that the work saw the light of day at the end of the
13th century. The fascinating literary problems connected
with the Zohar have been extensively investigated. Comprehensive summaries are provided by Scholem and by
Tishby. Orthodox kabbalists still believe that the true author of the work is Rabbi Simeon bar Yoḥai (or his disciples), but the majority of modern scholars accept the
argument of Scholem as conclusive that de Leon himself
was the author. This does not necessarily mean that de
Leon was engaged in pious fraud. The work bears all the
marks of a pseudepigraphic production, i.e., Moses de Leon

used the figure of Rabbi Simeon bar Yoḥai as the vehicle for the transmission of his own ideas. It has also been noted that many of the ideas found in the Zohar go back to a much earlier period than that of de Leon.

While the Zohar can be read in its plain meaning as a profound mystical commentary to the Pentateuch, it is important to appreciate that it is written in a kind of code: a rich variety of symbols is used to denote the *ten Sefirot*—the powers or potencies in the Godhead that are an emanation from the impersonal Ground of Being, *En Sof*, the Limitless, God as He is in Himself. The term *Sefirot*, originally meaning simply "numbers," is used by the kabbalists for these powers in the Godhead. According to some kabbalists the *Sefirot* are, as it were, a part of *En Sof*. According to others, the *Sefirot* are only the instrument used by *En Sof*. According to still others, in a position of compromise, the *Sefirot* are the "bodies" to which *En Sof* bears the relation of "soul." All the kabbalists stress the basic unity of *En Sof* and the *Sefirot*. A favorite metaphor is that of water poured into bottles of various hues, which assumes, for the time being, the particular color of the bottle into which it is poured.

The ten *Sefirot*, in descending order, are:

1. *Keter* ("Crown")
2. *Ḥokhmah* ("Wisdom")
3. *Binah* ("Understanding")
4. *Ḥesed* ("Lovingkindness")
5. *Gevurah* ("Power")
6. *Tiferet* ("Beauty")
7. *Neẓah* ("Victory")
8. *Hod* ("Splendor")
9. *Yesod* ("Foundation")
10. *Malkhut* ("Sovereignty")

Scholem notes that the Zohar has little use for ecstasy in the mystical life and that the part ecstasy plays both in the descriptive and in the dogmatic sections of the work is en-

tirely subordinate. Even so, he has shown that there are al-
lusions to mystical ecstasy in the Zohar, such as the following two passages, dealing with the experiences of the High
Priest as he entered the Holy of Holies on the Day of
Atonement.

On the Day of Atonement the High Priest entered the
Holy of Holies and uttered there the special divine name—
the Tetragrammaton—in its secret pronunciation. The four
consonantal letters of the divine name—Y (*yod*)-H (*he*)-
V (*vav*)-H (*he*)—represent the *Sefirot* thus:

> *yod*=Ḥokhnah (*Keter* is represented by the point of the
>   *yod*)
> *he*=*Binah*
> *vav*=*Tiferet* and the other five *Sefirot* apart from *Malkhut*
>   (the numerical value of *vav* is six)
> *he*=*Malkhut*.

When the High Priest utters the divine name he becomes a link between the sefirotic realm and creatures
down below, so that the divine grace can flow through him.
His experience is here described as one of profound ecstasy
and rapture.

Text I is from the Zohar, 3:67a and Text II from 3:102a.

Text

I

Lev. 16:30   It was taught: "From all your sins before the Lord shall ye be
clean." Why does the verse say "before the Lord"? Rabbi
Isaac replied: It actually [i.e., esoterically] means "before
the Lord." For it has been taught: The books are opened
and the judges sit in judgment from the beginning of the
Lev. 23:32   month until that day called "the ninth day of the month."

On that day all judgments ascend to the Lord of Judgment and they prepare a Throne of Mercy for the Holy King. On that day Israel down below must rejoice before the Lord who is ready on the next day to sit in judgment upon them on His Holy Throne of Mercy, the Throne of Pardon. He then forgives them and purifies them from all the sins recorded in the books open before him. Therefore the verse says: "From all your sins before the Lord shall ye be clean," actually "from before the Lord."

Those who recited the verse only recited it thus far. The High Priest alone was permitted to say: "shall ye be clean." For he was engaged in the Temple service and was bound together with the Holy Name that was in his mouth. When he was bound to the Holy Name and recited the blessing with his mouth, that voice came down and smote him so that the word became illumined in his mouth causing him to say: "shall ye be clean." He carried out the order of service and all the supernal beings that remained there were blessed. He then bathed his body and consecrated his hands in readiness for another holy service and his intention was that he was to enter another place on high, holiest of all. Three rows, formed by his brethren the priests, the Levites and all the people, surrounded him. They all blessed him, raising their hands over him in prayer. A golden thread was attached to his leg. He took three steps forward but the others remained where they were and did not move forward with him. He took a further three steps turning toward his destination. He took a further three steps, closed his eyes and attached himself to the world on high. He then entered the place he had to enter where he heard the sound of the cherubim's wings as they sang and they beat their wings that were spread out above in unison. As he burned the incense the sound of their wings ceased and they came together in a whisper. If the Priest was worthy that there should be rejoicing on high, then here below, too, there came forth an illumination, expressing acceptance, sweetened from the hills of pure balsam on high. This pervaded the whole of that place. The fragrant odor entered into his two nostrils and his heart was made tranquil again. Then all was silent and no accuser was there found. The Priest, with concentration and joy, opened his mouth to pray and he completed his prayers. When he had finished, the cherubim again raised their wings and sang. Then the Priest knew that he had proved acceptable. It was a time of general rejoicing, the people being aware that their prayers had been *Isa. 1:18* accepted, as it is written: "Though your sins be as scarlet, they shall be as white as snow." He then recited his prayers as he went out backwards. Happy the portion of the Priest. Through him rejoicing upon rejoicing was found on that day both on high and here below. In connection with that *Ps. 144:15* hour it is written: "Happy is the people that is in such a case, yea, happy is the people whose God is the Lord."

II

On that day the Priest is crowned with supernal crowns. He stands between those on high and those here below as he makes atonement for himself, his household, the Temple and all Israel. It has been taught: When he entered with the blood of the bullock he had the "Head of Faith" in mind. He then did the sprinkling with his finger, as it is written: *Lev. 16:15* "and sprinkle it upon the ark-cover, and before the ark-cover." How did he do this? He dipped his fingertips in the blood and sprinkled the blood in a downward thrust towards the ark-cover. As he sprinkled he concentrated his thoughts and began to count: "One"; "One and One." This means: First the One by itself, the One that embraces all, the One that is the praise of all, the One towards which all are directed; then, "One and One," thus both are joined together in love and friendship and are never separated. After he had counted this "and One," the Mother of all, he began to count in pairs, saying as he counted: "One and Two," "One and Three," "One and Four," "One and Five," "One and Six," "One and Seven," in order to draw down by degrees the One that is the Supernal Mother to the Crown of the Lower Mother and in order to draw down from their place the deep rivers so that they flow into the Community of Israel. Therefore, on this day the two illuminaries shine as one, the Supernal Mother giving light to the Lower Mother. That is why it says: "the day of atonements," as we have said.

Rabbi Isaac said: A chain was tied to the leg of the Priest as he went in so that if he died there they could pull his body out. How could they know? They knew it by means of the scarlet thread. For if its color did not change they would know that the Priest had remained there in the state of sin. But if he was to emerge in safety they would know it because then the colored thread would turn white. When that happened there was rejoicing both on high and below, otherwise they were all distressed and all would know that their prayers had gone unanswered. Rabbi Judah said: When he entered he closed his eyes so as not to gaze where it was forbidden to gaze. He heard the sound of the cherubim's wings as they sang their praises. The Priest then knew that there was only rejoicing and that he would emerge in safety. In addition he would know it by the manner of his prayers. For if the words of his prayer came out in joy, there was acceptance and blessing. Then there was joy on high and among those here below.

Comments

I

The passage begins with the question, is it not obvious that Israel becomes clean *before the Lord*? Rabbi Isaac replies that the esoteric reference is to the *Sefirah Binah*. This is called "before the Lord" because the name "the Lord" (the Tetragrammaton when pronounced *Adonai*, "the Lord") represents *Tiferet* (and the *Sefirot* around it including *Ḥesed* and *Gevurah*). Hence the *Sefirah* that is "before" the Lord, i.e., higher than *Tiferet*, etc., is *Binah*.

The Zohar understands the High Priest's entry into the Holy of Holies as an ascent of his soul into the realm of the *Sefirot*. The reference to the books being opened is to the talmudic saying (*Rosh Ha-Shanah* 16b) that on Rosh ha-Shanah, the first day of the new year, the books of judgment are opened and they remain open until the Day of Atonement, the tenth day of the year. But, according to the Talmud, while the tenth day is a great fast day, the ninth is a feast-day. Here the Zohar interprets the whole process as taking place in the sefirotic realm. Here the judgments begin, ascending to *Binah*, the source of both judgment and mercy, on the Day of Atonement.

Only the High Priest was permitted to say: "shall ye be clean" because, in fact, it was not really his voice at all that spoke in his mouth the words of pardon. Rather is was the *Sefirot* speaking, as it were, through him, since by uttering the divine name he became linked to them. As his body walked towards the physical Holy of Holies his mind dwelt in profound contemplation on the mystery of the *Sefirot* so that each physical step meant for him a still higher ascent of soul. Hence he is said to have taken three sets of three steps, representing the nine *Sefirot* below *Keter*, which was eventually reached, as the highest of all, when his soul reached as far as it could. Or, possibly, the Zohar means that the nine steps include *Keter*, with *Malkhut* not being counted because this was in his mind as soon as as he began. When he closed his eyes, it is said, he attached himself to the world above. This probably means that at that moment his thought reached to the highest of the *Sefirot*. The reference to the cherubim coming together in a whisper is to the belief that the cherubim on the ark-cover, one male, the other female, were actually united in a miraculous way in order to give expression to the "sacred marriage" on high of *Tiferet* and *Malkhut*, known, respectively, as "the Holy One, blessed be He" and the *Skekhinah*. When this took place, the divine grace could flow to all creation. The "illumination from on high" is a ray of divine light sent to demonstrate that the High Priest's prayers had been accepted. The reference to the heart of the High Priest being made tranquil again is to his coming down to earth again after his ecstatic contemplation.

II

Though the theme is the same as that in the first passage, here further details are given of the High Priest's mystic contemplation. The Supernal Crowns are the *Sefirot*. The procedure described here is based on the talmudic account (see especially *Yoma* 53b). The High Priest had to sprinkle the blood eight times in the direction of the ark-cover but not onto the ark-cover. In order to avoid any mistake in the counting, the High Priest did not count: "One." "Two," "Three," and so on, but "One and One," "One and Two," "One and Three"; but he first said simply "One." The Zohar here gives its own mystical interpretation of this method of counting. It refers, in fact, according to the Zohar to the *Sefirot*. The "Head of Faith" is *Keter* together with Hokhmah and *Binah*, the three highest *Sefirot*, heading all the others. The Zohar means here that although the High Priest only sprinkled seven times, he thought of all ten *Sefirot*. When he said "One" he had *Keter* in mind. When he said "One and One" he had Hokhmah and *Binah* in mind. These are thus described because they are always united as if they were one. When he said "One and Two" he had in mind that *Binah* ("One") was united with Hesed and *Gevurah* ("and Two"). When he said "One and Three" he had in mind that *Binah* was united with Hesed, *Gevurah* and *Tiferet*. When he said "One and Four" he had in mind that *Binah* was united with Hesed, *Gevurah*, *Tiferet* and *Nezah*. When he said "One and Five" he had in mind that *Binah* was united with Hesed, *Gevurah*, *Tiferet*, *Nezah* and *Hod*. When he said "One and Six" he had in mind that *Binah* was united with Hesed, *Gevurah*, *Tiferet*, *Nezah*, *Hod* and *Yesod*. Finally, when he said "One and Seven" he had in mind that *Binah* was united with Hesed, *Gevurah*, *Tiferet*, *Nezah*, *Hod*, *Yesod* and *Malkhut*. The High Priest thus caused all the *Sefirot* to become united through his mystical thoughts.

Binah is the Supernal *Mother*. It is so called both because it is the female, the passive element (Hokhmah being the male element) and because it is *Binah* that gives birth to the lower *Sefirot*. *Malkhut*, the *Shekhinah*, is the Mother of all creatures beneath the sefirotic realm. Hence it is called "the Lower Mother." The "rivers" are the illuminations which flow from *Binah* to *Malkhut*. *Malkhut* is called "the Community of Israel" because it is the archetype of the community of Israel on earth and because *Israel* is the name for *Tiferet*. This, and the other *Sefirot*, are gathered together in *Malkhut* which thus becomes a *gathering* or *community* of Israel.

The Day of Atonement is, in the Hebrew, *Yom ha-Kippurim*, literally, "the Day of Atonements," in the plural. This the Zohar understands to mean that it is a day on which both *Binah* and *Malkhut* shine forth. Since all is harmony on this day, the *Sefirah Malkhut* is not darkened, as it is on the other days of the year, by the demonic powers, but shines as brightly as *Binah*.

Red is the color of judgment, white the color of mercy. The thread turning white symbolizes the harmony and grace that reigns on this day on high so that in the realm of the *Sefirot* there is no judgment, only mercy.

9

The Visions and Mystical Meditations of Abraham of Granada

৩৫

Introduction

On the title page of the work *Berit Menuḥah*, attributed to Abraham ben Isaac of Granada, the publishers quote, not quite accurately, the 16th-century kabbalist Moses Cordovero, in his book *Pardes Rimmonim, Sha'ar ha-Nekkudot*, chapter 1: "I observed the work *Berit Menuḥah*, a delightful work containing an exposition of the Tetragrammaton. It is certain that the contents of this book have been handed down by tradition from master to disciple [lit. "from mouth to mouth"], or else they were imparted by an angel since these are not subjects to be grasped as a result of profound speculation and subtle reasoning but can only be the fruit of wondrous comprehension by the aid of the holy spirit."

Scholem has described the literary problems connected with the book, including the identity of the author. Scholem concludes that the book was composed in Spain in the 14th century. As Cordovero states, the book is a treatise on the various ways of pointing the Tetragrammaton. Scholem notes that the thinking behind the book resembles that of Abraham Abulafia but with a much stronger emphasis on the practical Kabbalah, i.e., on the theurgic use of the divine names. Scholem points, too, to the obscurity of the larger portion of the work but adds: "The few clear passages reveal the author as a profound thinker and visionary."

The selection here given in translation speaks of "illuminations" (*orot*). These are spiritual influences on the material world coming from on high. They are represented by the vowel-points of the Tetragrammaton. Although the kabbalists are always at pains to deny that there is any physical light in the upper realms, they prefer the symbol of light for these spiritual entities since light is the most ethereal of all material substances. It would also seem, however, that the author of our text actually depicts to himself during his meditations the flashing of lights, spiraling, twisting, ascending and descending, so that he sees in his mind's eyes the detailed workings of the supernal forces.

It will be helpful to the understanding of our very complicated text if a skeleton outline is given of the processes it describes. The pointing of the Tetragrammaton referred to in the text is that of *segol*—the *eh* sound. This pointing is conventionally in the form of three dots. These are either in the form ∴ (when used as a musical notation above a syllable) or in the form ֶ (when used as a vowel sign under a consonant). This pointing is said to represent the unification of all things with their divine source. The creative power of the Tetragrammaton serves a unifying purpose when the divine name is pointed with the *segol*. The three illuminations represented by three dots are really one, but they become divided into three, the middle entity being the most powerful and the one that provides the unifying principle. Thus, the middle illumination first flashes upward and then it moves swiftly downward, drawing the other two along with it. Since the three points are separate and yet form a unity, they represent the redemptive principle at work. There is a constant move toward the ultimate cosmic harmony that will obtain in the messianic age when the scattered ones of Israel will be gathered in again. *Segol* is a short vowel and when applied to the Tetragrammaton in the various ways described by our author, it brings about the messianic impulses to be awakened in the most powerful manner, the divine name flashing forth, as it were, as these three powerful illuminations, all anxious for the culmination of human history to be realized.

The text then goes on to say that this method of pointing was used in Temple times when the High Priest entered the Holy of Holies on the Day of Atonement. When he uttered the divine name, pointed with the *segol*, the High Priest was granted a vision of the *Shekhinah* and the whole sefirotic Tree. The text then describes the method used by the High Priest.

The section reproduced here is the chapter on the seventh way of pointing the Tetragrammaton, found on pages 20d–22d of the edition of *Berit Menuḥah* printed in Warsaw, 1883.

Text

As for the seventh manner of pointing, who can speak of its profundity, power, wisdom and mighty wonders, of its processes and stages, great, choice and terrible, showing forth wisdom and knowledge? This, more than all the other illuminations we have previously expounded, points to the unity of the Holy One, blessed be He. For, as this illumination ascends on high, it combines the fire on high with the fire below and in turn it combines the fire on high with the power of its Source and so does it combine all things. And as it descends, it combines those on high with those below and joins form to form. For the truth is that man's form is that of the Supernal Form, Supernal Man. And so, too, vermin and creeping things and all things have their supernal forms, as I have previously expounded this wondrous topic. In its great brilliance, this illumination pushes away, at first, the other illuminations but then brings them near again by its great power, attracting them by its abundant splendor. This demonstrates how great it is, having neither beginning nor end.

When this illumination emerges to spread from the well-known beautiful and choice root, without any admixture, exceedingly clear and terrible, it ascends by way of the path leading to Beth-El. It gains power in its ascent, and is divided into three parts. These three parts join each creature with its source and thus dominion is ascribed to the Master of each. As for these three parts, the first attaches, each to its place (another version: each to its source), all the beings on high. The second attaches, each to its place (another version: each to its source), all the middle beings. The third joins together all the beings below, one by one, to the power of their source, so that all dominions become a single dominion. This dominion is bound to the One Lord so that the tent is joined to become one.

Two of these three illuminations ascend at the same pace but the third moves forward powerfully between the other, equally paced, two. The third, which should be higher, in fact turns its face downward, seizing hold of its two companions to draw them down, with the great power it possesses even when it faces downward.

These three illuminations are called the places of those illuminations which form that peculiar treasure with which *Ex. 19:5* Israel has been endowed, as it is said: "Ye shall be Mine own treasure from among all peoples." By the power of their holiness, the two illuminations, which proceed apace together with the third attached to them, go forth until they reach the place of Massah and Taberah (see Exodus 17:7 and Numbers 11:2). There they gain in strength until a further illumination proceeds from Him who brings all things into existence and this scatters the illuminations in all directions. At the end of a day and a watch (i.e., in the night) the third illumination, covered by Massah and still holding fast to the other two, seizes hold of them in order to gather them together again, restoring them so that they regain their previous excellence. Here, if only you can understand it, you will discover a profound mystery. For this illumination is situated among the scattered ones of Israel and as these are gathered together you will observe exceedingly profound wisdom, very plausible matters. The accents are *egol* and then *zarka segol*. You must prepare yourself to grasp a matter of exceedingly great wisdom and you will discover such a perfect unification that neither your fathers nor your fathers' fathers ever comprehended.

These three illuminations, bound all three one to the other, appear as three types of dominion, one joining energetically together the upper beings, the second the middle beings, and the third the lower beings. Since these three dominions are bound together they appear as a single entity bound to the First Cause. All the functions of these three illuminations are carried out energetically. Consequently, the vowel is a short one, moving energetically towards the First Cause. These are the three illuminations which rise on behalf of Israel to gather them together from the lands of their dispersion among their enemies. These are exceedingly significant illuminations. Another great illumination proceeds from these. From this latter, those forces of destruction and harm, which caused Judah and Israel to be scattered from their land, draw their nourishment. These three illuminations are not nowadays in operation and will not be until a day and a watch has passed, namely, the sign of the Redemption, shoutings of Grace, Grace unto it. For when that day comes Redemption will spread abroad to all the corners of the earth, from the rising of the sun to the going down thereof. The son of David will then come out of his place to visit upon Edom his iniquity and also to requite his recompense upon his head and to pay him as he deserves for his works done to the children of Israel his brother. Then there will be a great confusion among all kingdoms, with peace neither for those who come in nor those who go out, and He will be sanctified by those close to Him and He will gather in Israel. That illumination which dispersed them will have dominion for a day and a watch. Why is this? It is because the darkness becomes increasingly strong as the light is about to shine, for then the forces of destruction spread abroad. Here is a hint about the Redemption. As it is about to come the Exile will be even stronger. Many of the wise will stumble as they observe the confusions of Exile and the great tribulations and they will forsake the religion in order to escape the devouring sword. Regarding this it is *Jer. 30:7* written: "And it is a time of trouble unto Jacob but out of it he shall be saved." In His abundant mercies, the Holy One blessed be He, will save them and will not abhor them to destroy them and to break His covenant with them, for He is full of compassion and the Lord of hosts will deal graciously with the remnant of Joseph.

Happy the man who persists in his uprightness to walk in the good way, keeping far from the wicked in those days, peradventure he be saved from the troubles known as the birth-pangs of the Messiah. Of the time of the Redemption *Isa. 19:2* it is said: "And I will spur Egypt against Egypt; and they shall fight every one against his brother, and every one against his neighbor, city against city, and kingdom against kingdom." But afterwards there will be such peace and tranquility, such rest and quiet, that no generation prior to that of the Messiah could have imagined it, neither the generation of the wilderness nor the generation of King Solomon, on whom be peace. For it would have been right for Solomon to have been the Messiah, but Israel took at that time beautiful women as wives and so mixed that holy seed with Amon, Moab, Edom, the Amorites and the Canaanites and other idolators. This great sin of intermarriage with the pagan nations did they commit. But in all other matters they were whole, unblemished from head to foot. Because of their sin Israel was driven out of the land.

Who can speak of the wisdom, power and dominion of these three illuminations, which will gather in the dispersed of Israel at the time of the Redemption? How mighty are they! Even now they stand ready to save those who stumble, hearkening to prayers, giving victory of every kind, and answering the requests of them who know the source. The name of the first one is: YeYiYa. The name of the second is YeYaHW. The name of the third is: HeHaYW. These three names are mighty: they are effective without (prior) purification and without invoking an angel, but solely as a result of perfect meditation on them. Whoever makes use of them must meditate so that power is drawn down into them in the way I have described. At the time of the Redemption these three illuminations will spread abroad and will shine beneath the sun and the moon. Their light will be divided into two paths to illumine the inhabitants of the world and to spread wisdom, understanding and knowledge as they shine on all. Consequently, they will spread swiftly, The angels of destruction will fly to meet this great illumination and a great battle will be joined in heaven. Correspondingly, here below there will also be a battle, above as below, because of the great power that will proceed from these illuminations. They will come together in one place. Israel should know these things. This method of pointing achieves its object more speedily than any I have previously mentioned. This is as it should be, since a name that has short vowels achieves its aim more speedily than the others. Understand, therefore, this manner of pointing and you will witness exceedingly glorious wisdom.

Know, that the name the High Priest uttered on the Day of Atonement was pointed entirely with short vowels as you now see. He uttered the name very slowly. When he set the first consonant in motion he did so with force, bringing it to and fro, to east, north, south and west with incomprehensibly powerful movements. When he uttered the second consonant he drew all the illuminations together with an exceedingly great force. When he uttered the third consonant he did so hurriedly in order to prevent the quality of Power from becoming so strong that it would destroy the world. And when he uttered the fourth consonant he did so hurriedly in order to prevent the quality of Rest becoming so strong that there would be insufficient power for the world to continue to endure in its present form.

I shall explain to you the pointing used by the High Priest when he uttered the name on the Day of Atonement. Do not convey this to everyone for it is a great principle. It was with the seventh mode of punctuation. In it you will see limitless wisdom and perfect unification for, as you observe, it is all made up of short vowels. As the High Priest uttered the name, the Levite accompanied him with melody corresponding to the movements he made. When the Levite accompanied him in this manner his prayer was accepted at once. It was hearkened to because of the great effectiveness and dominion of this name.

Reflect now and observe this wise thing. For the truth is that when the High Priest came into the Holy of Holies with the incense in his hand, clothed in his pure garments, the turban on his head and the girdle around his loins, his appearance was like that of the celestial High Priest whose name is Michael. The shine upon his face resembled *Hashmal*, the breath of his mouth was like the seraphim, his tongue was like a sharp sword as he entered the Sanctuary. When he saw the ark covered by the cloud he would say: "Sovereign of all worlds! Pardon my sins and the sins of my household and the sins of the children of Israel." After this he would hear a voice, saying: "So-and-so, My son, bless Me." Then would the High Priest know that it was a time of grace. He would then shake his garments and the sound of the bells would be heard outside and Israel would know that it was a time of grace. Then the High Priest would pronounce the name as it is written YHWH together with its vowels, and, gently and mysteriously, he would meditate on it. Then the threshold of the Temple would tremble and the Temple be filled with a celestial light. The High Priest in the midst of this light would say: "Sovereign of all worlds! May it be Thy will that this year be a year of blessing and happiness," etc. When the priests who stood around in the courtyard would hear the name they would fall upon their faces and exclaim: "Blessed be the name of His glorious Kingdom for ever and ever." The High Priest would offer supplication to his Maker. When he uttered the name he raised the *yod* on high and caused it to go forth powerfully and with the sound of melody and so did he do with the other letters, as I have said.

How glorious was the High Priest when he emerged safely from the Holy Place, for the radiance of the *Shekhinah* was as a halo around his head until he reached his home. When the people saw the awesome radiance around the head of the High Priest they stood in dread and fear and then bowed the knee and prostrated themselves, saying: "Happy the people that is in such a case. Happy the people whose God is the Lord." The High Priest did not leave the Holy Place with his back to the ark, lest he be punished on the spot. A certain ray of light came from between the staves of the ark in the Holy of Holies. This was like a flash of lightning which embraced the High Priest to push him out in such a manner that his back was never turned to the ark where the *Shekhinah* was.

Who can possibly describe the wisdom attained by the High Priest when he saw the *Shekhinah* and the comprehension that was his! The great wisdom he comprehended was limitless and beyond imagination. For there he saw the Roots where all the Qualities grow, the mysteries of the Foundation of the World and the Great Constructions. He saw how the Roots were grafted onto a single Root, the Root of the Tree of Life. He saw the Tree of Life and the Branches and how the Branches cover the Root. He saw the Fruit of the Branches but did not eat of them and he did not know which fruit was sweet, which bitter. He comprehended those three illuminations as they are combined, as I have stated previously. After he had emerged from the Holy Place he would impart his skills to his son if the latter was worthy to be the high priest, or to another priest worthy of becoming High Priest, so that when he entered the Holy of Holies he would be adept in the knowledge of the illuminations and not stumble, causing Israel to stumble with him.

This was the procedure adopted by the High Priest in the Holy of Holies. The consonants and vowels of the divine name were engraved on the gates of the ark. If the High Priest saw that the gate of the ark was filled with white light he rejoiced exceedingly. But if he saw red it was a good sign neither for Israel nor for the High Priest himself. If the High Priest saw the red light he would take his courage into his hands and say: "Sovereign of all worlds! Turn from Thy fierce wrath and repent of this evil against Thy people." He would engage long in requests and supplications to the Holy One, blessed be He. There was a certain thread attached to the coat of the High Priest. It was made of white silk, the other end of it being tied outside in the courtyard. The High Priest would set the thread in motion, hinting to the people of Israel to cry out to the Lord and to return to Him with all their heart. When the priests and the people saw that the High Priest had set the thread in motion they would at once cry out in bitterness of spirit and beg for mercy from the Holy One, blessed be He. At once the red would turn to white and the High Priest would ring the bells in great joy.

Behold, I have told you some of the procedures of the Sanctuary when the High Priest entered the Holy of Holies. I have explained at length the pointing of *segol* because this is the pointing which represents the peculiar treasure (*segullah*) with which Israel, the holy seed, has been endowed. This is the second illumination, deriving from the Root of delight, gladness and beauty. As I have stated, those who lead the name derive from here. This is an exceedingly great topic. It is the illumination drawn down powerfully to extend this way and that. It embraces in its great power those above and those below to link them in unification. Because it is so powerful another illumination proceeds from it to push against it with great force. This is the *dagesh* in the second letter. This illumination extends on all sides and in every direction and by its great force compels all the other illuminations to do its bidding. This is the illumination that opens the gate to bring out in power and splendor all the other illuminations. It is the light that opens the windows of the east, bringing forth the sun from its place in order to fulfill its function. It is pointed with the vowel *pataḥ*, one of the shorter vowels which, as I have said, fulfill their aims speedily. It is an exceedingly great and effective pointing, of infinite discernment and beauty. It is the vowel under the first *he*, the second letter of YHWH, the terrible and glorious name. The name of this second illumination is *Elohim*. This is a great matter, that the letter which denotes rest should conduct itself with energy, as you will appreciate if you have understood what has been said.

The third illumination is most awesome to contemplate.

The High Priest would prolong his contemplation of this more than of any other illumination. He would draw it down to himself by means of the pleasant melody and that illumination would bring down to him tremendous sovereignty and dominion, as I have said. Its name is MLKYH and its vowel is *hirik*, the light which cools, as I have stated more than once. The fourth illumination is composed of all three together as they proceed energetically and its vowel is *shuruk* with its three points. They all have the single name: YHWDREYHW. This is a most powerful name. It has no place of derivation but is an illumination *sui generis*. As you can see it is a combination formed from YHWH.

Happy the man who delves deeply to attain to the knowledge and to grasp the wisdom contained in this name.

There were twenty-six steps from the innermost sanctuary to the place where the ark stood. The High Priest was not permitted to go higher than the fifteenth step lest his punishment be that he would never emerge alive. As he would ascend these fifteen steps he would sing songs and praises. In each song he referred to the derivations of the name and its various combinations. When he reached the fifteenth step he would recite the confession and then utter the name, as I have said.

The task of expounding the seventh mode of pointing is now finished in all its general principles and details, concerning the Quality of severe Power by means of which great power is drawn down through the short vowels. Now I shall begin to explain the eighth mode of pointing. Here you will see even greater and more powerful forces than in the seventh mode. I have already warned you that whoever has this name in mind should have in mind the vowel points under the consonants and if he does this he will achieve whatever he desires. There will be nothing he cannot do if he follows all these rules in the order in which they have been presented, missing nothing out. Now that you have witnessed the profundity of these matters your eyes will be opened.

Comments

Like many other passages in *Berit Menuhah* this section is obscure in some of its details but the general sense is clear enough or, at least, as clear as these matters can ever be. The remarkable description of the High Priest's meditation on the Day of Atonement resembles in some respects the passage from the Zohar on the same theme translated in chapter 8 of this book.

The accents *zarka, segol* are said to represent the scattering of the three illuminations (from the Hebrew root *zarak*, "to throw") and the gathering together of the three (the *segol* is written as three points). There is the further pun on *segol = segullah*. The interpretation of *am segullah*, "the people that is My treasure" (Deut. 26:18) is "the people of the *segol*," i.e., the people for whom the three illuminations shine forth. The remarks about short vowels mean that these vowels take little time to pronounce. There is no pausing but the tongue trips along "energetically." Since this name, or part of it, represents both Power and Rest, these must not be the occasion for a station as the name progresses, for if it were, then either undue Power or undue cessation from Power (= Rest) would result and the harmony required to sustain the world would be lacking.

The whole passage is typical of the combination in the *Berit Menuhah* of meditations on the divine name, the light flashing in the soul of the devotee, and the visions of its author. The reference to the "halo" is peculiar, although the *Shekhinah* is called the *Atarah*, the *Crown* (the word used here for "halo") in the Kabbalah.

10.

The Communications of
the Heavenly Mentor
to Rabbi Joseph Karo

ဢ

Introduction

Rabbi Joseph ben Ephraim Karo (1488–1575) was one of Jewry's greatest legal luminaries, author of the *Beit Yosef* and the *Shulḥan Arukh*. The latter is the standard code of Jewish law. Karo was probably born in Toledo, but after the expulsion from Spain in 1492 his family settled in Turkey where Karo lived for about 40 years. In 1536 he left Turkey for Safed where he headed a large academy. In Safed, Karo became a member of a circle of mystics that included Moses Cordovero, Solomon Alkabetz, and Isaac Luria.

Karo believed himself to be the recipient of a heavenly mentor. This phenomenon was not unknown among the kabbalists, who called the spirit which brought the revelation a *maggid*. Karo's *maggid* revealed itself to him in order to impart kabbalistic mysteries and to instruct and rebuke him. He identified the *maggid* both with the soul of the Mishnah and with the *Shekhinah*. The revelations of the *maggid* were in the form of automatic speech coming out of

Karo's mouth. Karo kept a diary—published in part under the title *Maggid Mesharim* ("Teller of Upright Words")—in which he recorded the *maggid's* revelations. Selections from this diary are given in translation in Texts II–VI below. Preceding them is a translation of a unique letter sent by Solomon Alkabetz from Safed to the mystic brotherhood in Salonika, containing an eye-witness account of the appearance of the *maggid* to Karo. Solomon Alkabetz (c. 1505–1576), who was brother-in-law of Moses Cordovero, is best known as the author of the hymn to welcome the Sabbath, *Lekhah Dodi* ("Come my beloved"), now recited in all synagogues on Friday night (see chapter 16). It is reported that the Safed mystics would dress in white and go out into the fields to welcome "Bride Sabbath," identified with the *Shekhinah*. Together with Cordovero, Alkabetz would "divorce" himself from his home (*gerushin*, "divorces") to prostrate himself on the graves of the saints near Safed in the belief that this made him a suitable vehicle for the transmission of mysterious communications from the Academy on High.

The translations are all based upon the first edition of *Maggid Mesharim* (Amsterdam, 1704), in which Alkabetz's letter appeared as the Introduction (without pagination). Text II can be found on pages 1a–b; Text III, on pages 1b–2a; Text IV, on pages 2a–b; Text V, on page 36a; and Text VI, on pages 59b–60a.

Text

I

Know that the saint (= Karo) and I, his and your humble servant, belonging to our company, agreed to stay up all night in order to banish sleep from our eyes on Shavuot.[1]

We succeeded, thank God, so that, as you will hear, we ceased not from study for even a moment. This is the order I arranged for that night. First, we read the Torah with a *Gen. 2:1–3* pleasant melody from the beginning until: "And the heaven *Ex. 19:1* and the earth were finished." Then we read: "In the third month" to the end of the section. Then in the section *Mish-* *Ex. 24:1* *patim* from: "And unto Moses he said" to the end of the section. Then in the section *Va-Ethanan* from: "And Moses *Deut. 5:1–6:9* called unto all Israel" to the end of the section: "Hear, O Israel." Then in the section *Ve-Zot ha-Berakhah* from: "And *Deut. 34* Moses went up" to "in the sight of all Israel." Then we read *Ez. 1* the *haftarah*: "Now it came to pass in the thirtieth year" and *Hab. 3* the *haftarah*: "A Prayer of Habakkuk." Then the Psalm: *Ps. 19* "The heavens declare" and the Psalm: "Let God arise." *Ps. 68* Then we read the alphabetic acrostic without the songs.[2] *Ps. 119* Then we read the whole of the Song of Songs, the whole of Ruth and the final verses of Chronicles. All this we did in dread and awe, with quite unbelievable melody and tunefulness. We studied the whole of the Order *Zera'im* in the Mishnah and then we studied in the way of truth [= the Kabbalah].

No sooner had we studied two tractates of the Mishnah then our Creator smote us so that we heard a voice speaking out of the mouth of the saint, may his light shine. It was a loud voice with letters clearly enunciated. All the companions heard the voice but were unable to understand what was said. It was an exceedingly pleasant voice, becoming increasingly strong. We all fell upon our faces and none of us had any spirit left in him because of our great dread and awe. The voice began to address us, saying: "Friends, choicest of the choice,[3] peace to you, beloved companions. Happy are you and happy those that bore you. Happy are you in this world and happy in the next that you resolved to adorn Me on this night. For these many years had My head been fallen with none to comfort Me. I was cast down to

the ground to embrace the dunghills but now you have restored the crown to its former place.[4] Be strong, My beloved
ones. Be courageous, My friends. Rejoice and exult for you
belong among the chosen few. You have the merit of belonging to the king's palace. The sound of your Torah and
the breath of your mouth have ascended to the Holy One,
blessed be He, breaking through many firmaments and
many atmospheres until it rose upwards. The angels were
silent, the seraphim still, ḥayyot stood without speech and
all the host of heaven heard, together with the Holy One,
blessed be He, the sound of your voice. Behold, I am the
Mishnah,[5] the mother who chastises her children, and I
have come to converse with you. Had you been ten in number you would have ascended even higher but you have
reached a great height nevertheless. Happy are those who
bore you, My friends, in that, by denying yourselves sleep
you have ascended so far on high. Through you I have become elevated this night and through the companions in
the great city, a mother-city in Israel.[6] You are not like those
who sleep on beds of ivory in sleep which is a sixtieth of
death, who stretch themselves out upon their couches. But
you cleave to your Creator and He rejoices in you. Therefore, My sons, be strong and rejoice in My love, rejoice in
My Torah, rejoice in the fear of Me. If you could only imagine one millionth of the anguish which I endure no joy
would ever enter your hearts and no mirth your mouths, for
it is because of you that I am cast to the ground. Therefore,
O My dear sons, be strong and of good courage and rejoice.
Cease not from studying, for a thread of mercy is stretched
out over you and your Torah study is pleasant to the Holy
One, blessed be He. Therefore, stand upon your feet and
raise Me up, saying in a loud voice as on the Day of Atonement 'Blessed be the name of His glorious Kingdom for ever
and ever.' "[7]

We then rose to our feet with the joints of our loins loosened and we proclaimed in a loud voice: "Blessed be the name of His glorious Kingdom for ever and ever." He then repeated: "Happy are you. Return to your studies, not interrupting them for one moment. Go up to the land of Israel, for not all times are opportune. There is no hindrance to salvation, be it much or little. Let not your eyes have pity on your worldly goods, for you eat of the goodness of the higher land. If you will but hearken, of the goodness of that land will you eat. Make haste, therefore, to go up to the land, for I sustain you here and will sustain you there. To you will be peace, to your household peace, and to all that is yours peace. The Lord gives strength to His people. The Lord will bless His people with peace."[8]

All these things did we hear with our own ears and much more of a like nature, all matters of wisdom and great promise. We all broke into tears at the great joy we had experienced and when we heard of the anguish of the *Shekhinah* because of our sins, Her voice like that of an invalid in her entreaties. We took courage so that our mouths did not cease from study in joy and dread until daybreak. In the morning we immersed ourselves, as we had done on the previous two days. There we met the sages who had not been present on that night and we rebuked them. We told them of all the good the Lord had wrought on our behalf so that their heart died within them. They smote their own faces and wept aloud. We persisted in our criticism of them since it was because of their absence that we failed to receive further revelations, as we said above. So we said: "Let us join one another this coming night and we shall be ten in number."[9] It was agreed. Now although we did not sleep at all, not even for one moment, on the first night, and athough we were unable to sleep even during the day, since the saint, may his light shine, expounded the Torah in the afternoon and we all listened, yet we girded our loins to repeat the program of the first night on the second. In the great rejoicing that we were ten in number, they did not wait until the time for the Mishnah reading nor did they wait until midnight (on the previous night it happened exactly at midnight) but no sooner did we begin to read the portion preceding: "Hear, O Israel" in Deuteronomy, then the voice of our beloved knocked at the door. It began to speak: "Hearken unto me, O my beloved ones, choice ones. Awake and sing you who dwell in the dust, according to the mystery of the supernal dust, the two letters *he*," etc.[10] And he spoke many words of wisdom. Afterwards he said: "Happy are you, My beloved ones. Happy are you in that you have elevated Me. I have become most elevated now that you are ten in number, the quorum for all sacred matters. Happy are you and happy those who gave you birth. Fear not the reproach of men and have no dread of their insults, for you have elevated the Community of Israel and know that you are the chosen few (so did he continue, as above). To Me you cleave and the glory is above your heads and there extends over you a thread of mercy. If permission had been granted for the eye to see, you would see the fire surrounding this house. Be strong, therefore. Do not allow the knot to be untied. Elevate Me by reciting in a loud voice: 'Hear, O Israel' and 'Blessed be the name' as on the Day of Atonement."

Thus did he speak many things for about half an hour and we then returned to our studies. At midnight the voice returned, speaking for over an hour, repeating the praises of our studies. The voice said: "See! Did any people ever hear the voice speaking as you did? Ask thy father and he will tell thee, thine elders and they will say, whether during these many hundreds of years they have heard or seen such a thing and yet you have been worthy of it. Therefore, let your eyes be upon your ways from now onward. Let each help his neighbor and say unto his brother, be strong. Let the weak say, I am mighty, and let each be great in his own eyes since you belong to the king's palace and have had the merit of entering the vestibule. Endeavor now to enter the great hall and do not leave the vestibule. For whoever leaves to go outside, his blood be upon his head. Awake, My sons, and see that I speak to you. Awake, My beloved ones. Be firm and valiant in battle. Be strong and rejoice and a thread of mercy will be extended over you daily. Observe how intoxicated you are with worldly desires. Awake, O drunken ones, for the day comes when a man must cast away his gods of silver, worldly desires, and his gods of gold, lust for wealth. Go up to the land of Israel, for so you are able to do if it were not that you are trapped in the mud of worldly desires and vanities. Whoever leaves your company and turns away, his blood be upon his head. See! How worthy you have been, that of which no others have been worthy" (and so he continued at length in this vein).

Now, my sons, hearken unto me. Incline your ears and your hearts to me. Who can be so foolish as to hear these things without resolving to return to the Lord with all his heart and with all his soul and with all his might? I call heaven and earth to be my witnesses that all I have recorded here and in the tract I composed is not even one hundredth of what actually transpired. And even with regard to the tract, you will sometimes note an asterisk after some words, to denote that here a mystery was revealed I could not allow myself to record in writing.[11]

O my brethren, my people! Hearken and let your souls be revived. For a new spirit entered into the perfect companions who witnessed all this. Also on the Sabbath the word returned to the saint and he spoke wondrous praises of our achievements on these two nights. He repeated that our companions should keep their promise. Now that they have entered the vestibule they must try to enter the palace and whoever tries to escape, his blood be on his head, the others being innocent. Then the saint rose to his feet before the morning meal. He gathered them all together and spoke to them, warning them to do as he had commanded. They all responded: "We will do and we will obey." They drew up numerous regulations, one of these being that the fourth day each week should be devoted to a reminder of the destruction of the Temple. For the whole twenty-four hours of this day no meat should be eaten and no wine imbibed unless it be for such exceptional circumstances as a religious feast or when hospitality is offered to a guest or when one is on his travels and so forth.[12]

And you, my brethren, awake. Be strong, be firm, and rejoice in the service of your Creator. Observe that the *maggid* mentioned some of you on the first night of Shavuot, when you resolved to serve the Lord, and yet you were not mentioned on the second night. Be careful, therefore, and set your hearts on all these things. Perhaps the voice will speak to you and you will then be astonished. Your eyes will be opened to the promise contained in this tract when, in the final vision, the saint and I are to proceed to dwell together with our companions in the holy land and the angels will come, etc.

Let each of you, therefore, pay heed. Have no pity on your worldly goods. Let there be no obstacle because of your desire for worldly things and because there is no firm guarantee. Otherwise you will regret it and when you do resolve to go you will be unable so to do. For the time of reaping has come and not every time will be so opportune. So open your eyes. As for me, I have no time to deal with the matter at length. My heart burns within me. Observe how many things God has wrought for me, things utterly incomprehensible to the human mind. I am a fool, having no knowledge. But it was His intention, blessed be He, to show me this great thing. You, too, be firm and encourage one another, taking it all to heart. Let the weak say I am strong. Let each help his neighbor. I have saved my own soul. Be strong and of good courage and let not your hands be weak. Observe the following. Eat no cooked dish on the eve of the fast of Av, not even a dish of lentils. This applies to the whole of that day. At the meal which precedes the fast, eat only dry bread and drink only a glass of water. Carry out many such practices. Have regard for the glory of your Creator and pay honor to Him. Be careful lest, God forbid, you regret it. I offer my supplication to Almighty God. May He put it into your hearts to have pity on yourselves and may He give me the merit of joining you in the holy land that we may there serve Him together. Amen. Thus speaks your brother, Solomon, the Levite, Alkabetz.

II

First of all you must take care never to allow your thoughts to dwell on anything other than the Mishnah, the Torah and the precepts. If any other thought enters your heart, cast it away. 2. Take care to have no other thought in mind during your prayers except the actual words of the prayers, not even thoughts of the Torah and the precepts. 3. Take care never to speak an unnecessary word, whether by day or by night. 4. Take care never to speak anything that leads to laughter and if you hear such, never laugh. This includes the admonition never to scoff at all. 5. Never lose your temper[1] over merely material things. 6. Take care to eat no meat at all for forty days. On the Sabbath you can eat a little. Do not eat horseradish. 7. Drink no wine during these days except one drink at the end of the meal. 8. Be gentle in your replies to all men. 9. Never be proud. Be exceedingly low in spirit. 10. Sleep in your own bed. When you have to have marital relations in order to fulfill the precept to be fruitful and multiply, rise up from her bed a half an hour after you have completed the act and return to your own bed. 11. Take care not to enjoy your eating and drinking and your marital relations. It should be as if demons were compelling you to eat that food or perform that act[2] so that if it were at all possible for you to exist without food and drink or to fulfill the duty of procreation without having intercourse you would prefer it. 12. Have your sins always in mind and be anxious because of them. 13. Do not eat for dessert more than one measure and no more than twenty of melons, grapes and raisins. Except on Sabbaths and festivals do not eat of more than one type of fruit. At the beginning of the meal cut three measures of bread and during that meal eat no more. Never drink your fill of water. 14. Train yourself to keep your eyes downcast so that you will never have cause to gaze at a woman forbidden to you. 15. Have the Mishnah in mind during the meal and study a chapter of the Mishnah before Grace. 16. Do not allow your mind to wander away from Me even for a single moment and have as little pleasure as possible. When you are at meals and experience a special longing for some food or drink, desist from it. If you do this, it will be as if you offered a sacrifice at each meal and your table will be a veritable altar upon which you slaughter the evil inclination. 17. Do not drink the wine at meals in one gulp and take care with regard to how you measure it. Be not afraid that this may affect your eyesight. On the contrary, both your eyesight and your strength will increase. 18. Have little further to do with the pleasures of eating and drinking. Do not make a habit of eating a particular food that you enjoy especially. Substitute for it, rather, another type of food from which you do not derive such enjoyment, as Al-Constantin did. . . .[3]

One who understands the mystery of *oneg* ("pleasure") and *nega'* ("plague"), namely, that the letters of one word are the same as those of the other, albeit in a different order, will understand that if a thing is in any way good, even when it reads backwards, it is good always, since the left hand must conform to the right.[4] For those who know "grace" this is a mystery.[5] How careful must one be regarding thoughts about women! You must burn out all such thoughts which enter your mind during prayer, especially during the *Amidah*. You know full well who it is that brings them into your heart. Take exceedingly great care in this matter and keep your eyes always open to it. If this you will do, you will be greatly exalted. Take great heed of the plague of leprosy, namely, never to soil too much the sign of the covenant of circumcision, even when it is permitted to you, unless it is absolutely necessary. Never touch it with your hand and never touch any part of your body below the navel. Of this take the greatest care, for you have no idea of the harm it causes.

Know that if you see your garments torn in a dream it means that there is something wrong with your deeds. It is a dream that Gabriel brings about. He extends throughout the world, even among the nations. If you will ask: Why is it that a man grieves over a calamity seen in a dream more than over one which befalls him while he is awake? It is because in man's waking life the soul is clothed by the body. No sense of urgency is experienced because the body acts as a shield. But the harm seen in a dream oppresses the naked soul so that it experiences far greater anguish. This will help *Gen. 41:8* you to understand the verse: "And his spirit was troubled."[6] Keep yourself from eating too much meat, for this flaws the soul. As for drinking wine, you have no idea how much harm it does and how great the flaw in the soul it causes. Be far, therefore, from these and be very careful. The masses imagine that this world is all it appears to be so that there is no one to see when they eat and drink in order to satisfy their evil inclination. Woe to them. For they are fooled by the world. The hand writes it all down up above and they are obliged to pay for it severely. Therefore, it is written:

"What will you do on the day of visitation?" Happy are you   Isa. 10:3
in that you have been warned. Reveal it to your friends and
they, too, will wake up. Was it a good thing that you failed
to read the Mishnah yesterday? Was it good that you have
been so careless lately about thinking on the Torah? You
have seen what happened to the business in which you were
engaged. Note how the Holy One, blessed be He, punishes
measure for measure, and take greater care in the future.

How can you wish me to converse with you when you
eat horseradish? Be careful, therefore, to eat only a little. I
have already hinted to you the mystery of the good smell
and the bad smell.

You did well to write to that sage regarding the Torah
scroll you are about to purchase. Observe how the Lord
your God is with you always. Note that for this past year
and a half you have had no nocturnal emissions. Be strong
and of good courage. Be not afraid and dread naught.

Do not speak to so-and-so. He is under the ban on high
because of the sins he committed in private, his mind not
being on God. You see how he is like the pig who declares:
"I am pure." Know his secret. He cannot deny it.[7]

If you will improve your behavior I shall reveal to you
the mysteries of reincarnation. I shall show you the previous
incarnations of all your friends and relatives and you will
witness wondrous things and be astonished. Be strong,
therefore at all times in the fear of God. Mortify your flesh
with all your might and burn out all the thoughts that enter
your mind during prayer and when you study the Mishnah.
Burn them out with the straw of reading the *Shema*, with
the breath of your mouth.[8]

Is it good that you fail to go early to the synagogue and is
it so bad for you to be among the first ten there? Consequently, from now onward be exceedingly careful in your
deeds and also in your words and do not fly into a rage as
you often do. Remember the saying of the rabbis that when

a man flies into a rage he is led into error. Bad temper derives from Samael and the serpent and it is not right for
you to listen to them. Pay them no heed when they try to
seduce you.

Do not eat of the meat they brought you this day, for it is
terefah. Therefore examine the slaughterers. Although they
have commited no sin, for it was done unwittingly, you stay
here with me and if you are a man of soul put a knife to your
throat.[9]

III

The eve of the Sabbath, 22nd Adar. The Lord be with you
but only if you cleave to Me and do not separate your
thoughts even for a single moment from My Mishnah. Eat
not and drink not for your own enjoyment at all. What
profit is there in the pleasures of this world? Rather your
thought should be: If it were possible to keep body and soul
together without having any pleasure, you would greatly desire such a state. In this way you will cleave always to God
and miracles will be performed on your behalf just as they
were performed on behalf of the ancient saints and people
will know that there is a God in Israel. For at this time the
name of heaven is not sanctified. Take heed, therefore,
against Samael and the serpent and the evil inclination who
pursue you in order to disturb your thoughts and interfere
with your prayers. Unify your heart in My service and come
unto Me. I have already told you how essential it is for you
to behave in a humble manner and never to lose your temper over anything at all. Go out and learn from Moses,
teacher of all the prophets, who fell into error whenever he
lost his temper. Do not lose your temper, therefore, over
anything in the world. Even in religious matters, where you
are obliged to pretend to anger, be careful never to allow

your thoughts to be separated from Me and from My Mishnah and from the fear of Me and from My Torah. For if only
you knew how many worlds go to waste whenever you fail
to think on the Torah, you would not cease from this for
even a moment. For when you go out into the street with
your thoughts on My Mishnah, My young ones proclaim before you: "Pay homage to the image of the King" and innu-
merable angelic beings accompany you. Above them worlds
without number tremble at this proclamation and ask:
"Who is this man whom the King delighteth to honor? He
is the head of the College in the land of Israel. He is the
great author of the land of Israel."[1] If you behave as I instruct you, I will give you the merit of completing your
books without error or mistake, your books, commentaries
and works in which you decide the law. I shall allow you to
print them and publish them in all the borders of Israel as
you have requested of the Lord your God. And I shall give
you and your sons the merit of having fulfilled for you the
verse: "This book of the Torah shall not depart out of thy   *Josh. 1:8*
mouth." And I shall give you from this modest and worthy
wife a saintly and wise son, for she deserves it because of all
she has suffered. As for you, if you will do as I have taught
you to separate yourself from all worldly pleasure and if you
will sanctify yourself in purity during the marital act, behav-
ing as it was said of Rabbi Eliezer, that he engaged in the act
as if a demon were compelling him to do it, then you will be
worthy of bringing down into the world a pure, holy soul
from the Garden of Eden and he will become a great sage
and saint. And when she will have departed this life you
will marry, one after the other, two women who had been
previously married and that is what I told you: "The vir-   *Ps. 45:15*
gins—her companions that follow her—shall be brought
unto her." From these you will have sons gifted with discernment, knowing His name and studying His Torah for its
own sake.[2] I shall increase the fame of your college in both

quality and quantity, etc. And after all this I shall give you the merit of being burned for the sanctification of My name. All your sins and faults will be purged by fire so that you will rise from there like pure wool. All the saints in the Garden of Eden, the *Shekhinah* at their head, will come out to meet you, welcoming you with many songs and praises. They will lead you like a groom who walks in front and they will accompany you to your canopy. I have prepared for you seven canopies, one within the other, and seven canopies, one higher than the other. Within the innermost and highest of the canopies there will be seven rivers of fragrant balsam. It is all there ready for you. And there will be a golden throne with seven steps, embedded with numerous pearls and precious stones. All the saints will accompany you and sing before you until you arrive at the first canopy. There they will clothe you with a precious robe and so on at each canopy so that by the time you arrive at the final canopy you will be clothed with fourteen precious robes. Afterwards, two of the saints who accompany you will stand, one to the right and one to the left, like groomsmen for a groom, and they will help you to ascend the throne. As you ascend the throne they will put another robe on you in addition to the fourteen so that as you sit on the throne you will be wearing fifteen precious robes. They will take a crown hanging there and place it upon your head. There you will sit with one to the right of you and one to the left. All the saints will sit around you and you will discourse on the Torah. This will continue for one hundred and eighty days, after the pattern

Esth. 1:4   of: "When he showed the riches of his glorious kingdom and the honor of his excellent majesty, many days, even a hundred and fourscore days." Afterwards, all the saints will arise to accompany you, with you in the front like a groom. They will walk behind you but some of them will go before you, proclaiming: "Pay homage to the son of the Holy, Supernal King. Pay homage to the image of the King." Thus they will sing until you arrive at the place where there are thirteen rivers of balsam. A garment will be removed from you as you immerse yourself in the first river and so on until thirteen garments will have been removed when you immerse yourself in the thirteenth river. Afterwards a river of fire will gush forth and as you immerse yourself in it the fourteenth robe will be removed. As you emerge a precious white robe will be made ready for you to wear and Michael the High Priest will be ready to bring up your soul to the Holy One, blessed be He. From this stage onward permission has not been granted to describe what will transpire. Eye has seen it not . . .[3]

The Holy One, blessed be He, and His Academy have sent me to tell you these mysteries in order that you might see yourself occupying such a stage. Sin not, therefore, not even in thought. Let not the evil inclination get the better of you and if he endeavors to do so rebuke him, saying: "Shall a man like me, destined for all this glory, sin in thought?" Concealed within these mysteries there are numerous higher ones. Open your eyes. Behold, all the sages of Israel plead for you to the Holy One, blessed be He, namely, Rabbi Isaac Alfasi, Rabbi Moses ben Maimon and Rabbi Asher ben Jehiel, because you are engaged in explaining their words and deciding in accordance with their opinions and you explain these and frequently decide in accordance with their opinions, For from the days of Moses, teacher of all the prophets, the Oral Torah was not recorded in writing until the days of Rabbi Judah the Prince. And from his day the whole Mishnah had not been explained until Rav Ashi came, collecting all the teachings and rendering decisions. And from his day there were only a few collections of decisions such as the *Halakhot Pesukot*, etc., until Rabbi Isaac Alfasi, Rabbi Moses ben Maimon and Rabbi Asher ben Jehiel came to render decisions in the whole of talmudic law. Rabbi Moses ben Maimon, especially, wrought great things in expounding the whole Torah. And from that time until the present no one bestirred himself to gather together all the material of the teachers as you have done.[4]

IV

The eve of the Sabbath, 29th of Iyyar, portion *Be-Midbar Sinai*. I ate but little and drank the same and I studied the Mishnah at the beginning of the night. I then slept until daybreak so that when I awoke the sun was shining. I was very upset, saying to myself: "Why did I not arise during the night so that the word should come to me as beforetimes?" Nevertheless, I began to rehearse the Mishnah and I studied five chapters. As I was reading the Mishnah the voice of my beloved knocked in my mouth and the lyre sang of itself. It began by saying: "The Lord is with you wherever you go, and the Lord will prosper whatever you have done and will do, but you must cleave to Me and to My Torah and to My Mishnah at all times, not as you have done this night. For, although you did sanctify yourself in your food and drink, yet you slept like a sluggard, for the door revolves upon its hinges but the sluggard is on his bed, and you did not follow your good habit of rising to study the Mishnah. For this you deserve that I should leave and forsake you since you gave strength to Samael, the serpent and the evil inclination by sleeping until daybreak. But in the merit of the Six Orders of the Mishnah that you know by heart and in the merit of the self-tortures and torments you engaged in in years past, and which you still practice, it was agreed in the Heavenly Academy that I should return to converse with you as in former times and that I should neither leave you nor forsake you. And so have I done as you can see. I speak to you as a man speaks to his neighbor. Your eyes can see that for many generations no one, with the exception of a few chosen ones, attained to such a degree. Therefore, My son, hearken to My voice and to that which I command you, to busy yourself with My Torah, unceasingly by day and night. Have nothing else in the world in your thoughts than words of Torah, the fear of Me and My Mishnah."

Afterwards, I slept for about half an hour and I awoke in great distress, saying, the word has ceased because I fell asleep. I read in the Mishnah and the voice of my beloved knocked in my mouth, saying: "Know, that the Holy One, blessed be He, and the whole of the Heavenly Academy send you greetings. I have been sent to inform you that all the acts of God are part of His providential care. Behold, you have taught the Torah in two of My communities and I saw that you left a great and holy community to dwell among those who pray in the ruin. It was agreed in the Heavenly Academy that all will be well with you. Let not your thoughts be separated for even a single moment from My Torah and the fear of Me and I shall give you the merit of ascending to the highest stages."[1]

Then slumber fell upon me and I slept for about half an hour. I awoke in distress in that He did not converse with me at length as in former times. I began again to rehearse the Mishnah and before I had completed two chapters, the voice of my beloved began to knock in my mouth, saying: "Although you imagined that I had forsaken you and left you, do not think I really will leave you before I have fulfilled My promise not to withhold good from your mouth. But you must cleave to Me and to the fear of Me, as I have said, and then you will be elevated, lifted up, and made high before all the members of the Heavenly Academy, all of whom send you greetings because you busy yourself all the time with the Talmud and the codes and combine the two. As I have said, you should also mortify your flesh in order to have the merit of seeing Elijah face to face while you are still awake. He will speak to you mouth to mouth and will greet you, for he will become your teacher to teach you all the mysteries of the Torah. Open your eyes, therefore, and dedicate all your thoughts to My worship and the fear of Me. Eat little and drink no wine, except for one, thoroughly diluted cup each night. Eat no meat, except once or twice during the week and then only a little. If you leave off soup it will be considered as if you had rejected an abominable thing. Let your thoughts be in My Torah. Even while eating, think on My Mishnah and your meals will then be considered as if they were sacrifices and offerings to the Holy One, blessed be He. Do not grieve that you left the Great Assembly.[2] It is for your own good that you have gone forth from there. For the Holy One, blessed be He, has decreed that the community be destroyed and it is good for you not to be there when it happens. Even though you will suffer greatly the sufferings will purge your soul so that you will be cleansed of your sins. The members of the Great Assembly will also be visited with great sufferings. The secret of the matter is . . . The secret of the matter is . . . The secret of the matter is. . . ."[3] (Thus he repeated for more than an hour, as if reluctant to tell me, until eventually he said:) "The secret of the matter is that the members of the Great Assembly have sinned by blasphemy, God forbid, in that they scoff at those who pray in the ruin. The Holy One, blessed be He, was exceedingly wrath, as it were, and He decreed, measure for measure, that you should not be among them until many days have passed. You see that I have given you another community in their stead and they will raise your college to a position of great fame. Grieve not, therefore, for all you lack is from the Holy One, blessed be He. You will witness how He arranges all things. He will order it so that the members of the Great Assembly will come to offer you their entreaties that you return to them to spread the Torah among them even if for only one day each week. Wait until the days I have mentioned have passed and you will witness the things of the Holy One, blessed be He, and you will be astonished. Grieve not at all, therefore, for the Holy One, blessed be He, will arrange your affairs while you study the Torah unceasingly. Know that very soon a large sum of money will arrive for you from the Diaspora so that you will be able to provide for your students. Your students will increase and will become great sages, rendering decisions in law. No student who has not studied in your college will have any reputation for learning at all. You will become elevated and lifted up on high, for I will make you great, I will raise you up. I will exalt you. I will make you a Prince over My people Israel. Your college will be greater than that of My chosen one, Isaac Aboab.[4] You will learn and teach and your children will be members of the Sanhedrin in the Chamber of Hewn Stone. You will yet see them teaching the laws of *kemizah*.[5] This son of yours will become a rabbi and a great man, a great sage in the Talmud and the Kabbalah. During his lifetime no greater kabbalist will be found, for he will attain to a knowledge of the Kabbalah greater than that of any other man these past five hundred years, ten times more than My beloved Solomon.[6] He will compose a commentary to the Zohar and will compose strictures on your book, for his soul derives from the Quality of Wisdom. He will, therefore, comprehend the secrets of Wisdom and will render decisions in law in Israel. Therefore, My son, busy yourself constantly and unceasingly in My Torah and devote all your thoughts to My worship. All your needs will be attended to by Me and I shall look after all your affairs. Only cleave to Me and to My Mishnah and let not your thoughts be separated from them for even one moment. Then you will become most elevated. Grieve not at all. Whatever the Holy One, blessed be He, does is for your benefit and for your own good. Open your eyes to My Torah and to My fear. Let your heart be a nest and sanctuary for My Torah. Sanctify yourself and all your limbs to My service by day and night. Let your limbs form a camp within which the *Shekhinah* can rest. And so peace to you. Peace to you, Peace to your teaching. Peace to your book. Peace to your learning. Peace to your life. Peace to your soul. Peace to your spirit. And to all that is yours, peace!"

V

Thus has it been decided in the Heavenly Academy and the Holy One, blessed be He, together with the members of the Academy, has sent Me to tell you new things hitherto unrevealed. All the sages of the generation, when they hear these things coming from your mouth, will praise you. Gaze at all the great love and goodness the Holy One, blessed be He, has wrought for you. He created you out of nothing to bring you into this world. Even though you have sinned He caused you to be reincarnated again and again until he brought you into this age. And He held your right hand even when you sinned. You returned to Him in those days but then you became lax in repenting. But now that you have drawn near to the fear of Him I have come to take delight with you, to speak in your mouth, not in a dream but as a man speaks to his neighbor.[1] Hold fast to Me, therefore and give up bodily pleasures. Drink no wine during the day and eat no meat. At night drink only one cup of wine and eat meat but not a great deal, only enough to keep you in good health. You are permitted to drink wine on the Sabbath and on festivals but yield not to your evil inclination to drink, as you wish to do, a great deal, except for the festival of Purim when you may drink limitless quantities. If you will do this, forsaking bodily pleasures so that your heart and mind become a constant nest for the Torah and if you never cease from thinking on the Torah, then the Holy One, blessed be He, will take delight in you. Busy yourself constantly with rendering decisions in Jewish law and with the Talmud, the Kabbalah, the Mishnah, the *Tosafot* and Rashi, as you are doing. For you combine them and fit one to the other bringing the hooks into the loops. Because you do this, the Holy One, blessed be He, loves you and at the time when you arise to offer your prayers and to study, the time when the Holy One, blessed be He, delights with the saints in the Garden of Eden, namely, at midnight, He takes delight in you, too, and extends over you a thread of mercy which kisses you with loving kisses and embraces you. And the *Shekhinah* converses with you and you become attached in such a way never achieved by even one in a generation, nay, by one in many generations. From it you can see how great is the love the Holy One, blessed be He, bears for you. He has stretched out His right hand to receive you as you repent. These days in which you have repented now shine for you. Your glory is upon them and theirs upon you. You will be worthy of being burned for the sanctification of the name. Then will your sins be completely erased, all the dross and rust being purged by fire. You will be clothed in a robe of light when you ascend to Heaven. There you will be among the saints of the highest degree. You will no longer be obliged to return to earth in a new incarnation for here you will rest, as it was said to Daniel, until the resurrection of the dead, when you will rise again together with the saints. Be strong, therefore, in separating yourself from bodily pleasures. For Samael and the serpent try to prevent you; their desire is to overcome you but you will prevail over them to reject them and subdue them and the Lord will be at your right hand. If they entice you to eat more meat and drink more wine than you should, whether on weekdays or on the Sabbath and festivals, pay them no heed. Also when they entice you with base thoughts, as they do, rebuke them and subdue them. Busy yourself constantly in the study of the Torah, for when you casuistically examined the opinions of the Rambam [Rabbi Moses ben Maimon] yesterday, the two views you expressed are correct and the Rambam is pleased that you have succeeded in uncovering his full meaning and he is pleased that you always quote his opinions and discuss his views casuistically. Your words are right except in the few instances I shall show you. When you die, the Rambam will come out to meet you because you have defended his decisions and, even now, he pleads on your behalf. And he is among the saints, not as those sages who say that he has been reincarnated, etc. For let it be that so it was decreed because of certain heretical views he expressed but the Torah he had studied protected him as well as his good deeds, for he was a master of good deeds, so he was not reincarnated, etc., but he was reincarnated and then he died and he is now among the saints.[2]

VI

The eve of the Sabbath, 14th of Elul. The Lord be with you, only cleave constantly to Me, the fear of Me, and My Mishnah. Cease not for a single moment from your thoughts. At all times let the chambers of your heart be filled with Torah and the fear of God and leave no room for those thoughts and images that Samael and the serpent and the evil inclination bring into your heart. Burn them out with the straw of the reading of the *Shema* and the fire of the Torah. Take care, as I have taught you, to the best of your ability, never to enjoy anything or have any longings for anything. I shall not forsake you until I have fulfilled My promise and will satisfy all your needs, only cleave to Me.

Deut. 21:10   Now the verse: "When thou goest forth to battle [against thine enemy and the Lord thy God delivereth them unto thy hands, and thou carriest them away captive]" hints at the Community of Israel. She wages war against your evil inclination and were it not for Her help, man would be incapable of overcoming the evil inclination. As the Rabbis of blessed memory say: "The evil inclination of man seeks to slay him each day and if it were not that the Holy One, blessed be He, helps him, man could never prevail, as it is said: 'The wicked watcheth the righteous and seeketh to slay him.'" If you will ask: In that case there should be no reward. For if the Holy One, blessed be He, did not help, the evil inclination would prevail? Therefore, the verse continues: "The Lord will not leave him in his hand, nor suffer him to be condemned." The Holy One, blessed be He, considers it as if man had achieved the victory by his own efforts without the assistance of the Community of Israel. Consequently, the verse says: "When [= *ki* = *Keneset Yisrael*]" goes forth to battle against your enemies, and *Tiferet* helps Her. Therefore it says: "And the Lord" = *Tiferet*, "your God" = *Binah* or *Paḥad*. Or the meaning may be that He will conduct Himself according to His quality of mercy to deliver the evil inclination into your hands, as it is said: "and the Lord thy God delivereth into thy hands, and thou carriest them away captive," the evil inclination will be held captive by you. "And seest among the captives a woman of goodly form." This means that even when you have conquered the evil inclination he will not give in but will try to make worldly things attractive to you. As the holy Zohar says: The evil inclination resembles a beautiful woman.[1]

Suk. 52b

Ps. 37:32

The eve of the Sabbath, 11th of Elul. Be strong, etc. "When thou goest forth to battle against thine enemies," namely, the evil inclination. "And the Lord thy God delivereth them into thy hands," etc. But beforetimes you saw among the captives "a woman of goodly form." This refers to the evil inclination, compared, as the holy Zohar says, to a beautiful woman. "And thou hast a desire unto her," as one who desires a loose woman. And at that time you took

Deut. 21:11

her to wife and at that time you brought her home to your house and shaved her head—in order to adorn her—and she remained in your house. But now that you have repented she weeps for her father and mother for a full month. This means that you must weep for a full month, a *Deut. 21:13* complete cycle, over the sins of your youth. "And after that thou mayest go in unto her." That is to say, you are bound to have recourse to the pleasures of the evil inclination in order to keep body and soul together, but do not bring her into your house, for if you do she will become the dominant *Deut. 21:13* partner. Rather cast her out of your house and when you need her "thou mayest go in unto her, and be her husband." This means: Do not stay with her but behave like a man who cohabits with a woman in stealth. As soon as he has completed the act he departs from her. So, too, you should not take pleasure in the evil inclination except when it becomes absolutely necessary for the body to survive. But since stolen waters are sweet, it follows that by having only *Deut. 21:13* occasional recourse to the evil inclination its blandishments become even sweeter. Therefore, the verse says: "and she shall be thy wife." This means, in connection with this matter, the relationship should be that of a man with his wife where familiarity has blunted the edge of pleasure. And peace to you.[2]

Comments

I

This epistle of Solomon Alkabetz was also printed in the section *Shavuot* in Isaiah Horowitz's *Shenei Luhot ha-Berit* (the *Shelah*), published in Amsterdam, 1649. For further bibliographical information, see Werblowsky, 19–22 and 108–12. Karo was living at the time in Nikopol and Alkabetz's epistle was evidently addressed to the mystic brotherhood in Salonika. Werblowsky (p. 111) suggests either the year 1530 or 1534 as the date of the events recorded in the epistle.

1. The festival of Shavuot is traditionally the anniversary of the revelation at Sinai. The night-vigil on this festival had been adopted by Turkish and Safed mystics but Alkabetz here refers to the program of readings and studies he had drawn up for the occasion. The vigil took place in Karo's house. The mystics believed that on Shavuot the *Sefirah Tiferet* ("the Holy One, blessed be He"), the King, is united with His Bride, the *Shekhinah*, the *Sefirah Malkhut*. The "sacred marriage" is assisted by the devotions of the mystics, "the sons of the palace."

2. Ezekiel chapter 1 is the *haftarah* for the first day of Shavuot, Habakkuk chapter 3, the *haftarah* for the second day. The reference to "without the songs" is obscure; perhaps it means without reciting the Songs of Ascents, the following series of Psalms.

3. "Choicest of the choice" (Hebrew: *mehaderin min hamehaderin*) is a rabbinic expression for the especially pious and observant.

4. In this epistle the *maggid* is clearly identified with the *Shekhinah*, fallen to the ground as a result of man's sins and ready to be raised up again by the deeds of the pious. It must be noted that in the Kabbalah, the *Shekhinah* is the counterpart on high of the Community of Israel here on earth and is, in fact, called "The Community of Israel." Israel's exile, particularly acute after the expulsion from Spain at the end of the 15th century, was said to mirror the "exile of the *Shekhinah*," that is to say, disharmony in the sefirotic realm as a result of human sin. When the *Shekhinah* is in exile She is attacked by the demonic forces, the *kelippot* ("shells" or "husks"), hence the reference to Her embracing the dunghills.

5. As in other parts of the book, the *maggid* is also identified with the Mishnah.

6. The reference to the companions in the great city is probably to the brotherhood in Salonika, to whom the epistle is addressed.

7. The recital of: "Blessed be the name of His glorious Kingdom" is based on the identification of the *Shekhinah* with *Malkhut* ("Sovereignty"). That the *maggid* is the Mishnah as well as the *Shekhinah* is no doubt based on the identification of the Oral Torah with *Malkhut* (see Werblowsky, 267–69).

8. The companions are urged to go to the holy land; in fact, both Karo and Alkabetz eventually did settle in Safed.

9. The reference to "ten in number" is to the quorum for the most sacred prayers—the *minyan*—but which in the Kabbalah also represents the ten *Sefirot*. When all ten *Sefirot* are mirrored on earth, then the unification is complete.

10. The two letters *he* are two of the four letters of the Tetragrammaton. *He* also has the numerical value of "five"; hence twice "five" corresponds to the number of the *Sefirot* in the "eternal dust" on high.

11. From the reference to the "tract," it appears that a special tract was composed containing further revelations of the *maggid* which Alkabetz sent together with his epistle to the brotherhood in Salonika (see Werblowsky) but it is just possible that the tract and the epistle are one and the same.

12. For the "regulations," see Schechter's essay on the Safed regulations.

II

These are the rules of conduct ordered by the *maggid*. The numbers of the first 18 items are in the text.

1. The reference to bad temper is repeated frequently in the book.

2. "As if a demon . . ." is in the Talmud, *Nedarim* 20b. But the Talmud states that it was in order to avoid having thoughts of another woman. The kabbalists extend it to mean that no pleasure should be had when performing the act and Karo extends it further to mean that no pleasure should be had from food or drink.

3. The identity of Al-Constantin is uncertain (see Werblowsky, 164).

4. The point about *oneg* and *nega'* is that these two Hebrew words have the same letters. The "mystery" to which Karo alludes is that the demonic side can also serve the good, the sinister side being converted to good when man enjoys the world with his thoughts only on God.

5. "Grace" is *ḥen*, the initial letters of *ḥokhmah nistarah*, "the secret science," the Kabbalah.

6. Gabriel is the angel of judgment. The verse from Genesis is interpreted to mean that Pharaoh's *spirit* was troubled because in the dream the soul alone is affected and there is a strong sense of urgency.

7. The reference to the "pig" is to a rabbinic saying that the pig has cloven hooves but does not chew the cud. He has only one of the two marks which distinguish a clean animal from an unclean one. The pig displays his cloven hooves as if to say: "See, I am clean" while hiding the fact that he does not chew the cud.

8. The reference to the "straw" contains a pun. *Kash* is "straw" and also the word formed from the initial letters of *keri' at Shema*, "the reading of the *Shema*."

9. The reference to the "knife to the throat" is to the rabbinic rule (see *Ḥullin* 6a) that one should refrain from questionable food and drink.

III

1. From the reference to the land of Israel it is obvious that this section was written after Karo had settled in Safed.

2. For information on Karo's several wives, see Werblowsky, 131.

3. For the river of fire see *Ḥagigah* 13b–14a based on Daniel 7:10 (as above); and for Michael as the High Priest who brings the souls of the saints to God, see *Ḥagigah* 12b and *Zevaḥim* 62a.

4. Rabbi Isaac Alfasi (1013–1103), Rabbi Moses ben Maimon (1135–1204) and Rabbi Asher ben Jehiel (d. 1327) were the three great codifiers of Jewish law prior to Karo. Karo's *Beit Yosef* is a commentary to the *Tur*, the code compiled by Asher's son, Jacob. In this work, Karo summarizes all the opinions of the earlier codifiers and then renders his decision. The *maggid* here compares Karo to the successive compilers of the Oral Torah, from Rabbi Judah the Prince, the editor of the Mishnah, in the early third century, to Rav Ashi, the traditional editor of the Babylonian Talmud in the 5th century, down through the medieval codifiers. The *Halakhot Pesukot* is an early code compiled before that of Rabbi Isaac Alfasi.

IV

1. The reference to the two communities is clearly to Safed where evidently Karo at first taught in a large synagogue but was later compelled to teach in the "ruin." The *maggid* reassures him. The members of his former congregation will beg him to give them some of his time.

2. The "Great Assembly" is the larger of the two congregations.

3. On the stutterings of the *maggid*, see Werblowsky, 261–63.

4. Isaac Aboab (1433–1493) was a famous Spanish talmudist of whom Karo may have been a discile in his youth, though this is unlikely (see the discussion in Werblowsky, 87).

5. The reference to the Sanhedrin is to the messianic restoration when the Sanhedrin will function once again in the Chamber of Hewn Stone adjacent to the Temple. Karo was involved in the controversy between Jacob Berab and Levi ibn Ḥabib on the restoration of "ordination" (*semikhah*) as a prelude to the restoration of the Sanhedrin, and Karo was himself ordained by his teacher Berab. This passage contains echos of the controversy. *Kemiẓah* is the manner in which the priest smooths out the meal of the meal-offering in the Temple; from *komeẓ*, "a handful." With the Temple rebuilt, the Sanhedrin will teach the priests how to carry out the sacrificial system.

6. Werblowsky identifies the "beloved Solomon" with Solomon Alkabetz (see pages 101, 119).

V

1. The reference to "as a man speaks to his neighbor . . .", indicated that the *maggid* did not come when Karo was in a state of trance but while he was fully awake.

2. See Werblowsky, 170, note 2, that the original reading was to Maimonides being reincarnated "as a worm," which the printers deleted because of its offensiveness, substituting "etc."

VI

1. The "Community of Israel" is the *Shekhinah* (see Comments to Text 1 above). In kabbalistic symbolism, the *Shekhinah* =

Malkhut = Keneset Yisrael ("The Community of Israel") and the initial letters of Keneset Yisrael form the Hebrew word ki. This is the word which appears in Deuteronomy 21:10 and is translated as "when." The Tetragrammaton ("the Lord") represents Tiferet; "God" represents either the Sefirah Binah ("Understanding") or the Sefirah Gevurah ("Power") or, as Karo here calls it, Pahad ("Dread"). In rabbinic thought, wherever the Tetragrammaton is used in the Bible it means God in His quality of mercy.

2. In this final paragraph, the maggid advises Karo to treat worldly pleasures as shameful. He should have recourse to them in stealth and with embarrassment as if he were consorting with a loose woman. But complete consistency here would add the allure of the forbidden. Consequently, paradoxically, he should, at the same time, treat the evil inclination as a lawfully wedded wife where strong allure is lacking owing to familiarity.

It will be seen from these selections that Karo had a longing for martyrdom. Although, of course, Judaism has had its martyrs throughout the ages, Jewish law demanded martyrdom only when the alternative was apostasy; thus, the desire expressed by Karo to become a martyr and his yearning for martyrdom as a sacrifice of the highest merit are extremely unconventional. It has frequently been suggested, with much probability, that Karo's unusual desire to be burnt at the stake for the glory of God was influenced by the fact that this death was the tragic fate of a man he admired, the kabbalist and pseudo-Messiah, Solomon Molcho (c. 1500–1532).

The list of ethical maxims imported to Karo by his maggid bears a striking resemblance to the similar lists produced by the Safed mystics as recorded by Solomon Schechter in his study of the Safed circle. The members of this circle sought to hasten the advent of the Messiah by their holy lives. These ascetic exercises were all part of their messianic aim.

II.

The Visions of
Rabbi Ḥayyim Vital

ᔐ

Introduction

Rabbi Ḥayyim Vital (1542–1620) was chief disciple in Safed
of the great kabbalist Isaac Luria, and also propagated his
teachings at length in voluminous writings. Vital wrote his
Sefer ha-Ḥezyonot ("Book of Visions") while he was in Damascus between the years 1609 and 1612. As its name implies, the work contains his dreams and visions and those of
others about him. The following translation is from the edition published in Jerusalem in 1954 by A. Z. Aescoly. The
division into parts and numbers is the original manuscript,
written in Vital's own hand. Selection I can be found on
pages 1–3; selection II, on pages 6–8; selection III, on pages
50–55; selection IV, on pages 141–50; and selection V, on
pages 170–72.

Text

I

The following are the events which befell me from the day of my birth, on the first day of the month Ḥeshvan in the year 5303 from the creation (= 1542).

1. While my father of blessed memory was still in the Diaspora, before he came to the land of Israel, he had as his guest a great sage by the name of Ḥayyim Ashkenazi, who said to him: "Know that you are destined to reside in the land of Israel. There a son will be born to you. Call him Ḥayyim after my name. He will be a great sage, without peer in his generation."

2. The year 5314 from the creation (= 1554). I was twelve years old at the time. A great expert in the interpretation of the palms of the hand, gazing at the lines in my palms, said to me: "Know that at the age of twenty-four the thought will perforce enter your head to be indifferent to the study of the Torah for two and a half years. Then two ways will present themselves to you, one leading to heaven, the other to hell. The choice will be yours. If you choose the path to hell no more wicked person than you will be found in your generation, but if you choose the path to heaven you will be beyond measure superior to all the members of your generation in wisdom and piety." And nothing that he said has failed to be realized.

3. The year 5317 from the creation (= 1557). In the name of the angel, the *maggid*, who spoke through him, our master, Rabbi Joseph Karo of blessed memory, ordered my teacher, Rabbi Moses Alshekh, to take care to instruct me to the best of his ability since the role I am to play in this generation is that of successor to our master, Rabbi Joseph Karo.

4. The year 5325 (= 1565). The sage, Rabbi Lapidot Ashkenazi of blessed memory, a true prognosticator, was in Safed. His art was based on the fact that the soul of a living person or one dead, even from ancient times, would come to him to tell him all he wished to know. One day I visited his home on some errand but he treated me with no respect at all since he did not know who I was. When I returned to his house on the morrow he rose to his feet as soon as he saw me and paid me great honor, saying: "Forgive me for not paying respect to you yesterday but until last night, when they told me of it, I did not appreciate the high state of your soul. I now give you this counsel. Remove all worldly matters from your thought. Let all your thought be directed towards the elevation of your soul to its rightful place, for you do not belong to the souls of this generation but to the souls of the early *tanna'im*. If you so desire, you can ascend to the most tremendous and immeasurable stages because of the great power of your soul. It is essential, therefore, that you do not imagine you have a lowly soul but that you have a very lofty soul since this is the truth. As a result you will be encouraged in your service, as we find it

2 Chron. 17:6   said of Hezekiah: 'And his heart was lifted up in the ways of the Lord.' Know, furthermore, that you have no sins, apart from one, which you committed again a day or two ago. If you put this right you will be elevated beyond measure." After a time, when I came before my master the Ashkenazi of blessed memory, he spoke to me in the same manner. I then told him what Rabbi Lapidot had said to me, which was the same as he had said, and he was very pleased.

II

11. The year 5338 (= 1578). On Sabbath morning I was preaching to the congregation in Jerusalem. Rachel, the sis-

ter of Rabbi Judah Mishan, was present. She told me that
during the whole of my sermon there was a pillar of fire
above my head and Elijah of blessed memory was there at
my right hand to support me and that when I had finished
they both departed. Also in Damascus in the year 5362 (=
1602) she saw a pillar of fire above my head when I conducted the *Musaf* service in the Sicilian community on the
Day of Atonement. This woman is wont to see visions,
demons, spirits and angels and she has been accurate in
most of her statements from the time she was a little girl
until now that she has grown to womanhood.

13. Jerusalem the year 5339 (= 1579). One morning I was
visited by an Arab who was the custodian of a mosque. He
was a Jew-hater, yet he kissed my hands and feet and entreated me to bless him and to write in my own handwriting
whatever two or three words I would choose so that he
could hang them around his neck as a kind of amulet. I
asked him why the sudden change of heart and he replied:
"I now know that you are a godly and holy man. For I am
the custodian of a mosque. Last night at midnight I went
out of the door of the mosque to relieve myself. The moon
was shining so brightly at the time that it was as clear as
noon. I raised my eyes and saw you flying through the air,
floating for an hour above the mosque—you yourself, without any doubt."

14. The year 5340 (= 1580). A man by the name of Rabbi
Abba came from Assyria to Safed and inquired of my
whereabouts. They told him that I was in Jerusalem, whereupon he related to them all that he later related to me, as I
shall tell. From thence he came to Jerusalem and he entered
my house and kissed my hands and feet. He said to me: "Behold, before I left Assyria, namely, the town of Mosul, a
great and venerable sage who resided there, whose name is
so-and-so (I have forgotten the name he gave)—he is a famous saint, living as a hermit in an upper room, seeing no

man, and visited frequently by Elijah of blessed memory—
ordered me to greet you in his name and to inform you that
all that your master Rabbi Isaac Ashkenazi has told you regarding the successive incarnations of your soul and its
great worth is all firm and true. If you were only aware of
the greatness of your soul you would be astonished. Therefore, let not the words of your master depart from before
your eyes, for great goodness will come to Israel through
your efforts. If you are small, you are the head of the tribes
of Israel. All his days he has had a great yearning to see your
face but he lacks the strength to visit you. He is in constant
anguish that he is unable to visit you to converse with you
mouth to mouth about your affairs but he has had to be
content with the delivery of his message by me."

15. The year 5350 (= 1590). A man by the nane of Rabbi
Shealtiel Alsheikh came from Persia. He is a man who sees
visions even while he is awake, a man of discernment; a sage
and saint who spends all his days in fasting. He told me that
they always show him that the redemption of Israel depends
on me, as does the return of Israel in repentance. They tell
him of the high state of my soul. Even until now, in the year
5370 (= 1610) he writes letters to me regarding his visions in
the matter of my soul and the matter of the redemption.

III

Part 2: 8. The year 5330 (= 1570). I had the following dream
on Sabbath night. It was either on Shavuot or Rosh Ha-
Shanah that I was sitting at table with my father and
mother and other relatives. In the south wall was a window
ledge upon which rested a serpent's egg, one end of which
was breaking open. I threw it outside so that it broke open
entirely and from it emerged two huge serpents, one male
the other female, attached to one another in the manner in

which males and females copulate. I took hold of a stone, white as snow, and cast it at one of the serpents, cutting off its head but that head still remained attached to the other serpent. The head that had been cut off then jumped away to flee from that house. As I went to find it I perceived a tent made of a very white cloak. I entered that tent to see if the serpent's head was there but did not find it. I said to myself, no matter, for undoubtedly it will only survive until sundown and will die completely once the sun has set. I then raised my eyes and saw inscribed on the cloak, partly in Aramaic partly in Hebrew, the words: "Whoever subdues and crushes the Other Side and whoever runs after sinners to cleanse them of that filth and conquer the Other Side, his throne will I elevate above that of My servant Metatron." It appeared to me then that this formula was actually a verse in the book of the Proverbs of Solomon so that I said: "If the reward of one who subdues the Other Side is so great, I shall go and slay the other serpent whose companion I have already slain." And then I awoke. This took place early in the morning.

9. That same year I had a dream in which it was the day of the Rejoicing of the Law and I was praying in the synagogue of the Greeks in Safed. Rabbi Moses Cordovero was there and another man, greater than he in degree. When I awoke I forgot whether it was the *tanna* Rabbi Phinehas ben Jair of blessed memory or our contemporary Rabbi Eleazar ben Yoḥai. They begged me to lead the congregation in prayer, reciting the *Musaf* aloud. But I arose and recited the morning prayer until the conclusion of the benediction: "Who causeth the strength of His salvation to spring forth." I then immediately stepped backwards three paces and recited: "He who maketh peace . . ." All the congregation protested, asking why I did not complete all the eighteen benedictions, whereupon the other two sages said to them: "Be silent. He knows what he is doing and that it is this that

the hour demands." After the prayers, Rabbi Moses Cordovero said to me: "Why do you torment yourself to such a degree to grasp the wisdom of the Zohar with utter clarity and why can you not be content with the comprehension of the Zohar I and the sages of previous generations have attained?" I replied: "I shall continue to acquire as clear a comprehension as I can. If they do not wish it in heaven, what more can I do?" He said to me: "If this is your desire to know the work to its very roots, more than the generations before you ever comprehended, I shall ascend to heaven to pray for you with all my might." Then the other sage with him said: "Who is this man that he should be able to attain to such comprehension?" Rabbi Cordovero replied: "Behold, he is very God-fearing. All his life he has striven with all his might to grasp this science so he is worthy of it." Whereupon the other sage said: "If that is the case, I, too, shall pray for him on high until he attains the comprehension he desires." Afterwards I left the synagogue and I saw many people strolling in the field, taking their food and drink there, for, as I have said, it was a festive day. I went along with them, not to eat there but in order to study the Torah. Robbers attacked us and took away all we had, taking from me my outer robe, a fine festive garment. I fled and entered the city where I went to the synagogue. There I offered the prayer: "It is known to Thee that I did not go out to take a stroll or to eat like the others but in order to study the Torah. Why, then, did this befall me?" And, behold, a man entered with my cloak in his hand, saying: "Your prayer has been answered. For you went out there for no other purpose than to study the Torah, so they have restored your cloak to you. Take it, it is your very own."

10. In that year some of the scholars, God-fearing and saints, in the city of Safed, resolved to meet weekly on the eve of the Sabbath to tell one another all their deeds, whether good or bad, of that week, in order to shame them-

selves out of sinning. But I objected: I cannot agree with you that it is right for a man to reveal his bad deeds to others. Their meeting took place on the eve of the Sabbath in the synagogue. That night, on the Sabbath, I had the following dream. I was going down from the khan of Safed by way of the stone steps leading to the marketplace and where, at the butchers' stalls, there is a crossroad. Behold, my father was coming to meet me along one road and Rabbi Moses Cordovero and Rabbi Moses Sagis both came to meet me along the other road which leads from the cemetery to the khan. Many of those who had departed this life came down to the road from heaven and they all came to meet me. Before they reached me I perceived from afar a ledger in their hands, containing a list of the names of many scholars, which they read out softly. Rabbi Solomon Sagis was the first name on the list, then I myself, Ḥayyim, then the other scholars. When they came close to me I abjured Rabbi Moses Cordovero to tell me the truth regarding the list. For if, God forbid, it contained the names of those who were to die during that year it would have been better for me to know it so that I could scrutinize my deeds and so have provisions for the way. He replied: "This is nothing else than a list of those scholars who are ready to repent and to serve the Lord. This day they were all gathered in the synagogue to examine their ways but you could not agree with them that it was right to perform this good deed." I repeated to him the reason I had given on the eve of the Sabbath, as above. Then I asked whether Rabbi Solomon Sagis is greater than I. "God forbid," he replied, "that is not the reason. It is rather out of respect for his father who was the first this week to fulfil that upon which they had agreed. That is why his son's name tops the list."

Then we all came to the Jewish quarter where I saw all Israel gathered. The sun had set at noontime and, behold, there was a thick darkness over all the world and all Israel wept bitterly. Now, behold, a man having the appearance of a hermit and dervish, his garments rent and his hair so long that it reached down to his legs, came to that quarter from the east, by way of the Aragon synagogue, and he sang a pleasant tune in a loud voice. The song was in stanzas, as is the manner of such songs, and its whole theme was that of levirate marriage, the Messiah and the Redemption, after the manner in which the Zohar explains the verse: "If he will redeem thee, well; let him redeem thee." But no one understood what he said and no one, apart from me, heard his voice at all. Thus he sang until he came near to me and then the sun shone once again as before.

Ruth 3:13

11. 5331 (= 1571). The New Moon of the month of Iyyar. At the time of the afternoon prayer I went into isolation by the means known to me of reciting three times the Mishnah text. I had it in mind to inquire about my previous incarnation. I fell into a trance and saw my master of blessed memory, who said to me: "Behold, this handsome young man standing beside us is my brother-in-law, my sister's husband, and you were his teacher." Then I awoke.

I recited the Mishnah once again and fell asleep. I heard a very loud voice calling "Ḥayyim! Ḥayyim!" and I was afraid and I awoke. I thought to myself that my master of blessed memory was Rabban Gamaliel, the brother-in-law of Rabbi Eliezer, disciple of Rabban Johanan ben Zakkai. I went to my master and related all this to him but he said: "This is undoubtedly a heavenly visitation, yet I do not wish to reveal to you the meaning of it because I do not wish you to know the previous incarnation of my soul."

12. On the Sabbath day, the 25th of Iyyar, while the reader was singing the *Kaddish* of the morning *yozer*, I fell into a trance. I saw my master of blessed memory who said to me: "Do you know that a certain person is on his way to your house carrying a valuable turban for your head and that man is called *El* and called *Yeho*?" And I awoke. I told

the dream to my master who explained to me that on that
Sabbath I had attained to a Sabbath addition to my spirit,
ready for me once I had perfected my soul.

IV

Part 4: The following are the matters concerning me and
the root of my soul and told to me by my master of blessed
memory.

14. One day I visited him, a whole month having passed
during which I had performed none of the *yihudim* (unifications) he had prescribed for me. Recognizing this by looking
at my face, he said to me: " 'If you leave me for a day I shall
leave you for two.' You cause great harm by failing to perform the unifications, for it causes the souls who wish to become attached to you to become separated from you." I
excused myself in that I desired only to study the Torah at
that time, especially since those souls did not come to me as
openly as they should have done. He replied that in spite of
this I must not fail to perform these unifications daily. It is
more important than the study of the Torah since it unifies
the upper worlds and so serves the dual purpose of Torah
study and unification. He warned me that when I perform
the unifications my intention should not be only for the
purpose of attracting the soul but in order to put things
right on high.

He also said to me, when I went with him to the sepulcher of Rabbi Akiva, that Rabbi Akiva had told him I was
to mention Rabbi Akiva's name ten times consecutively before each of the three daily prayers, evening, morning and
noon. As a result he will become impregnated in me and
will greatly assist me. He told me that there was no need for
me to say "Rabbi Akiva," only "Akiva."

He also said to me that until the festival of Tabernacles

in the year 5334 (= 1573) I shall require real assistance, that he should assist me whenever I perform unifications. But from then onward I shall require no assistance whatever, for then compensation will have been made for the two and a half years I had sinned by failing to study the Torah. Furthermore, until that time, even if he did assist me, it was only on occasion, for it could not then have been permanent, but that from that time onward it would be permanent, God willing.

15. He ordered me never to refrain from performing the unifications he had delivered unto me and that when I go to prostrate myself on the graves of the saints it should either be on the eve of the New Moon or on the fifteenth day of the month, for then it is more effective than at any other time. I should not go on the Sabbath or on the festivals or on the New Moon, for at these times the souls of the saints ascend to heaven and cannot be apprehended at the graveside. Once he sent me to the graves of the saints on *hol hamo'ed* to offer prayers there but I did not prostrate myself.

V

32. On the eve of the New Moon of the month of Elul in the year 5331 (= 1571) my master of blessed memory sent me to the sepulcher of Abbaye and Rava. There I prostrated myself at the grave of Abbaye of blessed memory and first performed the unification of the Mouth and Nose of the Holy Ancient One. Sleep fell upon me and then I awoke but I saw nothing. Then I again prostrated myself on Abbaye's actual grave and I performed the unification recorded in my master's own handwriting but as I was engaged in combining, as is well known, the letters of the Tetragrammaton with those of *Adonai*, my thoughts became confused and I was unable to combine them, so I ceased from reflecting on that combination of letters. It then

seemed to me in my thought as if a voice was saying to me:
"Retract! Retract!" many times and I thought to myself that
these were the words Akavyah ben Mahalalel addressed to
his son, as is well known. So I tried again to combine the
letters and this time I was successful. It then seemed to me
in my thoughts that they were saying to me: "God will pro-
vide Himself the lamb for a burnt-offering, my son" (*elohim*   *Gen. 22:8*
yir'eh lo ha-seh le-'olah beni) and it seemed as if they were explaining the meaning of the verse to me, namely, I was ap-
prehensive that I had not performed the first unification
adequately but it was not so. It had, in fact, been effective
before God, hence: "God will provide Himself the lamb."
And it seemed in my thoughts as if they were explaining to
me that the whole of the first unification I had performed
was hinted at in this verse. For the initial letters of *elohim*
yir'eh lo ha-seh have the numerical value of forty-six, the
same as that of the Tetragrammaton and *Eheyeh*. And the
initial letters of *ha-seh le-'olah beni* form the word *hevel*
("breath"), which refers to the mystery of the breath of the
Supernal Mouth which I had in mind while performing that
unification. And it seemed to me as if they were saying that
Hillel the Elder is hinted at in the initial letters of *lo ha-seh*
le-'olah but I failed to grasp the meaning of this. Behold, all
this passed through my mind. Then a great dread and trembling seized hold of all my limbs and my hands trembled. My
lips, too, were trembling in a highly exaggerated manner,
moving quickly and concurrently and with great speed as if
a voice was perched on my tongue between my lips. It said
with great speed more than a hundred times: "What can I
say? What can I say." I tried to steady myself and prevent
my lips from moving but was unable to still them at all.
Then I had in mind to ask for wisdom upon which the voice
broke out in my mouth and on my tongue, saying, more
than twenty times, "Wisdom. Wisdom." Then it repeated
many times: "Wisdom and knowledge." Then it repeated:
"Wisdom and knowledge will be given to you from heaven

like the knowledge attained by Rabbi Akiva." Then it repeated: "And more than that of Rabbi Akiva." Then it repeated: "Like that attained by Rabbi Yeiva Sava." And then it repeated: "And more than that of Rabbi Yeiva Sava." And then it said: "Greetings to you." And then it said: "They send you greetings from heaven." All this was said at a great speed, repeatedly many times, utterly wondrous, while I was in a waking state and while prostrated in the sepulcher of Abbaye.

Then I went to my master of blessed memory who said to me that I was most effective in performing these two unifications one after the other and that this was, indeed, the right way to perform them. The reason I had received no response after performing the first unification was because they were waiting until I had performed both. And my master of blessed memory said to me that when I returned from that place and entered my house he saw the soul of Benaiah ben Jehoiada going along with me. He told me that Benaiah did not belong to my soul root but the reason he accompanied me was that he is always revealed together with anyone who performs the supernal unification. For this was his habit during his lifetime on earth as we have stated elsewhere.

My teacher of blessed memory said to me at the time of the afternoon prayer that if I shall be worthy on the coming Sabbath, the soul of Rabbi Yeiva Sava will remain with me for ever, never to depart, as do the other reincarnations. Through him I shall be worthy of receiving powerful illuminations, especially during the *Amidah* prayer while reciting the benedictions "the years," "the shoot" and "hearkening to prayer." The reason for it is that Rabbi Yeiva Sava also reveals himself to the saints just as Benaiah does, as we have explained. Furthermore, he belongs to my soul root. Therefore, if I shall be worthy of having him reveal himself to me he will disclose to me, God willing, marvelous things.

Comments

I

2. The reference is to the fact that at the age of twenty-four Vital devoted himself to alchemy, a practice he continued to pursue for two and a half years instead of studying the Torah.

3. The *maggid* of Rabbi Joseph Karo is the subject of chapter 10 of this book. Rabbi Moses Alshekh (d. after 1593) was Vital's teacher in Talmud and the legal literature. (As Aescoly points out, the name given in the manuscript, "Rabbi Moses Alshaker," is a mistake.)

4. The identity of Lapidot Ashkenazi is uncertain. The later reference to "my master the Ashkenazi" is to Isaac Luria also known as Isaac Ashkenazi, because his family was of Ashkenazi, not Sephardi origin.

II

11. Rabbi Judah Mishan was a member of the Safed circle of mystics. After he had moved from Safed to Damascus, Vital was the rabbi of the Sicilian Jews in the latter city.

14. Mosul is a town in Kurdistan.

III

8. The "Other Side" (*Sitra Aḥra*) is the kabbalistic name for the demonic side of existence. For Metatron see Comments to chapter 3 of this book.

9. Rabbi Moses Cordovero was the leader of the Safed circle before his teachings were superseded by those of Luria, largely through the adherence of Vital to the latter. The identity of Rabbi Eleazar ben Yoḥai is uncertain but he was evidently a member of the Safed circle. Rabbi Phinehas ben Jair was a second-century Palestinian teacher. The report about Cordovero and the Zohar obviously reflects Vital's desire to substitute the Lurianic understanding of the Kabbalah for that of Cordovero.

10. The reference to levirate marriage (Deuteronomy 25:5–10) and to the book of Ruth in a messianic context is based on the

idea that Boaz acted as a levir, and from his marriage to Ruth there was born the ancestor of David, in turn the ancestor of the Messiah. The Zohar (actually the *Zohar Ḥadash* to Ruth) interprets the verse as referring to the two Messiahs, the Messiah son of David and the Messiah son of Joseph. Perhaps Vital means that he, or his master, was the Messiah son of Joseph.

11. Rabban Gamaliel was the famous first–second-century Palestinian teacher. Thus the "handsome young man" was his brother-in-law, Rabbi Eliezer, and hence Vital was the reincarnation of the latter's teacher Rabban Johanan ben Zakkai.

12. *El* and *Yeho* are the names of Metatron.

IV

14. "If you leave me . . ." Jerusalem Talmud (*Berakhot* 9:5; 14d): "Rabbi Simeon ben Lakish said: They discovered a scroll of the saints in which was recorded: 'If you leave me (the Torah) for a day, I shall leave you for two,'" i.e., if one does not persist in study one soon forgets. The unifications (*yiḥudim*) are the combinations of the various mystical divine names the adept has to have in mind. These bring about greater unity and harmony in the realms on high. The impregnation of the soul (*'ibbur*) is the residence of a departed soul of high degree in the soul of a living person for the purpose of assisting the latter to rise to greater mystical heights.

V

32. Abbaye and Rava are the two famous Babylonian teachers in the 4th century whom the Talmud mentions much. The reference to Akavyah ben Mahalalel is to the Mishnah (*Eduyyot* 5:7): "At the time of his death he said to his son: 'Retract from the four things I was wont to teach.'" Rabbi Yeiva Sava is a hero in the Zohar. For Benaiah ben Jehoiada see II Samuel 23:20–23; I Chronicles 11:22–25; Zohar 1:6a–b. The three benedictions are on pages 50 and 51 of the new edition of the *Authorized Daily Prayer Book*, by S. Singer (1967).

12

The *Maggid* of
Rabbi Moses Ḥayyim
Luzzatto

ᴗᴖ

Introduction

Rabbi Moses Ḥayyim Luzzatto (1707–1746), talmudist, poet, moralist, mystic and one of the most acute writers on the Kabbalah, was born in Padua into a wealthy family who saw to it that he was given a thorough general as well as Jewish education. He had a knowledge of Latin and Italian and became a religious genius of such a high order that he was admired and accepted as a teacher both by the Ḥasidim and by their opponents in the late 18th century.

While still a very young man and unmarried Luzzatto gathered around him in Padua a circle of mystically inclined students. One of them, Jekuthiel Gordon of Vilna, who came to Padua to study medicine at the University, reported Luzzatto's claim to be the recipient of a *maggid* from heaven to Rabbi Mordecai Yoffe of Vienna. This letter was sent to Rabbi Moses Ḥagiz, a staunch opponent of Shabbateanism, who came to suspect the young master of Shabbatean leanings and who was scandalized at the alleged sinister activities in the Paduan circle. As a result, Luzzatto was compelled to desist from his mystical work. Eventually Luzzatto journeyed with his family to the Holy Land in the belief that there he would be free to recommence these activities. He succumbed to the plague, however, soon after his arrival, dying in the town of Acre.

Luzzatto was a prolific author. His kabbalistic work *Kelaḥ Pithei Ḥokhmah* is a comprehensive survey of the whole of the Lurianic scheme, described in great detail and with a complete mastery of the kabbalistic literature. His best-known book is the ethical treatise *Mesillat Yesharim*, "Path of the Upright," a statement of the path to holy living resulting in the attainment of the holy spirit. Although this work, too, is clearly based on kabbalistic ideas, the esoteric elements are consciously obscured and the book has served as a guide to Jewish ethical living even for those with no mystical pretensions.

Text I is a translation of Jekuthiel Gordon's letter to Rabbi Mordecai Yoffe, published by S. Ginzburg in *Rabbi Moshe Ḥayyim Luzzatto u-Venei Doro* (1937), pages 18–20. The letter is given in its entirety, except for the introductory, flowery titles with which Gordon endows Yoffe. These are based on subtle puns in the Hebrew and are untranslatable, sounding more ridiculous in English than they do in the original. Text II is a translation of a letter written by Moses Ḥayyim Luzzatto to Rabbi Benjamin ben Eliezer ha-Kohen Vitale, a famous kabbalist and the father-in-law of Luzzatto's teacher, Rabbi Isaiah Basson. The letter, written as a form of apologium for the mystical claims made on Luzzatto's behalf, was also published by Ginzburg in the same volume, pages 36–40.

Text

I

The fifth day of the week of the portion *Re'eh* in the year 5489 (= 1729), from the holy community of Padua to the holy community of Vienna to the great and famous lord, my friend . . . Rabbi Mordecai Yoffe, may the All-Merciful protect him and save him.

Although I do not know your honor personally I have heard of your fame and feel that it is right and proper to reveal to your honor the whole or the half of the secret of the Lord that is with those who fear Him. I said to myself: If I am to tell it all the page will be unable to contain it, especially since I have the brazen forehead of a harlot in daring to draw near to the holy to discuss with your honor previously unheard of matters. Who am I that I dare to come hither? I cannot therefore offer you this present in correct order but I shall tell my lord of it briefly.

I come regarding things of the Torah to inform my lord of the choice gift the Holy One, blessed be He, has granted to us from his treasure store. There is here a young man, tender in years, no older than the age of twenty-three. He is a holy man, my master and teacher, the holy lamp, the man of God, his honor Rabbi Moses Ḥayyim Luzzatto. For these past two and a half years a *maggid* has been revealed to him, a holy and tremendous angel who reveals wondrous mysteries to him. Even before he reached the age of fourteen he knew all the writings of the Ari by heart. He is very modest, telling nothing of this even to his own father and obviously not to anyone else. It was by the counsel of the Lord that I discovered it by accident, here is not the place to describe how. For the past month I have been ministering to him, drawing water from his well, happy the eye that has seen all this and happy the ear that has heard of it. He is a spark of Akiva ben Joseph. Eight months have passed since the time that the holy and tremendous angel was first revealed to him. He delivered to him numerous mysteries and imparted the methods by means of which he could summon to him the members of the Heavenly Academy. With the approval of the Holy One, blessed be He, and His *Shekhinah*, he ordered him to compose a Book of the Zohar, called in Heaven, the Second Zohar, in order that a great *tikkun* known to us should be carried out.[1]

This is what happens. The angel speaks out of his mouth but we, his disciples, hear nothing. The angel begins to reveal to him great mysteries. Then my master orders Elijah to come to him and he comes to impart mysteries of his own. Sometimes, Metatron, the great prince, also comes to him as well as the Faithful Shepherd, the Patriarch Abraham, Rabbi Hamnuna the Elder and That Old Man and sometimes King Messiah and Adam. He has already composed a marvelous and tremendous work on the book of Ecclesiastes. Now he has been ordered to compose seventy *tikkunim* on the last verse of the Torah: "And in all the mighty hand" in the same manner. He has also composed three works on the Torah, all three commenting no further than up to the portion *Va-Yeze*, all in accordance with the great mystery and in the language of the Zohar. He knows all men's previous incarnations and all the *tikkunim* they have to carry out and he knows the science of reading the lines of the hand and face. To sum up, nothing is hidden from him. At first permission was only granted to reveal to him the mysteries of the Torah but now all things are revealed to him. But no one outside our circle knows of it. He told to me personally a great secret regarding why I have come here to study under him, for nothing occurs without reason. He told me about my soul and the *tikkunim*, I have to perform.[2]

It is usual for the Faithful Shepherd and Metatron, prince of the Presence, to expound various biblical verses as referring to him and to the author of the Zohar, Rabbi Simeon bar Yoḥai, comparing him in all matters to Rabbi Simeon bar Yoḥai of blessed memory. As, indeed, he has demonstrated to all, that no one has hitherto had this kind of merit since the time of Rabbi Simeon bar Yoḥai. I, too, because of my great love for the Torah, decided to forsake the external sciences but he informed me through the *maggid*: "Take hold of this but withdraw not thy hand from the other, for a reason known only to me."[3]

Now all this has been kept a close secret from all except the members of our circle. Had I decided to tell everything about our above-mentioned master and teacher, time itself would come to end before I had finished. If your honor desires further information and wishes to be informed about the state of your soul and the *tikkunim* it requires, please forgive me and let it be written and I shall then convey the information to you little by little and you will be pleased. For one does not converse of these things in public, especially since this is the first time and I cannot know whether this letter will ever reach you. Let not my lord think, God forbid, of causing a blemish in sacred things by comparing this to false matters and to those who follow error, for the truth is its own witness. On the contrary, he knows of all that happens under the sun, all the events of the past and the root of all things. I must be brief for time presses. May the Lord prolong your days and years.[4]

Thus speaks your faithful servant who conveys these matters in a whisper, for permission has not as yet been granted to reveal them.

Jekuthiel, son of the Saint, our Master Rabbi Leib of Vilna, who studies the Torah and also studies in order to receive his diploma as a physician, God willing.

II

To the fount of living waters, the spring of sacred origin from the house of the Lord, the great and mighty tree, angel of the Lord of Moses, may the All-Merciful protect him and save him.

The Lord who is righteous and who searches all hearts is my witness in heaven and my testimony on high why I have kept it secret from your honor from the time I first saw your holy face as one sees the face of God. It was only due to my desire to keep it secret that I kept it from you, but now that the matter is public knowledge—in accordance with the word of the Lord, for when He speaks it comes to pass and when He commands it becomes firmly established—I am very pleased to hear that you know of the matter through the sage, like an angel of God, your son-in-law, my master the Rabbi, may the All-Merciful protect him and save him. I am especially glad to know that your honor, in his goodness and integrity, accepts it as true and reliable. And, now as I live, your honor, I want very much to see your holy face but it is not possible until the forthcoming fair. Then shall I come to bow to the splendor of your honor's Torah, God willing, for these matters have only just now been published abroad and have hitherto been kept a guarded secret by the members of our circle, may God preserve them.[1]

Praise to the God of Israel, many of the people now give up their sins to seek the Lord. All the God-fearing come daily to me to hear the new things the Lord tells me. The young men who had previously walked in the ways of youth's vanities, now, thank God, have turned from the evil way to return unto the Lord, each of them coming to me to receive *tikkunim* for his past deeds. Only yesterday did they come; shall I, then, forsake them by going to another country? Such a thing cannot be right! I have the obligation to encourage them until their feet have become firmly planted, as I hope, in the way of the Lord. Furthermore, it is impossible to rely on a miracle by bringing my book with me because of the danger from the censor.[2] Nevertheless, I am obliged to reveal to your honor, whose soul is so dear to me, the mysteries of God to the extent I am permitted so to do and within the confines of this letter. With the eye of your great and pure intellect you will see how profound these matters are, for deep are the thoughts of the Lord.

The gates of divine grace, open wide when the Temple stood, were shut when it was destroyed, the "Other Side" taking its power, then, from the sins of our ancestors. From that year onward events take place in accordance with the stages which require *tikkun* so that each day has its own illumination. Events are brought about in this world to correspond to the nature of this illumination, the flaws that have been made in it and the special *tikkun* it requires. Many *tikkunim* have been ordered for Israel during the exile. These are the *tikkunim* of the Mishnah, the *Gemara* and the *Midrashim*, each a special *tikkun* required at that time. Each of these operates during the time a certain illumination shines forth upon which that particular *tikkun* depends. But superior to them all is the *tikkun* of the Zohar. The secret of the Zohar is that it is all inwardness, unlike all plain meanings which belong to the external. Since the control of the world is through inwardness it follows that the chief *tikkunim* are performed through the Zohar.[3]

I shall explain this in greater detail. The Zohar belongs in the category of the seminal drop which comes from *Yesod*, hence it is called "the brightness (*zohar*) of the firmament." Now it is well known that all providence proceeds by means of copulation so that everything depends on the influence of the seminal drop. When it is merited that the category of this seminal drop comes down into the lower world, all is put right by means of a great *tikkun*, for by means of that drop are all things perfected in every way. Now Rabbi Simeon bar

Yohai was worthy of becoming the instrument by means of which this *tikkun* was performed, hence he composed the Zohar. However, the truth is that only a part of that illumination has emerged, for the purpose of allowing Israel and the world as a whole to survive during the exile. But for the real *tikkun* to be accomplished it is necessary for the thing to be permanent and unceasing so that the divine grace is constantly renewed, as is the mystical meaning of: "They are new every morning." For this is the mystery of the manna which came down in the merit of Moses whose soul embraced all six hundred thousand souls of Israel and who was able to draw down the grace provided by the copulation by a power equivalent to all these.[4]

This is the mystery. Every *tikkun* depends for its effectiveness on the degree of preparation undergone by the recipients. It can only become permanent when the recipients have made adequate preparations. It can happen that, according to the degree that is awakened, there is so powerful an increase of supernal illumination that those down below are insufficiently prepared to receive it. When this happens, it still achieves its purpose but does not remain in permanence. It departs, reserving the full *tikkun* for its revelation after a long time. The proof is from the Exodus from Egypt.[5] Consequently, after Rabbi Simeon bar Yohai, the illumination was blocked. When new degrees of illumination were afterwards ready to appear, new *tikkunim* were necessary. These appeared until the Ari came, when the illumination shone once again in the category of that original illumination which shone in the time of Rabbi Simeon bar Yohai on whom be peace. Permission was then given to the Ari to expound the Zohar of Rabbi Simeon bar Yohai on whom be peace and this was the means of bringing the original illumination to its complete expression.

Your honor will see that the amount of preparation required by Rabbi Simeon bar Yohai cannot be compared to that required by the Ari. The one required a cave and had to flee for his life and it happened in his old age; the other lead an ascetic life, of his free choice, and while he was still a young man. Many others led more ascetic lives, tortured themselves more and were more saintly than the Ari of blessed memory, yet they could not compare with him or approach near him. The truth is that just as there are numerous times of redemption—for the redemption comes in many stages, as the Ari himself observes in a comment on "And when the Lord saw that he had turned aside to see," the stages of redemption depend on the stages of those to be redeemed—so with regard to every illumination. In proportion to the degree which shines forth so is the amount of preparation required. Now great men have arisen in Israel from the time of the Ari, all of them by the power of that illumination, which departed then, and so it has proceeded from generation to generation.[6]

Now I shall tell your honor true things the Lord has revealed to me concerning yourself. You are chief of the tribes of Israel. The Lord has granted you the merit of having your fame extended to the ends of the earth. And yet you have no special disciples. All is from the Lord, whether great or little things. Since one does not praise a man too much to his face, I can only tell you the main things, those that are essential if you are to acknowledge the truth of that which I tell. That illumination from the time of the Ari of blessed memory has come down to your honor. Your honor is from the soul-root of Cain and of the prophet Ezekiel and since through you the original illumination finds its fulfillment you are obliged, for our sins, to suffer on our behalf and to carry our burdens. Because you were born under Mars it has been given you to remove the foreskin. As I have stated, you belong to *Gevurah*. Since this original *tikkun* has now been realized you were not required to have disciples, for there is no need for that illumination to spread further. At this time the Lord, in His desire to be good to His people, wished to reveal a new light in the category of the Zohar,

which, as mentioned previously, is the illumination provided by the seminal drop. For this, in His mercy, he chose
me. If you ask me about the state of my preparation, what
can I say? The truth is that it is by the Lord's grace alone
and has little to do with the state of my preparation for it.
However, it is also true that I have been assiduous for years
in carrying out *yihudim*. I perform a different *yihud* almost
every quarter of an hour and I do this even now, thank God.
I have also tried to worship in purity although I have not
engaged over much in fasting. I did, however, perform
yihudim. The root of all is that illumination depends on the
degree prevailing at a given time. And the Creator now uses
me as the instrument for the fulfillment of His purpose.[7]

In brief, this is what happened. On the first of Sivan in
the year 5487 (= 1727), as I was performing a certain *yihud*,
I fell into a trance. When I awoke, I heard a voice saying: "I
have descended in order to reveal the hidden secrets of the
Holy King."[8] For a while I stood there trembling but then I
took hold of myself. The voice did not cease from speaking
and imparted a particular secret to me. At the same time on
the second day I saw to it that I was alone in the room and
the voice came again to impart a further secret to me. One
day he revealed to me that he was a *maggid* sent from
heaven and he gave me certain *yihudim* that I was to perform in order for him to come to me. I never saw him but
heard his voice speaking in my mouth. He then allowed me
to put questions to him. Later on, after about three months
had passed, he gave me *yihudim* to perform so as to be worthy of having Elijah of blessed memory reveal himself to me.
It was then that he ordered me to compose a work on
Ecclesiastes on the basis of the mystical meaning of its
verses that he had imparted to me. Then Elijah came and
imparted his own secrets to me. And he said that Metatron,
the great prince, will come to me. I will know that it is he
because of what Elijah had said. From that time onward I
came to recognize each of my visitants. Souls whose iden-

tity I do know are also revealed to me. I write down each day the new ideas each of them imparts to me. All these things happen while I am prostrate with my face to the ground and I see the holy souls in human form as in a dream.

I can honestly and sincerely affirm that I have not as yet attained to the half of that which the Ari of blessed memory had attained. It is only that he was not ordered to record it in writing whereas I was. The *maggid* revealed to me, thank God, the innermost meaning of the kabbalistic science, wondrous things hardly known to others. For the words of the Ari are very obscure, especially on the problem of how the Column of *Ein-Sof* penetrates the World of Action. In general there are three main topics discussed in this science: the operation of providence; the descent of the illuminations by degrees; and the way in which the illuminations are combined. For all the images we use to describe these refer to quality, not to quantity, and from them all corporeality has to be negated. For the whole of this science is concerned with the manner in which the whole world is governed through the commingling of *Ḥesed, Din* and *Raḥ-hamim*.[9]

Your honor will see that all these topics are implied in the letter I sent to my master and teacher, our Rabbi, your son-in-law, may the All-Merciful protect him and save him. What the end will be I am not allowed to disclose at all, for it is secret and sealed.[10]

Now I take leave of your honor, prostrating myself with face to the ground and kissing the souls of your feet in great love and with yearning. May God fulfill your desires and long may you live. Amen. May it be His Will.

Your everlasting servant,
Moses Ḥayyim Luzzatto
The night following the Sabbath, the third day of Ḥanukkah, in the year 5490 [= 1729], Padua.

Comments

I

Mordecai Yoffe was a learned businessman in Vienna, evidently a patron of learning. Gordon, for reasons that are not altogether clear, sees fit to choose Yoffe to be the first to learn of Luzzatto's activities.

1. The Ari ("Lion:) is Isaac Luria, whose ideas had been recorded by Ḥayyim Vital (see chapter 11 of this book) in the so-called "writings of the Ari." A "spark of Akiva ben Joseph" means that a spark of the soul of the famous rabbinic teacher of old had entered Luzzatto's soul. The "members of the Heavenly Academy" are the famous personages—mentioned later—who came to Luzzatto when summoned. The word *tikkun* (plural: *tikkunim*) is a kabbalistic term denoting the "putting right" of things. According to the Kabbalah all is now in a state of disarray and the upper realms have to be "put right" by the good deeds of man, especially by various mystical meditations and special acts performed in a spirit of dedication. A part of the Zohar, known as the *Tikkunei Zohar*, takes the form of comments to the first verse of Genesis. Luzzatto's work referred to here is in the similar form of comments to the final verse of the Torah.

2. For Metatron, see Comments to chapter 3 of this book. The Faithful Shepherd is the name used (in Aramaic) for Moses. Rabbi Hamnuna the Elder is a hero of the Zohar, as is That Old Man. In the Zohar they both appear from time to time to impart mysteries to the circle of Rabbi Simeon bar Yoḥai. *Tikkunim* in this paragraph also means special written meditations, after the pattern of the *Tikkunei Zohar*.

3. Gordon wished to give up the study of medicine ("the external sciences") but the *maggid* dissuades him.

4. In the original, the expression "one does not speak in the field" is the idiomatic way of saying "one does not converse of these things in public." "Comparing this to false matters" almost certainly means that Yoffe should not suspect Luzzatto's circle of being Shabbateans, a suspicion that in fact was behind Ḥagiz's opposition to Luzzatto.

II

1. It appears from the letter that Luzzatto was being advised to leave Italy in order for the pressure on him to be removed.

2. "Danger from the censor" means from the Christian authorities who might see the book as offensive to the Christian faith and confiscate it.

3. The "Other Side" is the usual kabbalistic form designating the demonic side of existence. The *tikkunim* have the aim of frustrating the evil designs of the other side. The "plain meanings" are the meanings of Mishnah, *Gemara*, etc.; the "inward meanings" are the purely spiritual interpretations found in the Zohar since these do not deal with this world at all but with events in the realms of the spirit, the upper worlds.

4. *Yesod* is the *Sefirah* of that name, symbolized in phallic terms, because it is the source on high of all the creative processes. Through *Yesod* the "sacred marriage" of *Tiferet* and *Malkhut* takes place (see Comments to chapter 8). In the Zohar "the firmament" is the name for *Tiferet* and "the earth" for *Malkhut*. Hence the "seminal drop" of *Yesod* is "the brightness of the firmament." Hence, too, the reference here to "copulations." Naturally, Luzzatto, as, indeed, all the kabbalists, understands this in purely spiritual terms, for which the grossly physical images are only powerful symbols, or, rather, it would be more correct to say, the physical details on earth are the final form the spiritual entities on high assume once they have descended from world to world until they come down to this material world.

5. The "proof" from the Exodus is that even so powerful a manifestation did not last and Israel sinned later by worshiping the golden calf and later suffered a further exile.

6. According to the Talmud Rabbi Simeon Bar Yoḥai spent 13 years in a cave when he was obliged to flee for his life from the Romans. This became the basis of the notion that Rabbi Simeon composed the Zohar while in the cave. Luzzatto seeks to demonstrate that illuminations do not necessarily depend on the degree of sanctity of the recipients, so that while he acknowledges that he is unworthy and far from being a saint, God could still choose him as His instrument. The opponents of Luzzatto, in

fact, argued that a bachelor who had no beard and did not engage in fasting and ritual immersions could not possibly be the recipient of the revelations he claimed. It is interesting to note that these opponents, as can be seen from their letters published in Ginzburg's collection, did not deny that Luzzatto had a *maggid* but they maintained that it was not a holy angel but a demonic force.

7. Luzzatto tries to demonstrate to Benjamin that the *maggid* is reliable since he has given Luzzatto a detailed account of the role Benjamin has had to play in the scheme of things. From Luzzatto a new *tikkun* is required but Benjamin's task has been to complete the *tikkun* begun by Luria. Hence Benjamin has founded no school because those who come after him need to "put right" things in a different manner, namely, that of Luzzatto himself. *Gevurah* is the *Sefirah* of that name, the source on high of all sternness and judgments. Hence those, like Cain and the prophet Ezekiel, have a stern character requiring great control if it is not to burst its bonds and do harm. Benjamin was an invalid and Luzzatto sees something messianic in Benjamin's role as a sufferer since that particular *tikkun*, which Benjamin is now in the process of completing, is a stage in the advent of the Messiah and the coming complete redemption. The suffering Messiah is, of course, a well-known theme, referred to in the rabbinic literature and to which Luzzatto here alludes. *Yihud* means "unification" (plural *yihudim*). The reference is to a meditation on a particular combination of divine names (the Lurianic Kabbalah is full of these) which has an influence on the higher worlds. "Foreskin" here represents forces of evil which are to be removed.

8. The *maggid's* declaration: "I have descended . . ." is, in the original, in the Aramaic of the Zohar.

9. According to the Lurianic Kabbalah, the first stage in God's self-disclosure is for *Ein-Sof* to "withdraw" (the act of withdrawal is called *zimzum*) leaving an "Empty Space" in which there eventually emerge the Sefirotic realms and those beneath them until this World of Action is reached. But since something of *Ein-Sof*, as it were, is required for anything to exist, there are references to the "Column" (*kav*) of infinite light which penetrates the

"Empty Space." The great problem which remains is how the infinite can produce the finite or, in Luzzatto's words, how the "Column of *Ein-Sof*" can penetrate the World of Action. The "illuminations" in this passage are the various descents and combinations of the Sefirotic lights. The three *Sefirot* which are the particular cause of all creative activity down below are those of *Hesed*, *Gevurah* and *Tiferet*. The first is naked love as it were; the second naked power; the third the harmonizing principle. Nothing can happen without all three being brought into play but in some events there is more emphasis on one of these, in others more emphasis on another. Luzzatto uses, instead of *Gevurah* and *Tiferet*, the substitute names, also found frequently in the Kabbalah, *Din* ("Judgment") and *Rahamim* ("Compassion").

10. The reference to the end being secet is probably a hint at the messianic role reserved for Luzzato.

13

The Mystical Epistle
of the Ba'al Shem Tov

༄

Introduction

Israel ben Eliezer, known as the Ba'al Shem Tov ("Master of the Good Name") was the founder of the ḥasidic movement. The Ba'al Shem Tov (c. 1700–1760) left hardly any writings, but this remarkable epistle to his brother-in-law, Rabbi Abraham Gershon of Kutow, who was then in Palestine, is considered authentic by the majority of experts. The epistle first appeared in the work *Ben Porat Yosef* by the disciple of the Ba'al Shem Tov, Jacob Joseph of Polonnoye. This work was published in Korets in 1781, i.e., some twenty years after the death of the Ba'al Shem Tov. The letter was originally given by the Ba'al Shem Tov to Jacob Joseph to be delivered to Abraham Gershon in Palestine. Jacob Joseph, however, failed to realize his plan to journey to the Holy Land and the epistle was thus never delivered. The caption to the letter in the Korets edition of *Ben Porat Yosef* reads: "This is the letter which the Rabbi, Israel Ba'al Shem Tov, his memory be for the life of the world to come, gave to our teacher, the author of this book, Rabbi Jacob Joseph ha-Kohen, to deliver to his brother-in-law, Rabbi Gershon Kitover, who was at that time in the Holy Land. But through a hindrance brought about by God, blessed be He, he did not journey to the land of Israel so that it remained with him in order to bring merit to our people the children of Israel."

A facsimile of the letter printed in *Ben Porat Yosef*, together with the epistle in bolder type with notes, was published by A. Kahana, *Sefer ha-Hasidut* (1922), 73–77. Another version was published from manuscript by D. Fraenkel, *Mikhtavim me-ha-Besht ve-Talmidav* (1923). A more accurate version of the latter has been published with notes by M. S. Bauminger in *Sefer Margaliot* (in memory of Reuben Margaliot; 1973), 153–74. (*Cf.* the critique of A. Rubinstein in the same volume, 175–88.) Professor G. Scholem in a communication to me states that he is convinced that Bauminger's version is from a manuscript which definitely dates back to the time of the Ba'al Shem Tov. The translation here follows the version as printed in the *Ben Porat Yosef* (pages 100a-b), since this was the version known to the Hasidim.

Text

To my dear friend and brother-in-law, whom I love as my own self, wondrous Rabbi and Hasid, renowned in knowledge of the Torah and fear of God, his honor our teacher, Rabbi Abraham Gershon, may his light shine. Greetings to all and to his modest wife, mistress Bluma, and all their offspring. May they all be blessed with life. Amen. Selah.

I received the letter written by your holy hand at the Lyck fair in the year 5510 (= 1750) which you sent by the hand of the envoy from Jerusalem. The letter was very brief but you state therein that you have written to everyone in letters sent by the hand of a man who was traveling from Egypt. Unfortunately, these lengthy letters never arrived and I am greatly distressed not to have had the lengthier epistles written in your holy handwriting. For our sins, the reason for it is, undoubtedly, the confused state of communication among the countries. The epidemic has spread to all lands, reaching near to the place where we reside; to the holy communities of Mogilev and in the lands of Volhynia and the Tartar lands. You also remark that the new ideas and mysteries I recorded for you by the hand of the scribe, the Rabbi and Preacher of the holy community of Polonnoye, did not arrive. Over this, too, I am greatly distressed for you would undoubtedly have derived much satisfaction from them. Now, however, I have forgotten many of these matters yet I shall write to you very briefly those details I do recall.[1]

For on the day of the New Year of the year 5507 (= September 1746) I engaged in an ascent of the soul, as you know I do, and I saw wondrous things in that vision that I had never before seen since the day I had attained to maturity. That which I saw and learned in my ascent it is impossible to describe or to relate even from mouth to mouth. But as I returned to the lower Garden of Eden I saw many souls, both of the living and the dead, those known to me and those unknown. They were more than could be counted and they ran to and fro from world to world through the path provided by that column known to the adepts in the hidden science. They were all in such a state of great rapture that the mouth would be worn out if it attempted to describe it and the physical ear too indelicate to hear it. Many of the wicked repented of their sins and were pardoned, for it was a time of much grace. In my eyes, too, it was a great marvel that the repentance was accepted of so many whom you know. They also enjoyed great rapture and ascended, as mentioned above. All of them entreated me to my embarrassment, saying: "The Lord has given your honor great understanding to grasp these matters. Ascend together with us, therefore, so as to help us and assist us." Their rapture was so great that I resolved to ascend together with them.[2]

Then I saw in the vision that Samael went up to act the part of accuser because of the unprecedented rapture. He achieved what he had set out to do, namely, a decree of apostasy for many people who would be tortured to death. Then dread seized me and I took my life in my hands. I requested my teacher to come with me since there is great danger in the ascent to the higher worlds and since from the day I attained to maturity I had never undertaken such high ascents.[3] I went higher step by step until I entered the palace of the Messiah wherein the Messiah studies the Torah together with all the *tannaim* and the saints and also with the Seven Shepherds. There I witnessed great rejoicing and could not fathom the reason for it so I thought that, God forbid, the rejoicing was over my own departure from this world. But I was afterwards informed that I was not yet to die since they took great delight on high when, through their Torah, I perform unifications here below. To this day I am unaware of the reason for that rejoicing. I asked the Messiah: "When will the Master come?" and he replied: "You will know of it in this way; it will be when your teaching becomes famous and revealed to the world, and when that which I have taught you and you have comprehended will spread abroad so that others, too, will be capable of performing unifications and having soul ascents as you do. Then will all the *kelippot* be consumed and it will be a time of grace and salvation." I was astonished to hear this and greatly distressed that it would take such a long time, for when will such a thing be possible? Yet my mind was set at rest in that I learned there three special charms and three holy names and these are easy to grasp and to expound so that I thought to myself, it is possible by this means for all my colleagues to attain to the stages and categories to which I have attained, that is to say, they, too, will be able to engage in ascents of the soul and learn to comprehend as I have done. But no permission was given to me to reveal this secret for the rest of my life. I did request that I be allowed to teach it to you but no permission at all was given to me and I am duty bound on oath to keep the secret.[4]

However, this I can tell you and may God be your help. Let your ways be set before the Lord and never be moved, especially in the holy land. Whenever you offer your prayers and whenever you study, have the intention of unifying a divine name in every word and with every utterance of your lips. For there are worlds, souls and divinity in every letter. These ascend to become united one with the other and then the letters are combined in order to form a word so that there is complete unification with the divine. Allow your soul to be embraced by them at each of the above stages. Thus all worlds become united and they ascend so that immeasurable rapture and the greatest delight is experienced. You can understand this on the analogy of the raptures of bride and bridegroom in miniature in the physical world. How much more so at this most elevated stage! God will undoubtedly be your help and wherever you turn you will be successful and prosper. Give to the wise and he will become even wiser. Also pray for me, with this intention in mind, that I should be worthy of being gathered into the inheritance of the Lord (= the Holy Land) while still alive and pray, too, on behalf of all the remnant still in the diaspora.[5]

I also prayed there, asking why the Lord had done this and why this great wrath, to hand over so many Jewish souls to be slain by Samael, among them many souls who had apostatized and had still been killed. Permission was granted to me to ask this of Samael himself. I asked Samael why he did this and what could have been his intention in having Jews become apostates and yet still be killed afterwards. He replied that his intention was for the sake of heaven. And afterwards, for our sins, so it happened, that in the holy community of Izyaslav there was a blood libel against many people, two of whom became apostates and yet they still killed them. But the others sanctified the name of heaven in great sanctity, dying by terrible torture. Afterwards there were further blood libels in the holy communities of Shebitovka and Dunayevtsy. But there none of them became apostates having seen what happened in the aforementioned holy community of Izyaslav. They all resisted temptation, suffering martyrdom and sanctifying the name of Heaven. By their merit the Messiah will come to avenge us and to gain atonement for God's land and His people.[6]

On the New Year of the year 5510 (= September 1749) I made an ascent of the soul, as you know I do, and I saw a great accusation so that permission was almost given to destroy whole lands and communities. I took my life in my hands and prayed: "Let us fall into the hands of the Lord but let us not fall into the hands of man." This they granted to me, that there should be great sickness and an epidemic of unparalleled proportions in all the lands of Poland and in other lands adjacent to ours. And so it came to pass. Sickness spread over all so that it could not be counted and also epidemics in other lands. I discussed with my company whether to recite the portion regarding the making of the incense in order to nullify the above-mentioned judgments but they revealed to me in a vision of the night: "Behold, you yourself chose the alternative of falling into the hands of the Lord [as above] and now you wish to nullify it. An accuser cannot become a defender." So I then desisted from reciting the incense portion and from praying for this. But on Hoshana Rabba I went to the synagogue together with all the company, uttering the while many conjurations in great dread, and I recited the incense portion just once so that the epidemic should not spread to our districts, and thank God I was successful.[7]

It was my intention to write at greater length and discuss matters in detail but I am unable to continue because of the tears which flow when I reflect on our parting. But I do beg you to repeat the words of reproof I have said to you again and again. Have them always in your thoughts, meditate on them and take note of them. You will undoubtedly find numerous sweet things in every word, for that which I have told you is no empty matter. For God knows that I have not abandoned the hope of journeying to the land of Israel, God willing, to be there together with you. It is only that the time is not yet opportune. And please do not take it amiss that I have not sent you any money but there is no money left and we have been left penniless because of the treacherous way time has dealt with me. There have been epidemics and famine and I have been obliged to support and sustain many children belonging to our family as well as other poor Jews. Please God, when the Lord will enlarge our borders then I shall certainly. . . .

My grandson, the worthy bridegroom Ephraim, is a great genius in his complete devotion to study. It would undoubtedly be very fitting, if it can be arranged, for you to come here that we can see one another face to face and rejoice, as you have promised, at our celebrations.

With regard to the famous Rabbi, the Ḥasid, our teacher Joseph Katz, the servant of the Lord, I beg you, please welcome him with both hands and help him in every way possible for his deeds are acceptable to God, blessed be He, and all that he does is for the sake of heaven. Please write on his behalf to the wealthy that they provide him with a generous allowance and support him adequately, for you will certainly find great satisfaction if it can be arranged for him to be with you.[8]

These are the words of your brother-in-law who longs to

see you face to face and who offers his prayers for your long life and for your wife and offspring and who desires your well-being every day, including the night. Long may you live. Amen. Selah.

Israel Ba'al Shem Tov of Medzibezh

Comments

1. Abraham Gershon of Kutow was a famous talmudist, at first bitterly opposed to his sister's marriage to the Ba'al Shem Tov but later becoming a disciple of the Ba'al Shem Tov. The "Preacher" of Polonnoye was Aryeh Leib, another disciple of the Ba'al Shem Tov. Jacob Joseph was Aryeh Leib's successor as the Preacher of Polonnoye.

2. The Ba'al Shem Tov evidently engaged frequently in such ascents of soul and is aware that Gershon knows of this. The two ascents recorded both took place on New Year's Day, i.e., on the traditional judgment day of the year when the fate of the people is determined on high. The Talmud (*Berakhot* 18b) refers to a saint ("Ḥasid") who remained in the cemetery on New Year's Eve and there learned the decrees in heaven to be issued during the coming year. No doubt this well-known passage was in the mind of the Ba'al Shem Tov. The "day I attained to maturity" (lit. "the day I stood on my own mind") means the day on which he began to pursue his own mystical way. The "lower Garden of Eden," as opposed to "the higher Garden of Eden," is a kabbalistic expression for a spiritual state close to the material. The "column" is the means by which the souls ascend by climbing and the "hidden science" is the Kabbalah.

3. The teacher of the Ba'al Shem Tov referred to is Ahijah of Shiloh (I Kings 11:29f.). The legend that Ahijah was the Ba'al Shem Tov's teacher is referred to by Jacob Joseph in his *Toledot Ya'akov Yosef* (1881) in a number of places, e.g., in the list of sayings at the end of the book (416).

4. The "palace of the Messiah" is the place in Paradise where the Messiah resides until he is ready to come down to earth. The

"*tannaim*" are the teachers whose views are recorded in the early rabbinic literature down to the year 200. The "Seven Shepherds" (based on Micah 5:4 and *Sukkah* 52b) are: Adam, Seth, Methuselah, David, Abraham, Jacob and Moses. The Ba'al Shem Tov imagined that the rejoicing was due to the fact that he had died in ecstasy and was being welcomed to the heavenly halls. The "unifications" (*yiḥudim*) are the various combinations of divine names, as mentioned previously a number of times in this book. By studying the Torah in complete devotion and by having these names in mind, the Ba'al Shem Tov brought all things together so that the unity of God became established throughout all creation.

5. The advice given to Gershon by the Ba'al Shem Tov is typical of the latter's approach to the devotional life. The letters of the Hebrew alphabet are far more than mere symbols. They are the material form on earth which the spiritual forces on high assume and are thus the source of all creative activity. When man utters the letters of the prayers in Hebrew he assists the creative acts of God and brings down the flow of divine grace into all creation. In each letter there are worlds, souls and divinity, i.e., in the letters is mirrored that process whereby human souls are united with God and through them all worlds are united with God. An illustration of the joy inherent in such unification is given from the act whereby bride and bridegroom are united.

6. The Ba'al Shem Tov asks Samael what purpose was served by allowing Jews to be persuaded to apostatize, i.e., to be converted to Christianity, when arrested for the blood libel, in order to save their lives, since, in fact, those who allowed themselves to be converted were still slain. Samael replies that he did it "for the sake of heaven," i.e., to demonstrate to Jews the futility of conversion, since conversion to Christianity does not, in fact, save the lives of the accused. There was a blood libel in Izyaslav in the year 1747 and some Jews did try to escape, without avail, by converting to Christianity. See Dubnow, 61–62, note 1. Dubnow also notes that the libel in Dunayevtsy (or Dunograd) took place in 1748 but the records show that the accused received neither a death nor a prison sentence. Dubnow also notes that there was a blood libel at Shepetovka in 1748 in which two Jews were sentenced to death and suggests that this is the name of

the third town (Sebitovka) which is given incorrectly in the letter through a slip of the pen. For further details of these libels see Dubnow's *History of the Jews in Russia and Poland* (1946), vol. i, 177–8.

7. The Ba'al Shem Tov, in his second ascent of soul, pleads that if sufferings are to come upon Israel they should be by an act of God and not through blood libels and other machinations of wicked men. The reference to the "incense portion" is to Exodus 30:34–38 recited each day in the early morning service and by the Hasidim in the afternoon service. For the incense as the means of averting the plague, see Numbers 17:11–15 and *Sabbath* 89a.

8. The "bridegroom Ephraim" is Moses Hayyim Ephraim, the son of Adel, daughter of the Ba'al Shem Tov. He lived later at Sudylkow and was the author of *Degel Mahaneh Efrayim* in which are recorded many of the Ba'al Shem Tov's teachings. The "celebrations" are no doubt those of Ephraim's wedding at which Gershon had evidently promised to be present. "Joseph Katz" is Jacob Joseph, the proposed bearer of the letter whose intention it was at that time to settle in the Holy Land.

14

The Mystical Meditations of Shalom Sharabi and the Kabbalists of Bet El

∽∾

Introduction

The kabbalistic meditations (*kavvanot*, "intentions") of the school of the famous Safed mystic Isaac Luria are an extremely complicated series of reflections during prayer on the mysterious process in the Godhead as described in the writings of Ḥayyim Vital, Luria's chief disciple. For the *mekhavvenim*, as those who use these meditations are called, the words of the standard liturgy do not mean what they appear to be but are, in reality, symbols of the divine processes. The mystical adept allows his mind to dwell in profound meditation on each of these stages and so repeat, as it were, on earth the processes on high, with the result of helping God to restore cosmic harmony and the flow of divine grace.

A special circle of *mekhavvenim* was formed in Jerusalem in the year 1737 by Rabbi Gedaliah Ḥayon. This came to be known as Bet El. Ḥayon was succeeded in the leadership of the circle by the famous kabbalist Shalom Sharabi (1720–1777). Sharabi was born in the town of San'a in Yemen and emigrated to Palestine in his youth. After the initial letters of his name he is known as *Reshash*, *R*abbi *Sh*alom *Sh*arabi. Sharabi produced a prayer book, *Nehar Shalom* (Salonika, 1806), which contains all the Lurianic *kavvanot* as practiced in Bet El. Two selections from this prayer book illustrating the use of *kavvanot* at Bet El are given in translation in texts III and IV below. Text II is a translation of a pact drawn up in 1754 and again in 1758 by certain members of the Bet El circle, called Ahavat Shalom, in which they bound themselves to specific forms of religious practice. At first there were only 12 members, corresponding to the 12 tribes of Israel, but others were added later, as can be seen from the additional signatures appended to the note. Text I is an unusual description of the Bet El circle written by Ariel Bension, the son of one of the later members of the circle. Bension recorded the pattern of worship at Bet El and his impression of the life style of its members in a work, written in English, entitled *The Zohar in Moslem and Christian Spain* (1932). The description can be found on pages 242–46 of the book. Despite Bension's flowery style, his peculiar transliterations and spellings (reproduced here exactly as he wrote them) and his bias against the Ashkenazi "Chassidim," i.e., the Ḥasidim in Europe who followed the Ba'al Shem Tov's teachings (some of his generalizations border on the ridiculous), Bension's personal account, as a son of a member of Bet El, is unique.

Texts II–IV have been translated from the multivolume work by M. Y. Weinstock, *Siddur ha-Geonim ve-ha-Mekubbalim*, 1970–73. Text II is from vol. 1 (1970), 24–39; Text III, from vol. 3 (1971), 668; and Text IV, from vol. 7 (1973), 37.

Text

I

The Sephardi Mystics of Beth-El in Jerusalem

In the mystical group that centred around Beth-El in Jerusalem the Sephardi tradition remained an underlying principle, even though the centre was also directed by the teachings of HaAri, as expounded by his pupil Vittal. For the heavy and sombre spirit that went with this system was somehow eliminated. Practical Kabbalah was completely prohibited. In its place came the insistence on the living of a pure and holy life underlying which was a joy as sincere as it was silent; a silence which was helpful and productive; a brotherly love. There was no pilgrimage to graves, no use of amulets. The seal of the true Sephardi tradition marked the spiritual centre in Beth-El.

The centre consisted of a small group of the intellectual élite, whose mystic joy lay in the heart of the silence which enveloped them in its seven veils for centuries. Living in a retirement that screened it off from the vulgar gaze of the public the group pursued its upward course, striking the synthesis between conviction and action. It was a community agreed to live in unity and sanctity. Of those who sought to enter its portals it demanded the attainments of the scholar and the self-abnegation of the ascetic. Thus it missed the masses.

Although Beth-El held the same Kabbalistic-pantheistic conceptions as other mystical groups, the form of its manifestation, as exemplified in synagogue, home and life, was different. While Ashkenazi Chassidim glorified the individual—the wonderworking Rabbi—and occupied themselves with practical Kabbalah, such as the performance of miracles, the distribution of amulets and blessings [,] the chant-

ing of special prayers on behalf of those rich enough to ex-
pect material favours from the Lord, the Sephardi Chassidim of Beth-El—while their faith was similar—demanded
of their followers the living of a pure and harmonious life,
based on the sense of personal responsibility for the discord
in the universe, coupled with the use of *Kavanoth* for its redemption, as commanded by HaAri.

That joy which is an essential of Chassidism—for only
through joy can man recognize the Infinite—was attained
by the Ashkenazi Chassidim by means of the stirring sing-
song, the dancing, the body-swaying, the hand-clapping and
the shouting, reminiscent of certain mystic Christian sects,
such as "The Jumpers" and "The Shakers." To such practices the mystics of Jerusalem had shown an aversion in
their rejection of Sabbatai Zevi, the pseudo Messiah, when
he sought the seal on his Messianic pretensions in Jerusalem. For that which attracted the masses everywhere
to his standard repelled the mystics of Jerusalem. They
refused to accept the worship of a divine leader, the me-
chanically-aroused ecstasy, the pretensions of performing
miracles, and the rest of the well-known devices.

In Beth-El joy was attained by no artificial means, but by
silent meditation, by introspection in an atmosphere in
which music, blending with men's thoughts, induced a forgetfulness of externals. Each man's eyes were turned inwards. Seeking to mine the wealth of his own soul he found
there the soul of the universe. Amazed at his own discovery
of this hidden treasure the mystic pursues his course upwards until he attains the ecstasy that brings him to the
mystery of creation, where sits Joy enthroned. In a silence
in which alone the soul may meet its god, destroyed worlds
are reconstructed and restored to their pristine perfection.
And this is the aim of the *Kavanoth*—the meditation on the
mystic meaning of certain prayers with intention to bring
restoration.

In a song which follows the meaning-full word, continuing and deepening its meaning—even as a pause in the rendition of a symphony is but the continuation of the music—this wordless song attains that which cannot be reached through the medium of words. And the word of prayer, arising at a given moment from the throats of all Israel, attains its highest form in the silence of Beth-El, imaged in song by the Master seated on his divan and surrounded by silent, thought-inspired mystics.

The members of the mystical group in Beth-El were known under the name *Mechavenim*, i.e., those who make prayers with meditation. The harmony that ruled Beth-El followed the *Mechavenim* into their public as well as their private lives. At home and abroad Beth-El was at peace. While Ashkenazi Chassidim were involved in controversies and animosities with the Rabbinists, for whom was coined the characteristic name *Misnaggdim* (opponents), Beth-El opened its doors to both the Rabbinists and the Chassidists, but regarded the latter as having a higher degree on the ladder of Truth. The Chassidists of Beth-El did not look upon the Rabbinists as opponents but rather as fellow-seekers after Truth. And that union of groups and sects, which had not been found possible elsewhere in Jewish life, was accomplished in Beth-El, where all were able to meet in mutual respect and appreciation. In this way Beth-El's power and influence outside its own walls were greatly enhanced. At one time the whole Jewish community was influenced by Beth-El and governed by the same spiritual head, the *Rav HaChassid* being at the same time the Chief Rabbi of Jerusalem and the whole of Palestine.

A unique historical document may still be found in the old city of Jerusalem—a pact of friendship drawn up and signed by the great Sepharadi Rabbinic and Chassidic authorities of the day. Filled with expressions of the deep and abiding love of man for his neighbour, of the readiness of each to sacrifice himself for the others not only in this life, but in all lives to come—it shows the striving after complete union. Among the signatories are Algazi, the famous Azulai, and the Master Sharaabi.

Beth-El exists down to the present-day—though at present its state is on the decline—but it is enveloped, as it has always been, in a mystery of silence which the uninitiated cannot but fail to penetrate. The books which its members have written—*The River of Perfection, The Perfume of Joy, The Words of Greeting*—were books meant to light their own path to Kabbalistic understanding. The casual visitor could not but be baffled by the mystery of silence that walls Beth-El in.

Beth-El, a Holy Order

The group in Beth-El, founded by the descendants of some of the exiles from Spain, was at first small and but loosely held together, lacking cohesion and unity. As time went on, however, and under the guidance of devoted leaders, the group was transformed into a co-ordinated body possessing both authority and strength. And through the harmony thus brought into its spiritual life the Holy Community of Beth-El was created. Dominated by what may be called the categorical imperative of HaAri's teachings, the prayers were made with *Kavanoth*. This helped to bring together all the *Mechavenim* in a unison of prayer and meditation—the mystical practice of universal love which came to distinguish the Sephardi Chassidim of Beth-El.

The doors of Beth-El were open to all who came prepared to live in holiness, according to the high standards set by the Order. To the poor and to the exalted, to the downtrodden and to the illustrious, it restored the mystical tradition in which the Creator and the created thing, in which man and a grain of sand, meet together and are essential to each other.

Beth-El also introduced something new to Jewish liturgy: melodies to mark the period of meditation. The meditation

is sung aloud by the *Rav HaChassid* to stimulate and in-
spire the silent meditation of the *Mechavenim*. At first it
had been the custom to carry on the meditation in a deep
silence—the meditation on a single word, sometimes lasting
for fifteen minutes. But with the introduction of the musical interludes the *Kavanoth* began to be performed during
the intoning of a melody that was at the same time sugges-
tive of the form which the meditation was to take. So true
are these tunes, in searching out and expressing the emotions of souls dwelling on the mystic meaning of the prayer,
that even the listener, uninitiated though he may be, feels
himself transported into the realms of thought, where dwell
those who commune with the Infinite. Under the magic of
these tunes *Mechavenim* and listeners, animate and inanimate objects, become one in the true pantheistic sense.

Thus, on hearing the Master sing the *Umevi Go'el* ("And
He will bring a Redeemer unto their children's children for
His Name's sake in love")—hearing his voice rise in tri-
umphant rapture to the words—"In Love"—when the *Mec-
haven* must be prepared to die for the sanctity of the
Ineffable Name "In Love"—the listener feels himself a
heroic spirit ready to do battle for pure love. And he is able
to understand the ecstasy of saints and martyrs as they joy-
fully gave themselves to the flames of the stake "In Love."

And hearing the Master sing the *Shmah* ("Hear, O Israel,
the Lord our God, the Lord is ONE!"), it is as if a great
music had come into the soul washing away all its imperfections, bringing man nearer to his fellow-men: his hates
transformed, his world unified and ennobled. Thus it came
about that the *Kavana*—sent forth in the hope of bringing
together the conflicting fragments of the shattered *Sephiroth*
and of re-creating them into the perfect UNITY—first
pours its healing balm into men's souls, bringing them into
unity with things eternal.

The life of the Sepharadi Chassidim of Beth-El was a life
of beauty, of sanctity, of melody, of silence. And it was in

this fashion that Beth-El in Jerusalem kept alight the flame of Sepharadi mysticism down to the present day.

And we see that the long, golden chain of Jewish mysticism which had its beginnings in the days of the birth of the nation, which passed through the highroads opened up by the Bible, the Apocalypse, the Talmudim, the Midrashim, the Gaonate Literatures, etc., which broadened and deepened its course in the Spanish Peninsula, found its eternal expression in the *Book of the Zohar* and pursued its own peculiar, yet well-marked course down to our own generation.

II

By the help of God.

Since the Lord desires the return of those who repent, the spirit took hold of us, the young ones of the flock, the undersigned, to become as one man, companions, all for the sake of the unification of the Holy One, blessed be He, and His *Shekhinah*, in order to give satisfaction to our Creator. For this purpose we have made a pact and the following conditions are completely binding upon us.

First, we the undersigned, twelve of us, corresponding to the number of the tribes of Judah, agree to love one another with great love of soul and body, all for the purpose of giving satisfaction to our Creator through our single-minded association, although we are separated. Each man's soul will be bound to that of his associate so that the twelve of us will be as one man greatly to be admired. Each one of us will think of his associate as if the latter were part of his very limbs, with all his soul and all his might, so that if, God forbid, any one of us will suffer tribulation all of us together and each one of us separately will help him in every possible way. The main principle is that each of us will rebuke his associate when, God forbid, he hears of any sin the latter has committed. This embraces the obligation of the undersigned to

bind ourselves together in the mighty bond of love. We take
it upon ourselves from now onward, even after we have departed this life and gone to the world to come, that each
one of us will endeavor, both in this world and the next, to
save, perfect and elevate the soul of each one of our circle
to the best of his ability and with every kind of effort to do
everything possible for the others' eternal bliss. Each of us
agrees to save his associate in the event it has been decreed
in heaven, God forbid that one of us should receive the
goodness that belongs to his neighbor, on the basis of the
idea that there are occasions when a man receives both his
own portion in Paradise and that of his neighbor who has
sinned. In return for the advantage each of us has received
from the others, we hereby resolve to participate in that associate's tribulations, may they never come. With firm resolve, we take upon ourselves the obligation, with all the
formulae required to make it binding both according to the
laws of men and according to the laws of heaven, to relinquish that goodness that is to come to us for the benefit of
that associate for whom it has been decreed that it be taken
Num. 5:10 from him. We shall have no benefit from it "and every man's
hallowed things shall be his," as our master the Ari of
blessed memory said when commenting on the passage in
the liturgy: "and let our portion be with them." Following
this idea we have taken the above-mentioned obligation
upon ourselves.

To sum up, from now and for everafter we are met together, we are associates, we are joined, we are bound to the
others as if we were one man, we are companions in all matters of every kind. Each of us resolves to help, encourage
and give support to his associate, helping him to repent, re-
buking him and participating in his tribulations, whether in
this world or in the next, and all in the ways of faithfulness
and even more so.

We further take upon ourselves the obligation to follow

every enactment, rule or good custom agreed upon by the majority of our circle, both as a group and as individuals, unless we are prevented by forces beyond our control.

We take upon ourselves the obligation never to praise one another even if it is clear to everyone that one associate is superior to another both in age and in wisdom. None of us will rise fully to his feet before any other associate but we shall merely rise a little as a token of respect and we shall not say much about it. We shall conduct ourselves as if we were one man, no part of whom is superior to any other part. Though we have eyes of flesh, our heart knows our own worth and the worth of our associates and there is no need to give expression to it in words.

We further take upon ourselves the obligation never to reveal to any creature that we have resolved to do these things.

We further take upon ourselves the obligation never to be annoyed with one another in any way, whether because of his rebuke to us or because of anything else and if one of us offends his associate the latter will forgive him at once with all his heart and with all his soul.

All this have we taken upon ourselves under the penalty of the ban and by an irrevocable resolve in accordance with the laws of our sages of blessed memory. We are resolved to keep all these things, and we give them the full force of all the regulations that have been issued from the days of Moses our teacher, on whom be peace. And let the pleasantness of the Lord our God be upon us, and establish Thou the work of our hands upon us: yea, the work of our hands establish Thou it. Help us, O God of our salvation, for the sake of the glory of Thy name. As an indication of our sincerity we hereby sign this in the holy city of Jerusalem, may it be speedily rebuilt and established, on the week of the *sidrah*: "Behold, I give unto him My covenant of peace." *Num. 25:12* May the Lord bless His people with peace. All this is lasting and firm, the thing is right, true and established.

Shalom Mizraḥi di-Ydi'a Sharabi, pure Sephardi
Yom Tov Algazi
Samuel Alhadif, pure Sephardi
Abraham Belul, pure Sephardi
Aaron Bacher Elijah ha-Levi, pure Sephardi
Menaḥem ben Rabbi Joseph
The Young Ḥayyim Joseph David Azulai, pure Sephardi
Joseph Samanon, pure Sephardi
Solomon son of my master and father Bejoash
Jacob Biton
Raphael Eliezer Parḥi, pure Sephardi
Ḥayyim De La Roza

Now we have met together and the majority of the members of our circle have agreed to add to our circle the undersigned as well as the two golden flutes who add their signatures and bind themselves with every kind of formula so that it is all irrevocable.

Abraham Ishmael Ḥayyim Sanguinetti

And afterwards we met at the request of Rabbi Jacob Algazi who wished to join our holy circle. Since I agree to keep all these matters with a firm resolve and with full acceptance of the terms, I append my humble signature, lowly as a worm.

Israel Jacob Algazi
Raphael Moses Gallico, pure Sephardi

I, too, accept all these terms and conditions willingly,

The Young Abraham ben Asher, pure Sephardi

I, too, accept all these terms with the utmost willingness, behold I am a young man.

Saul, son of our master Rabbi Abraham,
our master of blessed memory

III

This is a short introduction to the idea of perfecting (*tikkun*) the *Beard* of *Arikh Anpin*. Know that the 13 qualities mentioned in Micah: "Who is a God like unto Thee . . ." are the innermost influx of the *Beard* which stem from the Concealed Head of *Arikh Anpin*. But the 13 of the portion *Ki Tissa*: "God, merciful and gracious . . ." are the channels which bring the *Pure Oil* to the *Beard*.

Know, too, that these 13 perfections of the *Beard* are divided into the *Sefirot* as follows: The first eight *tikkunim* represent the eight *Sefirot* of *Hokhmah*, from the *tikkun* of *El* ("God") the *Malkhut* of *Hokhmah*, down to "keeping mercy" which is *Binah* of *Hokhmah* (the order being in reverse). The last five *tikkunim* represent the five *Sefirot* of *Keter*, from "unto the thousandth generation" which is the *Hod* of *Keter* down to "and clearing the guilty" which is the *Hesed* of *Keter*. All this is in the category of surrounding lights and they are counted in reverse order. But with regard to the inner lights the opposite is the case[;] these are counted from above to below. This is from the first *tikkun El*, which is the *Binah* of *Hokhmah* down to "keeping mercy" which is the *Malkhut* of *Hokhmah*. And so, too, with regard to the *Sefirot* of *Keter*, they are counted from *Hesed* down to *Yesod*.

IV

All this applies to the weekdays. But afterwards, on the Sabbath, as a result of the prayers, those *berurim* that have been refined and put right (*tikkun*) on the weekday now emerge once again in order to be refined and put right through the Supernal *Parzufim* ("Configurations") more than could be achieved during the weekdays, each prayer proportionally, until the *Minhah* prayer (of the Sabbath). Then *Ze'eir Anpin* ascends to the place of *Arikh Anpin* and

This is the arrangement of the 13 qualities both of the verse "God, merciful and gracious" and of the verse: "Who is a God like unto Thee" and of both the surrounding light and the inner light:

THE FIRST EIGHT TIKKUNIM ARE OF HOKHMAH

	MICAH (7:18–20)	EXODUS (34:6–7)	SURROUNDING LIGHT	INNER LIGHT
1	Who is a God	God	Malkhut	Binah
2	Pardoneth the iniquity	Merciful	Yesod	Ḥesed
3	Passeth by transgression	Gracious	Hod	Gevurah
4	Remnant of His heritage	Long	Neẓaḥ	Tiferet
5	Retaineth not His anger	Suffering	Tiferet	Neẓaḥ
6	Delighteth in mercy	Abundant in goodness	Gevurah	Hod
7	He will again have compassion	And truth	Ḥesed	Yesod
8	He will subdue our iniquities	Keeping mercy	Binah	Malkhut
		FROM NINE TO THIRTEEN KETER BEGINS		
9	And Thou wilt cast	Unto the thousand	Hod	Gevurah
10	Faithfulness unto Jacob	Forgiveth iniquity	Neẓaḥ	Tiferet
11	Mercy to Abraham	Transgression	Tiferet	Neẓaḥ
12	Hast sworn unto our fathers	And sin	Gevurah	Hod
13	From the days of old	And clearing the guilty	Ḥesed	Yesod

then all the *berurim* ascend to become combined and put right by means of the *Av* of the *Av* and the *Av* of the *Sag* of *Adam Kadmon*.

Comments

II

This is the document referred to by Bension in the previous section. Sharabi signs first as the leader of the circle, the *Rav he-Hasid*, as the leader of the group who also acted as the prayer leader is called. The idea of unity is stressed in the Lurianic Kabbalah; hence the reference to the members becoming as one man.

III

These meditations on the details of the Lurianic scheme illustrate the type of mental activity the *Mekhavvenim* at Bet El engaged in, allowing their minds to dwell on the processes on high as reflected in each particular prayer. These are the meditations on the portion of the liturgy in which the 13 qualities or principles of mercy are rehearsed. There are two versions of these, one in Exodus (in the portion *Ki Tissa*) and the other in Micah. The text in Exodus 34:6–7 reads: "The Lord, the Lord, God, merciful and gracious, long-suffering, and abundant in goodness and truth; keeping mercy unto the thousandth generation, forgiving iniquity and transgression and sin; and clearing the guilty." The text in Mica 7:18–20 reads: "Who is a God like unto Thee, that pardoneth the iniquity, And passeth by the transgression of the remnant of His heritage? He retaineth not His anger for ever, Because He delighteth in mercy. He will again have compassion upon us; He will subdue our iniquities; And Thou wilt cast all their sins into the depths of the sea. Thou wilt show faithfulness to Jacob, mercy to Abraham, As thou hast sworn unto our fathers from the days of old." By referring to these processes in his mind the mystic assists in the restoration of cosmic harmony. According to the Lurianic Kabbalah, after the cosmic catastrophe known as the "breaking of the vessels" (i.e., of the seven lower *Sefirot*) the process begins, assisted by man, of restoration by means of "Configurations," *Parzufim*, that is to say, associations of *Sefirot*. There are five main *Parzufim*: 1) *Arikh Anpin*, "Long Face" = "Long Suffering"; 2) *Abba*, "Father"; 3) *Imma*, "Mother"; 4) *Ze'eir Anpin*, "Little Face" = "Impatient"; 5) *Nukba*, "Female." These five correspond to the *Sefirot*, e.g., *Arikh Anpin* = *Keter*; *Abba* = *Hokhmah*; *Imma* = *Binah*; *Ze'eir Anpin* = the six *Sefirot* from *Hesed* to *Yesod*; *Nukba* = *Malkhut* but in each there are all ten *Sefirot* and in each *Sefirah* there are all ten. The highest of the *Parzufim* is *Arikh Anpin*. From here pure mercy and grace, without any sternness or judgment, flow. Thus the 13 qualities of mercy derive from here and the symbol of the "beard" is used because the hairs of the beard denote the channels of the divine grace just as the beard has various strands. The "Concealed Head" of *Arikh Anpin* means the most hidden mysterious aspect of the Deity. From here the 13 qualities of mercy proceed in two different ways. The first can best be compared to the organic growth typical of the hairs of the beard. The second is more outward, as it were, and is best compared to the fragrant oil poured onto the beard. Hence Sharabi's symbolism, that the 13 qualities mentioned in Micah represent the more inward flow represented by the *Beard* of *Arikh Anpin*, while the 13 of Exodus represent the more outward channels symbolized by the *Pure Oil*.

We have noted that each of the *Parzufim* contains all the ten *Sefirot*. The illuminations which flow from *Arikh Anpin* do so in the form of "surrounding light," i.e., light which pervades the *Sefirot* from without and "inner light" pervading them from within. "Surrounding light" always proceeds "from below to above," i.e., in reverse order, beginning with the lowest *Sefirah*, *Malkhut*, while "inner light" always proceeds in descending order. Now since *Arikh Anpin* represents *Keter* in particular and is near to *Hokhmah*, the 13 qualities of mercy which flow from the *Beard* are divided into two groups of *Sefirot*, eight of *Hokhmah* and five of *Keter*. This explains Sharabi's detailed scheme in the diagram he presents. Thus the mystical adept is to dwell on all these details when he recites the 13 qualities of mercy in his prayers. By knowing what he is doing, what his meditations are intended to achieve, he does, in fact, achieve the "perfection." the *tikkun*, that is required of him and so he assists the divine processes.

IV

This text is part of Rabbi Shalom Sharabi's comments on the Afternoon Prayer (*Minḥah*) of the Sabbath. Prior to the section given in translation, Sharabi states that the weekday prayers have the effect of refining (*berurim*) the various stages in the divine process but only as a beginning. On the Sabbath these find their more complete "refinements" as they ascend even higher. He then continues with the translated comments.

The *Parzufim* have been explained above in the comments to Text III. The final reference to Av, etc., needs to be explained here. According to the Lurianic Kabbalah everything that happens does so by means of the power of the divine name, the Tetragrammaton. But this can be spelled in four different ways, i.e., if each letter is spelled out in full. These four ways of spelling has each its numerical value. Briefly, the scheme is as follows. 1) The Tetragrammaton is spelled out in full as: *yod* (= *yod*, 10, *vav*, 6, *dalet*, 4), *he* (= *he*, 5, *yod*, 10), *vav* (= *vav*, 6, *yod*, 10, *vav*, 6), *he* (= *he*, 5, *yod*, 10); we have a total of 72 and this is the 72-letter name (the name of Av = 72, *ayin*, 70, *bet*, 2). The Tetragrammaton is spelled out in full as in 1 but with *alef* as the middle letter of the *vav* instead of *yod*. Since *alef* = 1, this means that there is 9 less than Av. This is the 63-letter name, the name of Sag (*samekh*, 60, *gimmel*, 3); 3 and 4 where two other spellings are used resulting respectively in the names Mah = 45 and Ben = 52. Now just as the *Parzufim* are divided into *Sefirot* and contain all the *Sefirot*, so do they contain all the four names and each of these names contains all the others. In addition to the five *Parzufim* of *Azilut*, The World of Emanation, there are the five *Parzufim* and the four divine names of the even higher world known as that of *Adam Kadmon*, "Primordial Man," the nearest to *Ein-Sof*, the Limitless. Thus the Av and Sag of *Adam Kadmon* each has all four of the names. Hence Sharabi speaks here of the Sabbath afternoon prayer as reaching to the very highest stages and drawing up with it, as it were, all the potential *berurim* of the weekday. These highest reaches are the Av of the Av and the Av of the Sag of *Adam Kadmon*. All this the mystical adept has to have in mind when he recites the *Minḥah* prayer, or rather, before he begins to recite it. During the prayer itself various other complex associations in the realm of the *Parzufim* are the theme of his meditation.

15.

The Mystical
Experiences of the
Gaon of Vilna

ოი

Introduction

Elijah ben Solomon Zalman of Vilna (1720–1797), known as
the Gaon of Vilna, is generally acknowledged as the greatest
master of the whole range of rabbinic and kabbalistic studies. The Gaon of Vilna was a fierce opponent of Ḥasidism
but it is a severe error to depict him as a rationalist hostile
to the Kabbalah and to the mystical life. The opposite is
true, as the report here given in translation demonstrates.
The report was written by the closest disciple of the Gaon,
Rabbi Ḥayyim of Volozhin (1749–1821), the founder of the
famous yeshivah of Volozhin. It appeared as the Introduction to the Commentary written by the Goan to the book
Sifra De-Zeniuta, published in Vilna in 1820. The translation
is by R. J. Z. Werblowsky.

Text

God, in His mercy and to perform His good word that the Law would not be forgotten, sent us a watcher and a holy one, a man in whom there was the spirit of God, our great master, the Gaon and light of the world, whose learning and piety proclaimed his holiness from one end of the earth to the other, our pious and holy master and teacher Elijah of Vilna, from whom no mystery was hidden and who illumined our eyes in exoteric and esoteric lore . . . For there are few only that can study the sources of our exoteric Torah . . . the Babylonian and Palestinian Talmud . . . let alone the innermost mysteries of the Torah . . . and the writings of the Ari . . . For even the saintly disciples of the Ari could not penetrate the innermost depth of the meaning of this holy one of the most high, the Ari, except R. Ḥayyim Vital . . . Until He, for His righteousness' sake, to magnify the Law and make it honorable and to show us marvelous things from His Law, made His merciful kindness exceedingly great over us; and behold one like the son of man came with the clouds of heaven, to him glory was given, unique was this great man, none had been like him for many generations before him . . . all the ways and paths of exoteric and esoteric wisdom were clear to him . . . this is the *gaon* of the world, the *ḥasid* and saint, our great and holy master . . . whose way in holiness always has been to study and meditate and labor with great and incredibly mighty effort . . . and with a mighty and marvelous adhesion (to God), and a wonderful purity, until he was granted to penetrate to the full understanding of all things. And in his writings . . . he illumined for us the way . . . which none had been able to tread for many generations.

And whilst I am speaking of the great and marvelous holiness of the Torah of our great master, I am reminded of something that . . . makes my heart burn as a flaming fire

... (namely) the rumors (spread) by ignorant and vain men in parts far away, who have never seen the light of his Torah and his saintliness . . . dead flies which cause the fragrant ointment . . . of our great master to send forth a stinking savor, by saying that the holy Rabbi . . . held the Ari in low esteem . . . Others went even further . . . saying that the holy Zohar was not found worthy in his eyes . . . let the lying lips be dumb that speak iniquity concerning the righteous . . . For their eyes can behold . . . this commentary (on the Zohar), . . . woe unto the ears that have to hear (such slander), wherefore I found myself obliged faithfully to proclaim to the tribes of Israel his complete and mighty mastery of the whole Zohar . . . , which he studied with the flame of the love and fear of the divine majesty, with holiness and purity and a wonderful *devekut*. And I heard from his holy mouth that he rehearsed the *Raya Mehemna* many and many times . . . until he could count its letters . . . He also dreamed that our master Moses came to his house and disappeared again. . . .

Also concerning our holy master, the awesome man of God, the Ari, my own eyes have seen the glory of the holiness of the *Ari* in the eyes of our great master, for whenever he spoke of him his whole body trembled . . . and also on his holy writings he meditated . . . Concerning the *Sefer Yezirah* ("Book of Creation") he said that the Ari's text was as good as faultless, but for one mistake that had crept into the printed editions. When I said to him that in that case it should now be easy to create a *golem* (with the aid of the faultless text of the *Sefer Yezirah*), he answered, "Once indeed I started to create a *golem*, but whilst I was engaged on it I saw an apparition above my head and desisted, saying to myself that Heaven wanted to prevent me on account of my youth." When I asked him how old he was at the time, he answered that he had not yet reached his thirteenth year.

But the most mighty and awesome of his virtues was this,

that he did not allow himself to enjoy any good thing but that which he had labored to acquire through wisdom and understanding . . . and with great effort. And whenever Heaven had mercy upon him, and the fountains of wisdom, the most hidden mysteries, were revealed to him, he regarded it as a gift of God and did not want it. Also when Heaven wanted to deliver unto him supreme mysteries without any labor or effort . . . through *maggidim*, masters of mysteries and princes of the Torah, he did not desire it; it was offered to him and he refused it. I heard from his holy mouth that many times *maggidim* from Heaven appeared to him, requesting to deliver unto him the mysteries of the Torah without any effort, but he would not hearken unto them . . . When one of the *maggidim* insisted very much . . . he answered "I do not want my understanding of the Torah to be mediated by any (mediators) . . . my eyes are towards God: that which He wishes to reveal to me, and the share He wants to give me in His Torah through my hard labor (of study, these alone I desire). He will give me wisdom . . . and understanding . . . and thus I shall know that I have found favor in His eyes." Once it happened to me that our master sent me to my younger brother—though greater than me in virtue—the pious and saintly *gaon* Rabbi Solomon Zalman, in order to transmit to him his command on no account to admit any angel-*maggid* that might come to him, for he would soon be visited by one. He added that although our master the *Beit Yosef* (i.e., Joseph Karo) had a *maggid*, this was more than two hundred years ago when the generations were in a proper condition and he himself resided in the holy land. But today, when there was so much looseness, and more particularly outside the holy land, it was impossible that (a celestial revelation) should be (all) holy of the holiest without any admixtures. More particularly revelations without Torah were an abomination to him and he would not consider them at all.

He went even further than that and said that the wonderful insights obtained by souls during sleep, when the soul ascends to enjoy supernal delights in the celestial academies, were not highly esteemed by him. For the important achievement is what a man acquires in this world through his labor and efforts in choosing the good and devoting his time to the study of the Torah, for thereby he pleases his Creator. . . . But the insights obtained by the soul during sleep, without labor and without choice and free will, this rather belonged to the categories of rewards which God grants a man in this way by way of anticipation of the Hereafter. The implication of his words was that he experienced such ascents of the soul every night . . . and one of his disciples confirmed to me that he had actually heard him admit this. . . .

Once, on the first day of Passover, two of his senior disciples were sitting near him—and they knew that it was his holy habit to rejoice exceedingly in the gladness of the Lord, rejoicing in the most marvelous manner on the festival days as we are commanded by the Law. But when they saw that his rejoicing was not as full as was his wont, they asked him about it. At first he refused to answer, but when they insisted he could no longer refrain himself and said, "I must needs tell it to you, though it is not my way to do so; but by fulfilling the verse 'if there be anxiety in the heart of man, let him tell it to others.' For last night Elijah visited me—[if I remember rightly my informants did say in his name that it was Elijah, but possibly it was some other messenger from the celestial academy (bracketed text by Hayyim of Volozhin)]—and revealed awesome things . . . and in the morning, because in the excess of my joy I immediately meditated upon them before reciting the benediction over the study of the Torah, I was punished and forgot everything. . . ." Then they comforted him and wished him, "May God make good to our master his loss." Some time later one

of them asked him whether what he had lost had been returned to him (to which he answered, "Yes . . .) even as I
know why it was taken from me, I also know why it was revealed to me a second time. . . ."

To him these things were as "natural," and he did not require any special meditations or yihudim. And forsooth, this
stands to reason, since all his words and thoughts . . . were
given only to the study of Torah . . . and everything he did
was with a marvelous holiness and piety. Man is shown (in
his dreams) according to what is in his heart; so what need
was there in his case for special meditations and yihudim?
He used to say that God created sleep to this end only, that
man should attain the insights that he cannot attain, even
after much labor and effort, when the soul is joined to the
body, because the body is like a curtain dividing. But during
sleep, when the soul is out of the body and clothed in a supernal garment . . . one reveals to him (these insights).

Truly, from all his . . . wonderful deeds, as well as from
what I have seen with my eyes in his writings, it appears
that . . . holy mysteries were revealed to him by the Patriarch Jacob and by Elijah. In other places where he wrote in
a general way that "it had been revealed unto him" I am not
quite sure whether these were waking revelations or ascents
of the soul to the celestial academy during his sleep. There
can be no doubt that he certainly experienced ascents of
the soul every night . . . as said before; but concerning the
revelations in his waking state I have nothing certain from
him, for he kept these things secret . . . and the little that I
know about it is what he would tell us incidentally, on rare
occasions, in the course of our conversations. However,
from one amazing story which I heard from his holy mouth I
inferred that he also had great revelations when awake. My
Father in Heaven is a witness that once I heard from his
holy mouth that there was a man in Vilna who dreamed
dreams, awesome dreams that frightened all who heard

them, for he told everyone his innermost thoughts and deeds so that people greatly feared him. (Once) he was brought before (the Gaon) and said to him: "Rabbi, permit me to say one thing to your honor. A fortnight ago Thursday you sat in this place and expounded these and these verses from the portion *Ha'azinu* (Deuteronomy 32) and Rabbi Simeon ben Yoḥai was sitting at your right hand and the Ari at your left hand." Our master was amazed whence this mortal knew all this, and said, "But I remember that (on that day) I even sent my servant away from the house (so that nobody should know)." Then our master said to him, "It is true that I expounded awesome mysteries on that occasion," and as he said this his face waxed very pale— which shows that these must have been truly wonderful things and exalted mysteries, worthy of being expounded in the presence of Rabbi Simeon ben Yoḥai. Then our master looked at the dreamer and recognized that he was suffering from melancholia, and melancholics at times have correct and true dreams. Then he ordered his servant to chase the man away.

But in truth all these wonderful things are not wonderful at all in my eyes . . . for this is Torah and this is its reward. . . . We have a tradition from the *tanna* Rabbi Meir to the effect that (he who studies Torah for its own sake) "is vouchsafed many things"—this is a hint at those wonderful things and exalted revelations . . . And our eyes have seen how all these gifts were fulfilled in our master. . . . To him permission was granted . . . to behold the inner light . . . the most exalted and hidden mysteries . . . and all the celestial gates were open to him . . . as our Sages have said, "He who studies Torah even in distress . . . the curtain will not be closed before him," for he communes with God—for God and the Torah are one.

Comments

This text is largely self-explanatory. Rabbi Ḥayyim of Volozhin believes that the mystical revelations of which he speaks were vouchsafed to the Gaon because the latter devoted his life to the study of the Torah. The *Sefer Yezirah* is an ancient mystical text dealing with numbers and the letters of the alphabet. It was believed that by means of this book it was possible to create a *golem*, a figure in the form of a human being who was animated but did not possess the gift of speech. There are many tales told of famous rabbis creating a *golem*. From this text it is clear that such tales of wonders performed by the masters and revelations made to them were by no means confined, as is sometimes thought, to the ranks of the Ḥasidim.

16.

The Prayer Meditations
of Alexander Susskind
# of Grodno

೧೪

Introduction

Alexander Susskind of Grodno (d. 1793), Lithuanian kabbalist and ascetic, lived a secluded life in the town of
Grodno. Few details of his life are known. Joseph Klausner,
a descendant of Alexander Susskind, records some family
traditions but, beyond the fact that he was held in high esteem by his contemporaries as a holy man, there is very little known about him. He seems to have held himself aloof
from the ḥasidic-mitnaggedic struggles of his time, though
ḥasidic legend tells of a meeting between him and the *maggid* of Mezhirech just before the latter died. Rabbi Naḥman
of Bratslav is reported to have said of him that he was "a
Ḥasid before Ḥasidism."

Alexander Susskind's major work is his *Yesod ve-Shoresh
ha-Avodah* ("The Foundation and Root of Divine Worship"), first published in Nowy Dwor in 1782. The work is a
guide to the meaning of the prayers and especially the intentions the worshiper should have in mind. These "inten-

tions," although based largely on the Zohar and the writings of the Ari, are somewhat different from the standard Lurianic *kavvanot* in that they are far less in the nature of prolonged meditations on the *Sefirot* and the *Parẓufim* and far more individualistic reflections on the significance of the various items in the liturgy as a means of, in Alexander's words, "enflaming the heart in the service of God." The term he uses for this—*hitlahavut*—is the term popularized by the ḥasidic movement. It is none too clear whether he was, in some ways, influenced by early ḥasidic teaching. The work became extremely popular. In some circles, down to the present day, regular courses in it were conducted for the benefit of those who wished to offer their prayers with intense devotion.

The following five selections from *Yesod ve-Shoresh ha-Avodah* have been translated on the basis of the Jerusalem 1965 edition. Text I is from the section *Sha'ar ha-Gadol*, chapter 11, 33–35; Text II, from *Sha'ar ha-Shir*, chapter 1, 68–69; Text III, from *Sha'ar ha-Shir*, chapter 3, 73–75; Text IV, from *Sha'ar ha-Elyon*, chapter 2, 216–19; and Text V, from *Sha'ar ha-Iton*, chapter 13, 230–32.

Text

I. MARTYRDOM IN THOUGHT

I have seen fit, as I complete this gate and begin to open the following gates, to close this gate with an account of a particular form of divine worship of the most exalted kind. By means of this form of worship a man performs tremendous *tikkunim* in the holy worlds on high. Since I shall have occasion to refer repeatedly to this elevated form of worship on numerous occasions in this work, it is fitting to set it out at the end of this first gate so that this gate will be one in which the righteous enter so as to understand the following gates. The result will be that whenever I refer, in brief, to this form of worship the reader will know from the beginning its great advantage and how to depict it so that man will be energetic in fulfilling it so as to give satisfaction to our Maker and Creator, blessed be His name and may it be exalted for ever.

I refer to the worship of martyrdom, even though he only suffers it potentially, not in actuality. The great significance of this type of worship is attested to in many places in the Zohar and the *Tikkunim* and in the writings of the Ari of blessed memory. The Ari states how elevated is this form of worship and notes the passages in the liturgy where a man should have it in mind, as we shall record in due course when, with the help of God, I shall quote passages from the holy Zohar on the verse: "Hear O Israel." This type of worship comes to the man who has a great longing and love for his Maker and Creator, may He be exalted, which burn in his heart so that he expresses, *in potentia*, that is, in his thoughts, his willingness to suffer martyrdom, whether in those passages of the liturgy in which God, may He be exalted, is praised and thanked or in those passages which speak of the absence of God's glory in this bitter exile. As a result of this martyrdom, albeit only *in potentia*, in his thoughts, with great rapture and with the intention of sanctifying God's name throughout all the worlds, the great Name of our Maker and Creator, may He be exalted, is elevated and sanctified in all worlds, both those on high and those here below. By these means he humbles and brings very low the *Sitra Aḥra* ("the Other Side") and all the holy worlds on high are magnified and elevated exceedingly and he gives incomparable satisfaction to the Creator, may He be exalted. This is the main aim of all the *mitzvot* we perform.

Now it is obvious that this martyrdom of man, even

though it is only *in potentia*, must be whole-hearted and not with a remote heart. For the Creator, blessed be He and exalted, searches all hearts. For it is clear that a mere thought on man's part that he is ready to suffer martyrdom for the sanctification of God's name does not mean anything unless he really makes the firmest resolve that he will certainly survive the test, allowing himself to be threatened with every kind of death by torture rather than be false to his holy religion. And he should depict to himself that at this moment they are actually carrying out these forms of death and he should depict the pain and the sufferings that will be his and yet he survives the test. The Creator, blessed be He and exalted, who searches all hearts, sees his thoughts and the manner in which he depicts to himself the deaths and the tortures inflicted upon him and yet he survives the test. This is real martyrdom even though it is only *in potentia*.

This is as clear as anything to me, that every Jew, even the most lax, will, in fact, allow himself to be slain, in actuality, rather than be false to the holy Jewish religion. That is why in general we are called the holy people. In particular, one in whose heart there is the fear of God will certainly consider not to lose a permanent world that lasts for ever because of a world that passes away. He will certainly be ready to suffer torture and death for an hour in this lowly and despicable world and acquire thereby the world on high, endures for ever and ever. The Creator, blessed be He, delights in such a man in all worlds and He declares: "See, what a noble creature I have created, one who had no pity on himself and suffered terrible tortures in order to pay honor to Me and to suffer martyrdom for the sake of My name. Happy is he and happy his portion." I have heard of a certain saint in our own generation whose heart longed constantly for the opportunity of actually suffering martyrdom for the sanctification of the Name, for he longed to give satisfaction to the Creator, may He be exalted.

To revert to the subject, that a man should depict to himself in his thoughts the acceptance of martyrdom. This is how he should depict it. When thinking of death by stoning, a man should imagine himself to be standing on the edge of a tower of great height and facing him are many belonging to the nations of the world with an image in their hands and they say to him: "Bow to this image, otherwise we shall throw you off the edge of the tower." He replies: "I have no desire to bow to a graven or molten image, the work of men's hands, for our God is called the God of all the earth and He is the God of Israel. He is God in the heavens above and on the earth beneath; there is none else. To Him will I bow the knee and prostrate myself." He should then depict to himself that they cast him from the tower to the ground and he should also dwell on the terrible sufferings that will be his. This is how death by stoning should be depicted. He can, if he so wishes, depict to himself another way of being stoned to death, namely, that they cast huge stones upon him. For death by burning he should imagine that they want to compel him to bow to the image while they have a small pan filled with molten lead over a fire and they say to him: "Unless you bow down to this image we shall pour this lead down your throat." And he replies as above. And he should imagine how he opens his mouth of his own accord and how they pour the lead down his throat and the terrible sufferings he will endure. He can depict this form of death in another way, namely, that they cast him into a terrible fire. The method of depicting death by decapitation is: he should imagine that a sword is placed at his neck and he is told that unless he bows down to their image they will cut off his head. And he should imagine the terrible sufferings that will be his. And he can imagine other types of death of the same kind. As for strangulation, he should imagine that they tell him that unless he bows to the image they will strangle him or drown him in a river and he gives the same reply. And he should then imagine that they did strangle him until he expired or that they drowned him in a great river flowing there and he should imagine the great sufferings that will be his. This is death by strangulation. But a man must intend for this death of his, as if it were actually happening, to be for the sake of the sanctification of God's name in all the worlds. And He who searches out all hearts will know the truth. It is obvious that man can carry out this most elevated form of divine worship at every time and at every moment, for in a moment a man can depict to himself one of these forms of death together with its attendant sufferings. But his intention should be in order to unify God's great name and to give satisfaction to Him, blessed be He and elevated be His memory for ever. It all depends on the thoughts a man has. May God give us the merit of belonging to those who serve Him with wholeheartedness. Amen.

II. ON RAISING THE HANDS IN PRAYER

Before we begin to consider the Songs of Praise it is necessary to inform the reader of something he should know, having to do with worship in general in all the details of particular forms of worship. This is that there is a great advantage in raising the hands on high when offering prayer, thanksgiving or praise to God, blessed be His name. The great advantage of this form of worship, incomparable and boundless, has been stated in the holy Zohar, section *Yitro*, page 67a. The Zohar states: "'Ten potentates which are found in the city.' These are the ten who are appointed for those who spread out their hands on high to receive that prayer or that benediction and to endow it with the power of honoring the Holy Name that it be blessed here below. Since it has been blessed here below, because of those who

Eccl. 7:19

spread out their hands on high, it is blessed on high and is honored on every side. These ten are appointed to bring these blessings on high and pour them down on the one *Num. 6:27* who is reciting the blessing here below, as it is written: 'And I will bless them.' Consequently, a man must be careful when he lifts up his hands on high that it be only for the purpose of prayer or blessing or supplication. He should never raise his hands on high for no purpose because those ten are ever ready to be awakened to those who spread out their hands on high. And if it is for no purpose those ten curse him with two hundred and forty-eight curses, as it is *Ps. 109:17* said: 'As he loved cursing, so let it come unto him.' An unclean spirit rests upon those hands because that spirit rests upon every empty place whereas blessing can never rest *Gen. 14:22* upon an empty place. Hence the verse says: 'I have lifted up my hand unto the Lord, God Most High,' which the Targum renders 'in prayer.' In that spreading out of the hands on high there are supernal mysteries. When the fingers are spread out on high a man honors God with numerous supernal mysteries. He demonstrates the mystery of the ten *Sefirot* ('Words') as they are united and he blesses the Holy Name as it should be blessed. And he demonstrates the mystery of the unification of the inner Chariots and the outer Chariots so that the Holy Name is blessed on every side and all is united above and below. . . . Thus the whole side of the holy is elevated and all the 'Other Sides' are subdued so that they, too, acknowledge the Holy King."

My brothers and friends, how can a man fail to be on fire to perform this tremendous act of worship! It is so easy to carry out, yet there is no comparison and no limit to its worth. For all the holy worlds on high become united and sanctified as a result of this act of worship and all the "Other Sides" are subdued and denigrated. As a result the Holy Name is blessed and honored on every side, as the holy Zohar states, apart from the great and wondrous reward promised in the Zohar to the man who carries out this form of worship by raising his hands on high when he offers his prayers or gives thanks. However, a man must take great care that the palm of one hand should not be attached to the other. They should not be together when he raises his hands but slightly apart. This is stated in the holy Zohar, section *Naso*, page 146b. There on page 145a it is stated that the right hand should be held a little higher than the left when the hands are raised. A man should take great care never to raise his hands on high, God forbid, at other times than those of prayer, praise or thanksgiving for all can see, as above, the great penalty that results from it, as the holy Zohar says. But at the time of prayer a man should not be indolent in this matter. For the whole purpose for which the Creator brought man into this world was for man to do His will and give satisfaction to Him in every way he possibly can. King Solomon, on whom be peace, said in this connection: "Whatsoever thy hand attaineth to do by thy strength, that do." It is enough for the point to be taken.

Eccl. 9:10

III. MEDITATIONS ON THE MORNING SERVICE

My brothers and friends, it is obvious that no urging is required for a man to have proper concentration and burning enthusiasm (*hitlahavut*) so far as the Psalms and praises are concerned. For anyone who understands their meaning the words themselves set his heart on fire. Yet since one only urges devotion on those who are already devout I set myself the task now of hinting at the right kind of intention a man should have when reciting the praises. The wise man will know himself how to apply it to all the rest.

A Psalm, A Song at the Dedication of the House of David. According to the Ari of blessed memory a great

Ps. 30:1

tikkun is performed when this Psalm is recited before *Barukh she-Amar*. During the recital of this Psalm a man should have proper intention. For example, when a man has suffered some pain or has been sick, God save us, or when, God forbid, such has happened to a member of his family and, with God's help, he has been healed, then, when he re-

v. 3 cites the verse: "I cried unto Thee, and Thou didst heal me," he should give thanks and offer praise, with full concentration, to the Creator, blessed be He, who has sent him or his family healing from that pain or illness, God save us.

v. 4 When he recites the verse: "O Lord, Thou broughtest up my soul from the netherworld . . ." he should, with great joy in his heart, give praise to the Creator, blessed be He, for having made his portion and his lot among the holy people of Israel and not among any other people. And he should have in mind those intentions we have mentioned earlier for the benediction: "Who has not made me a Gentile." It is necessary for man to know that the whole of the book of Psalms was composed by King David, on whom be peace, by means of the holy spirit and he intended them to be applicable to all Israel. Even those words which suggest that he was speaking about his own experiences also hint at the experience of every Israelite, for every work composed under the influence of the holy spirit was composed on behalf of the Jewish people as a whole as well as on behalf of every

v. 10 single Jew. When reciting the verse: "What profit is there in my blood, when I go down to the pit?" a man should pray in thought that neither he nor one of his sons nor any person belonging to the holy people of Israel should die before his time. For it is certain that every one of the holy people of Israel praises and magnifies the Creator, blessed be He, while he is still alive, each one praising in accordance with his degree of understanding, and whether little or much there is

v. 10 no lack of God's praises. But once he has died: "Shall the
v. 11 dust praise Thee?" When he recites the verse: "Hear, O

Lord, and be gracious unto me" he should have the intention both of praying on his own as well as on behalf of all Israel.

Take this as a general rule. Whenever a verse speaks of prayer in the first person singular, a man, when reciting it, should not have in mind his own self alone but the whole of Israel. When reciting the verse: "O Lord my God, I will give *v. 13* thanks unto Thee for ever" he should take it upon himself with the truest resolve and with great joy to offer praises and thanks to the Creator, blessed be He, and that his sons, too, will do likewise since he resolves to train them so to do all their days. . . .

Then he should recite the great hymn of praise, *Barukh she-Amar*. A man should set his heart on fire to recite it with full concentration and exceedingly powerful joy, for this great hymn of praise was composed by the Men of the Great Synagogue on the basis of a missive that fell from heaven, as the *Turei Zahav* states in Section Fifty-one. The holy Zohar describes the great *tikkun* this hymn performs in the worlds on high, Zohar section *Va-Yakhel*, page 215b: "Prayer puts right (*tikkun*) many things. There are four *tikkunim*. . . . The first of these is the *tikkun* of man himself by means of the precepts of *zizit* and *tefillin*, and by reciting the passages dealing with the sacrifices and burnt offerings. The second *tikkun* is on behalf of this world in connection with the works of creation. This is performed by praising the Holy One, blessed be He, for each act of creation separately. For this reason, in the hymn *Barukh she-Amar*, the word *Barukh* ("Blessed be He") is repeated again and again so as to apply to all creatures. The third *tikkun* is on behalf of the world on high with all its hosts and it is performed through the Hallelujah hymns. . . . The fourth *tikkun* is provided by the *tefillah* [the prayer itself], the *tikkun* of the mystery of the Holy Name." Thus far the Zohar in brief.

Consequently, it is proper for every discerning man to re-

cite this great hymn of praise with great deliberation and
without haste. As he recites each particular praise beginning with the word *Barukh*, he should reflect on God's marvelous wisdom and power and give thanks and praise in his
thought to the Creator, blessed be He, as the holy Zohar remarks: "So as to apply to all creatures." He should rejoice
exceedingly on His greatness as it is exhibited in the works
of creation, on His great compassion for His creatures, and
on the majesty of His divinity for all eternity. This he should
have in mind when he recites: "Blessed be He who spoke,
and the world came into existence." When he recites:
"Blessed be He who made the world at the beginning," and
when he recites: "Blessed be He who speaks and performs,"
he should rejoice exceedingly at the greatness of His divinity in which He created the whole of creation merely by His
Gen. 1   word, as our holy Torah tells us: "And God said," "And He
said," "And He said." When he recites: "Blessed be He who
hath mercy upon His creatures" a man should also have
himself in mind, that God, in His great mercy, bears his sins
and is longsuffering to him and he should give thanks in his
thought to God for this, for showing mercy to him because
of His great compassion and not because of his merits.
When he recites: "Blessed be He who lives for ever, and endures to all eternity" he should rejoice exceedingly at His
divinity, enduring for all eternity. He should set his heart on
fire with great joy at the greatness of His divinity who endures for ever and so should he continue until he finishes
this great hymn of priase. This note is sufficient.

IV. MEDITATIONS ON THE
SABBATH EVE SERVICE

Evening time. The time after the *Minḥah* prayers have been
recited. And now the *Minḥah* has ascended, preparations

must be made for the Sabbath. Man must prepare to welcome the Sabbath Queen, to recite the Psalms for welcoming the Sabbath with exceedingly great joy. It is certain that the very words of these Psalms set the heart of man on fire for his Maker with great rapture when a man utters them with his mouth and recites them with all his might and with burning enthusiasm (*hitlahavut*). The holy Zohar states that man must serve his Maker and Creator, blessed be He and exalted, with all his might. We have already quoted this passage when we spoke of the Songs of Praise. The rule is this for proper intention: whenever a man recites those passages which speak of his love for God, he should offer himself in martyrdom in his thought so as to demonstrate the beauty of his true love for God. For instance, he should do this when he recites the words: "For He is our God, and we are the people of His pasture, and the sheep of His hand"; *Ps. 95:5* also in the second Psalm when he recites the words: "Give *Ps. 96:7* unto the Lord glory and strength. Give unto the Lord the glory due to His name." And in the third Psalm, the words: "And all the peoples behold His glory." And, especially, *Ps. 97:6* when he recites the verse: "Rejoice in the Lord, ye right- *Ps. 97:12* eous." And in the fourth Psalm, the words: "All the ends of *Ps. 98:3* the earth have seen the salvation of our God." And so on. How goodly is the thought of martyrdom when reciting these. This short note is sufficient.

"Give unto the Lord, O ye children of the mighty." Be- *Ps. 29:1* fore he begins to recite this Psalm let a man be ready to receive the additional Sabbath soul. Thus it is stated in the writings of the Ari of blessed memory. Now in the writings of the Ari of blessed memory there is stated the tremendous *tikkunim* performed in the worlds on high through the recital of this Psalm at the advent of the Sabbath. Through the recital of the three "Give unto the Lord" of this Psalm a special *tikkun* is performed in the worlds on high. Through the recital of the seven times "voice" mentioned in this

Psalm another special *tikkun* is performed. Through the eighteen times the divine name is mentioned in this Psalm, corresponding to which the Men of the Great Synagogue ordained that eighteen benedictions be recited, a special *tikkun* is performed, since there are seventy-two letters in all (4 times 18) and this corresponds to the seventy-two-letter name which has the same numerical value as *Hesed* ("Lovingkindness"). To be sure, happy is he whose intellect is keen enough to have the intentions of the Ari of blessed memory. But not every mind can grasp this. Consequently, a man should recite this Psalm with great deliberation and with a most powerful joy. He should have in mind that his intention in reciting this Psalm is in order to perform great *tikkunim* in the worlds on high and to give satisfaction to the Creator, blessed and exalted be He for ever. Then it will undoubtedly be accounted to him as if he had had all the intentions in mind. The All-Merciful desires the heart.

But you, O man of my stage, I shall explain for you in detail the simple intentions you should have when reciting this Psalm. Have it in mind that it should be as if you had reflected on the *Sefirot*. Imagine it as if your thought had entered the holy of holies of the Ari of blessed memory. These are the simple intentions for the children of Israel, the holy people. When reciting the words: "Give unto the Lord, O ye children of the mighty" a man should allow powerful joy to enter his heart at the thought that we are called "the children of the mighty," the children of Abraham, Isaac and Jacob, who are called "the mighty ones of the earth," as Rashi comments. The verse means that it is our duty as the holy people, the children of Abraham, Isaac and Jacob, to give glory and strength to the great name of our Maker and Creator, blessed be He, as the following verse *Ps. 29:2* states: "Give unto the Lord the glory due to His name," and man's heart should be full of rapture that we have this privilege. When he recites: "Give unto the Lord glory and strength. Give unto the Lord the glory due to His name" he should take it upon himself to suffer martyrdom, depicting to himself some type of death he would suffer, and all with great rapture, for his martyrdom brings great glory to the Creator, blessed and exalted be He, and His great name becomes sanctified in all the worlds, as we have said on numerous occasions. But let him not be, God forbid, as one who speaks falsehoods. And when he recites the seven "voices" in this Psalm, namely, from the verse: "The voice of the Lord is upon the waters," let him have in mind Rashi's comment to each verse and let him rejoice with great rapture at the greatness of His divinity, blessed be His name and exalted for ever. Undoubtedly, so great will be his longing for God and his love for Him that he will of his own accord come to accept martyrdom as he recites the verses of this Psalm. This general note is sufficient for the rest of the details which each man will supply for himself. He should also have Rashi's comment in mind when he recites the verse: "The voice of the Lord cleaveth flames of fire." We refer to it here only because a new idea is introduced, that Israel should rejoice in his Maker in that the holy people of Israel had the merit of seeing the "voices," the voice of the Lord cleaving flames of fire when the tablets of stone were engraved at the time when the Torah was given. And God has promised us that we will hear this once again when, in His great mercy, He will let us hear it in the eyes of all the living, when our righteous Messiah comes, speedily and in our days, so that we shall hear those wondrous words. These tokens of love are very precious to us. We long and yearn for the time when He will lead us as in former times, as Rashi explains in his comment to the verse in Song of Songs: "Let him kiss me with the kisses of his mouth." In his *Song 1:2* great longing he should take martyrdom upon himself in order to demonstrate his most powerful longing for God, blessed and exalted be He. . . .

As for the hymn: "Come, my friend," I have seen some of its meaning in holy books as follows. "My friend" is the Holy One, blessed be He. We pray here for the end of time when wonders will be performed and the *Shekhinah*, who is called the Bride, will be comforted. He will say to Her: "Shake thyself from the dust, arise . . . Be not ashamed, neither be confounded. . . ." Since on the holy Sabbath He is exalted as in the future time of redemption, we, therefore, recite on the Sabbath: "Come, my friend." So have I seen it written. But I shall now set before the reader of my stature the simple intentions he should have, in brief. "Come, my Friend," this refers to the Holy One, blessed be He, "to meet the Bride," the holy *Shekhinah*. This refers to the mystery of the Holy One, blessed be He, and His *Shekhinah*. During the days of the week the holy *Shekhinah* resides in the lower worlds for our sake but now, on the holy Sabbath, She ascends to the worlds on High so great is the holiness of the Sabbath. We, Her holy children, have an obligation to rejoice with Her in great rapture as She ascends on high. We say: "Come, my Friend, to meet the Bride" who now ascends on high to the upper worlds, go out to meet Her and welcome Her. And we, too, Her holy children, say: "Let us welcome the presence of the Sabbath," referring to the *Shekhinah*, also called, as the holy Zohar states, "Sabbath." Man should rejoice when he utters the words: "Let us welcome the presence of the Sabbath," with such powerful rapture that he takes upon himself the willingness to be martyred. And this is sufficient.

"Come in peace. . . ." This stanza a man should recite with the most powerful rapture, for as he recites this stanza man receives the additional soul of the Sabbath night. We call out to the holy *Shekhinah*: "Come in peace, Thou crown of Thy Husband . . . in the midst of the faithful of the chosen people." This means: Rest upon us, the holy people of Israel who are called "the chosen people," in accordance with the mystery of the additional soul. "Come, O Bride, Come, O Bride" and he should say a third time: "Come, O Bride," as the Ari of blessed memory states. After having recited: "Come, O Bride" three times, he should say: "Queen Sabbath." In his thoughts he should draw down into himself the additional soul of the Sabbath in these words: "I draw down into me and into all Israel the additional holy soul of the Sabbath night." This is stated in the holy Zohar that man has to make himself ready for it, to draw down upon himself the additional *nefesh, ru'ah* and *neshamah* of the holy Sabbath. We shall quote the passage later on. . . .

"A Psalm, Song for the Sabbath Day." It is fitting to recite this Psalm with boundless joy for it belongs, also, to the *tikkunim* in the upper worlds performed by prayer at this time. When he recites the verse "It is good to give thanks unto the Lord, and to sing praises unto Thy name, O Most High," it is proper to give the most powerful thanks, in thought, to the Creator, blessed be He, who created him with his portion of holiness and gave him the privilege of offering thanks and of singing to His great name. In great rapture at the thought of this privilege he should take martyrdom upon himself in order to demonstrate his great longing for God. "For Thou, O Lord, hast made me rejoice through Thy work." I have seen a wondrous and true explanation of this verse. By "Thy work" the holy precepts are meant, while "will exult in the work of Thy hands" refers to the Torah in general, which is the work of God's hands. Therefore, when he recites this verse man should rejoice exceedingly over this. "How great are Thy works, O Lord: Thy thoughts are very deep." The holy Zohar states that this refers to the Torah. Thus the *Zohar Hadash, Midrash ha-Ne'lam*, 9a, says: "If you will say that there are no mysteries in the Torah, you should know that in every word there are heaps and heaps of mysteries, laws and comments . . . Rabbi Levi said: It is written: 'How great are Thy works, O Lord:

Ps. 92:1

Ps. 92:2

Ps. 92:5

Ps. 92:6

Thy thoughts are very deep.' 'How great are Thy works, O Lord' refers to the work of creation, the work of the Lord. 'Thy thoughts are very deep' refers to the mysteries of the Torah." Thus far the Zohar in brief. Consequently, when he recites this verse a man should rejoice exceedingly over our marvelous holy Torah and with great rapture he should say to himself many times: "The wonders of God. The wonders of God," amazed at the thought that hidden mysteries are hinted at in every single point of our holy Torah, in every letter, every vowel point, every musical notation, heaps upon heaps of such tremendous mysteries that even the holy angels are incapable of grasping fully even a single let-ter of our holy Torah, as the holy Zohar states as we have quoted in the section on the study of the Torah. In great longing he should pray, in his thoughts, that the Creator, blessed be He, should show him wondrous things from His holy Torah in order that he might apprehend, through the Torah, the greatness of God, blessed be He. For the Torah and the Holy One, blessed be He, are one, as the holy Zohar mentions in a number of places. And this is suffi-

Ps. 92:14   cient. When he recites the verse: "Planted in the house of the Lord, they shall blossom in the courts of our God," which refers to the souls of the righteous after their death, who bask in the radiance of the Shekhinah, he should pray, in his thoughts, that he, too, should have the merit, after his death, of beholding the pleasantness of the Lord and basking in the radiance of the holy Shekhinah. When he re-

Ps. 92:16   cites the verse: "To declare that the Lord is upright: He is my rock, and there is no unrighteousness in Him," he should have in mind: "I believe in perfect and true faith that our Creator, blessed be He, is upright and there is no unrighteousness whatsoever in all his deeds and judgments, for the Lord is righteous in all His ways and gracious in all His deeds."

Ps. 93:1   "He should recite the Psalm: "The Lord reigneth; He hath robed Him in majesty . . ." with powerful rapture.

When he recites the verse: "Thy testimonies are very faithful" he should have in mind Rashi's comment and he should think to himself: "I believe in perfect and true faith in all the words of the prophets and even though they tarry, yet I believe that their prophecies will be fulfilled" and he should delight and exult in it.

V. MEDITATIONS ON THE *SUKKAH*

Here is a brief note to encourage a man to fulfill the *mitzvah* of sitting in the *sukkah* with powerful rapture when he observes how great is its reward and how terrible the punishment for failing to observe it, God forbid, and the idea of the seven guests who are invited to the *sukkah*, so that the result will be that his heart will long to fulfill it with profound joy. The great significance of the *sukkah* is stated in numerous passages in the holy *Gemara* and the *Midrashim* and the holy Zohar, too, describes it at great length. This is what the holy Zohar says in section *Emor*, page 103a: "Whoever sits under the shadow of faith inherits freedom for himself and his children for ever and is blessed with blessings from on high. But whoever removes himself from the shadow of faith inherits exile for himself and his children." And in that passage on the following page: "Come and see! When a man sits in this dwelling [the *sukkah*], the shadow of faith, the *Shekhinah* spreads out Her wings over him from above and Abraham and five of the righteous and King David stay there with him. . . . When Rab Hamnuna the Elder was about to enter the *sukkah* he would rejoice and would stand by the door of the *sukkah* saying: 'We invite our guests.' He would arrange the table and recite the benediction and then he would say: 'Ye shall dwell in *sukkot*. Please be seated, O ye supernal guests, please be seated! Please be seated, O ye faithful guests, please be seated!' He would then wash his hands and would rejoice, and would say:

'Happy is our portion. Happy the portion of Israel, as it is

Deut. 32:9 written: "For the portion of the Lord is His people." And he
would sit. . . . Therefore, a man has to make the poor happy
since the portion of those guests he invites belongs to the
poor. But if a man sits under this shadow of faith and he invites these supernal faithful guests without giving them
their portion (he means by inviting the poor to his table)

Prov. 23:6 they all go away from him, saying: 'Eat not the bread of
him that hath an evil eye.' That table he has prepared is his
own and not of the Holy One, blessed be He. Concerning

Mal. 2:3 him it is written: 'And will spread dung upon your faces,
even the dung of your festivals'—*your* festivals and not My
festivals. Woe to that man when these faithful guests depart
from his table. Rabbi Abba said: Abraham used to stand at
the crossroads to invite guests to his table. Now that he invites him and all the other righteous and King David and
yet does not give them their portion, Abraham arises from
the table and calls out: 'Depart, I pray you, from the tents of
these wicked men' and they all leave with him. Isaac says:

Prov. 13:25
Prov. 23:8 'But the belly of the wicked shall want.' Jacob says: 'The
morsel which thou hast eaten shalt thou vomit up.' And all
the other righteous say: 'For all tables are full of filthy
vomit, and no place is clean.' And King David says . . . A
man should not say: First I shall eat and drink well and I
shall give the remainder to the poor. But the first portion
belongs to the guests. If he makes the guests happy the Holy
One, blessed be He, rejoices with him and Abraham recites

Isa. 58:14 on his behalf the verse: 'Then shalt thou delight thyself in
Ps. 113:2–3 the Lord.' Isaac says: 'His seed shall be mighty upon earth . . .
Isa. 58:8 Wealth and riches are in his house.' Jacob says: 'Then shall
thy light break forth as the morning.' And the other right-
Isa. 58:11 eous say: 'And the Lord will guide thee continually, and satisfy thy soul in drought.' " This is what the Zohar says in
very abbreviated form.

My brothers and friends, beloved of the Most High and
dear friends, just think of the worth of those who keep this

precept. They inherit, and their children after them, everlasting freedom. The glory of the Lord hovers over such a man all the day. He sits there in the shadow of the *sukkah* and the holy ones who dwell on high, the holy Patriarchs, come to stay with him under the shade of the *sukkah*. They rejoice together with him when he gives of his bread to the worthy, needy poor scholars and when the poor that are cast off are brought into his house to receive the portion of those holy guests from on high. By them the God-fearing man is blessed with seven blessings. Where the opposite obtains, God forbid, the cloud of the *Shekhinah* turns away from the tent of the *sukkah*. Then, God forbid, he brings about that he and his children are exiled, God fobid, for ever and a curse comes to him instead of a blessing, God spare us, as the holy Zohar states. How, then, can man's heart fail to be set on fire and be warmed to keep all this with the utmost care. It is sufficient to note this passage from the holy Zohar.

Let his voice be heard at the entrance to the *sukkah* to invite the holy guests from on high. Let him call them all by name. For the holy books say, on the basis of this passage from the holy Zohar, that unless a man actually invites those holy guests by word of mouth, even if he is a completely righteous man, they do not come to his *sukkah*, for they have to be invited and each one called by name. The holy book describes at great length the order of invitation for the guests. But I have set forth for men of my spiritual stage the formula of invitation in short. He should issue this invitation whenever he enters the *sukkah* for the night meal or the daytime meal, as the holy Zohar states.

This is the form of invitation: On the first night of the holy festival, as soon as he comes home from the synagogue, he should stand at the entrance to the *sukkah* and recite the form of Rab Hamnuna the Elder, mentioned in the holy Zohar as above: "Enter O ye holy guests from on high. Enter ye holy fathers from on high to sit under the shadow of

faith, the shade of the Holy One, blessed be He. Enter
Abraham, and together with him, Isaac, Jacob, Moses,
Aaron, Joseph and David." He should at once sit down in
Lev. 23:42 the *sukkah* and say: "'Ye shall dwell in *sukkot* for seven
days.' Be seated, O ye holy guests from on high. Be seated,
O ye fathers from on high in the shadow of faith, the shade
of the Holy One, blessed be He. Happy is our portion and
Deut. 32:9 happy the portion of all Israel," as it is written: "For the portion of the Lord is His people." Then he should recite the
prayer printed in the prayer books. And so should he do before the meal on the first day.

On the second day he should say: "Enter, ye guests . . .
Enter Isaac, and together with him Abraham, Jacob, Moses,
Aaron, Joseph and David." Then let him sit down there at
once and say: "Ye shall dwell in *sukkot* . . ." up to "the portion of the Lord is His people." So should he do before each
meal of the day or night, only at each meal he should first
invite that guest who belongs to that particular day, in the
order we have arranged them, and then let him invite the
other six together with that one.

It is right and proper to recite the following short prayer
before eating in the *sukkah*: "Sovereign of all worlds. May it
be Thy will that this *mitzvah* of *sukkah* be acceptable to
Thee as if I had fulfilled it with all its details and with all the
613 precepts that depend on it and as if I had all the intentions (*kavvanot*) intended by the men of the Great Synagogue.

Behold it has been stated in the previous chapters of this
book that it is a great obligation for a man to study the
Torah at his table during the year. How much more so
should one study the Torah at the table on this holy feast in
honor of the seven holy guests. For the best way of paying
them honor is to study the Torah at the table and to sing
hymns and praises and to give pleasure to the poor and
needy at the table as above. And this note is sufficient.

Comments

I

For a similar longing for martyrdom, see the Text of chapter 10 containing the revelations of Karo's *maggid*. The four types of death described in this section are based on the rabbinic accounts of the four methods of capital punishment meted out by the court, stoning, burning, decapitation and strangulation. The details are based on those stated in the Mishnah, *Sanhedrin* 7:1.

The importance Alexander Susskind attached to martyrdom and to suffering the four death penalties is dramatically confirmed from two sources. One is an authentic account of Alexander Susskind visiting in prison a Jew who had been convicted of a trumped-up charge of ritual murder and who was told that if he converted to Christianity his life would be spared. Susskind urged him to be firm and taught him the benediction to be recited before the act of martyrdom. The martyr went to his death reciting the benediction and Alexander Susskind, who was standing nearby, gave the response, Amen. The second source is Alexander Susskind's will, containing instructions to the Ḥevra Kaddisha ("Holy Brotherhood"), those who were to wash and shroud his corpse. In this astonishing and very moving document, printed in full in the latest edition of *Yesod ve-Shoresh ha-Avodah*, he instructs his family to distribute various sums of money to the poor immediately after his death, and then he continues:

> And then, at once, the Holy Brotherhood should carry out on my corpse the four death penalties of the court. Since the most severe of these is stoning, they should stone my corpse seven times, corresponding to the seven holy *Sefirot*. They must take care that the stoning be carried out in accordance with the full rigor of the law, namely, the body must be thrown down from a height equal to twice the height of a man standing upright [Mishnah, *Sanhedrin* 6:4]. I have measured the height of my study from floor to ceiling and it is twice the height of a man standing upright. Consequently, if I expire in another room they must carry me into this room and there perform the actual penalty of stoning. Thus must they do. Many of the members [of

the Brotherhood] should lift me up to the ceiling and from there hurl me violently to the floor, there being upon it neither blankets nor straw. Thus must they do seven times, one after the other.

I decree by the ban of Josua son of Nun and by my own ban that the Holy Brotherhood must perform these seven deaths by stoning. Let them have no concern for the disgrace they will bring upon me, for it is really no disgrace but an honor seeing that thereby I shall be freed in some measure from the powerful judgment on high. On the contrary, it will be accounted as a great merit to whoever does this to me and I shall intercede on his behalf in the world on high. On the other hand, I shall be avenged on whoever tries to prevent this being done and sincerely hope that none will offend against the above-mentioned ban. Even after they have carried out the law of stoning, as above, they should not place my body upon straw but on the bare ground. I beg the Holy Brotherhood not to allow anyone to touch me unless he has first undergone immersion in a *mikveh* that is *kasher*.

II

The significance of the ten figures raised on high, according to the Zoharic passage quoted, is that these correspond to the ten *Sefirot* and so man's act "elevates all worlds" since he repeats the sefirotic process in which all ten *Sefirot* reached back, as it were, to *Ein-Sof*.

III

The recitation of a select number of Psalms forms the core of the *Pesukei de-Zimra*, the introductory section of the standard *Shaḥarit* ("Morning") service. This section begins with Psalm 30 and with the hymn *Barukh she-Amar* ("Blessed be He who has spoken"). The hymn is composed of a series of phrases, each of which begins with the word *Barukh*, "Blessed be He"; some of these are translated in full in the passage. The Psalm and the hymn can be found on pages 16–37 in the new edition of the *Authorized Daily Prayer Book* (1962) by S. Singer.

The *tikkunim* on high are the various "perfections" which take place as a result of man's actions on earth. This is a key idea of the Lurianic Kabbalah as we have noted more than once. The

Turei Zahav is one of the standard commentaries to the *Shulḥan Arukh*, the code of Jewish law composed by Joseph Karo.

IV

The Sabbath eve service, *Kabbalat Shabbat*, consists of the recitation of Psalms 95–99, 29, and the hymn "Come, my friend," *Lekhah Dodi*. In this hymn, the Sabbath is welcomed and re-ferred to as "Queen" and "Bride." In the translated passage, as in the Kabbalah in general, the Sabbath is identified with the *Shekhinah* and personified as the female aspect of the Deity. For a full description of Judaism as a mystery religion in the practices of the Lurianic school, see G. Scholem, *On the Kabbalah and its Symbolism* (1965), 118–157. For the full text of the *Lekhah Dodi* hymn, see Singer's Prayer Book, 146–47.

V

The seven guests, called the *Ushpizin*, represent the seven lower *Sefirot*, i.e., Abraham = *Ḥesed*; Isaac = *Gevurah*; Jacob = *Tiferet*; Moses = *Neẓaḥ*; Aaron = *Hod*; Joseph = *Yesod*; David = *Malkhut*.

17

Two Epistles in Praise
of the Hasidic
Ẓaddikim

∿

Introduction

There are a number of reasons why the opponents of Hasidism, the "establishment" figures in the Rabbinate, were so vehement in their criticism of the movement. It was alleged that the Ḥasidim neglected the study of the Torah; that they interpreted too literally the doctrine of God's glory filling the world; that they favored the Lurianic prayer book over the prayer book of their ancestors; that they had an irresponsible attitude to their families in journeying to the *ẓaddik*, the ḥasidic saint and leader. But prominent among the reasons for the fierce opposition was the idea of the *ẓaddik* itself, held by these opponents to be a foreign importation into Judaism. No intermediary is required, they protested, between man and God. No man needs a *ẓaddik* to pray on his behalf. Every man can come directly to God and God will hear his prayer. The elevated role given to the *ẓaddik* in Ḥasidism seemed to the critics to ascribe to him a semi-divine status. In some hasidic texts, the critics read an attitude bordering on worship of the *zaddik*. Implied, too, in the critique of zaddikism, is the accusation that in the new movement the Guru-like saint has taken the place of the traditional rabbi whose function it was chiefly to teach the Torah, not to set up subjective standards of divine worship. One of the disciples of the Maggid of Mezhirech said that he did not go to him in order to learn Torah from him but to see how he tied his shoelaces.

These two letters, the first by the son and the second by a disciple of the hasidic *zaddik* Rabbi Elimelech of Lyzhansk (1717–1787) are a defense of the hasidic *zaddikim*. Allowing for the obvious bias, these letters are important as examples of the very rare authentic reports of the spiritual life of the *zaddikim*.

Eleazar, author of the first letter, succeeded his father as the *zaddik* of Lyzhansk. Zechariah Mendel of Jaroslaw, author of the second letter, wrote his defense at the behest of his master. The letter is addressed to Zechariah Mendel's uncle, evidently a strong opponent of Hasidism who had upraided him for forsaking the ways of his ancestors by becoming a Hasid.

Both letters have been translated from the book *No'am Elimelekh*, a collection containing the sermons of Rabbi Elimelech arranged according to the weekly readings of the Torah, as well as letters and several short treatises.

Text

I

Your holy epistle has arrived in which you ask me to consult my father's holy mouth, may his light shine for ever.

I did ask my master and father, may his light shine, about
the controversy which surrounds that great *gaon*, the famous Ḥasid, head of the court of the holy community of
Zelechow, may his light shine.[1] This is what my father said:
Why do you imagine that this is in any way a new thing?
Things of this kind transpired from the earliest times. We
find that Nimrod cast our father Abraham, on whom be
peace, into the fiery furnace from which he escaped in
safety. When he came to Ereẓ Israel there was a famine in
the land and the inhabitants of that place declared that it
was because this heretic had come to live among them. He
therefore went to Egypt so that the rumor would not
spread. For otherwise he would not have gone to Egypt
since the Holy One, blessed be He, only told him to go to
the land of Canaan and this was one of the tests to which
Abraham was subjected. On the face of it, what kind of test
was this, an act practically contrary to the command of
God? But one must understand as we have said. Now it
is all very astonishing. Is it possible that inhabitants of
Canaan had not heard of the great miracle that was performed for him in Ur of the Chaldees? After all it happened
in Babylonia which is quite near to Ereẓ Israel. Secondly,
when Abraham came to Egypt, Pharaoh took his wife and
the Lord plagued the house of Pharaoh so that he gave her
up. Now two wondrous things are easily remembered so
that the house of Abimelech had undoubtedly heard of the
miracle since the two places were near to one another, as it
is said: "And God led them not by the way of the land of the
Philistines, although that was near," especially since it is the
case that kings inform one another of novel happenings, to
say nothing of such a great miracle unparalleled since the
world was created. We find, in fact, that Nimrod was not
punished until many years had elapsed. Pharaoh, too, was
not punished immediately and his main punishment was
with the ten plagues when Israel went out of Egypt. The

Ex. 13:17

reason Pharaoh was plagued at the time was only in order to prevent him from touching Sarah, God forbid. Abimelech was also not punished at once except that God closed all the wombs of his household and this was only so that they should not say that Sarah had conceived from Abimelech. All the males and females were closed so that all the people of the land could see that they were incapable of having children for they were closed in every way. These wicked men repented afterwards but Nimrod remained rebellious even though he witnessed the great miracle so that later on when he captured Lot his real aim was to capture Abraham, as it is implied. What will you reply to all these questions?

I shall tell you what it all means, and it is truly so. When the *zaddik* serves the Lord in fear and love, his love almost makes him insane, as it is said: "With her love be thou ravished always," as we find it said of King David, on whom be peace: "David leaping and dancing before the Lord."[2] The *zaddik* proceeds daily from stage to stage and the Holy One, blessed be He, renews His mercies for him daily, both on high and here down below, all in proportion to his stage. But the Holy One, blessed be He, does not renew His mercies without first testing the *zaddik*. The reason for this is because of the accusation made against him, as it is said: "For there is not a *zaddik* upon earth, that doeth good, and sinneth not." The accuser [Satan, the adversary who presents the sins of Israel before the Heavenly Throne] finds some pretext to accuse the *zaddik* and although the Holy One, blessed be He, pardons him (since it is the way of the *zaddik* to experience remorse immediately and he repents and is careful not to depart from the right way again even by an hairsbreadth so that he certainly repents, and how, then, can the accuser present his accusation?) yet the accuser ascends on high to declare that the *zaddik* only repents in order to win fame in the eyes of others. If, however, the accuser states, men rejected him he would be unable

Prov. 5:19

2 Sam. 6:16

Eccl. 7:20

to endure the temptation and the proof of it is that he did, in fact, sin. Therefore, the Holy One, blessed be He, brings the *ʒaddik* to the test to demonstrate that he is capable of withstanding temptation and then the Holy One, blessed be He, brings the *ʒaddik* into a superior spiritual stage each time.

Ber. 34b This is why the Talmud says that in the place where the repentant sinners stand the complete *ʒaddikim* cannot stand. This is very strange, that one who was a *ʒaddik* all his life and has never sinned should be unable to stand in the place of the repentant sinner who only repented later on. Why should the place of such a man be higher than that of the *ʒaddik*? But the Talmud must refer to the *ʒaddik* who serves the Lord with love and who is very careful in his conduct, repenting at every moment of his life, and for whom the Holy One, blessed be He, shows His mercies by tempting him so that he can rise to ever greater heights. In the place of this kind of *ʒaddik* who, as above, is a repentant sinner, the complete *ʒaddikim* cannot stand. By complete *ʒaddikim* here is meant those *ʒaddikim* who are unaware of the light sins they commit so that they do not repent every moment. They cannot stand in that place for since they do not repent for the light sins they committ, they are not given temptations, since for them the accusation has an opportunity to take effect.[3]

Now in the vast majority of cases the temptation to which the Holy One, blessed be He, subjects the *ʒaddik* is to confront him with evil men. For defects are brought about through those who are defective, as the Rabbis say and as

Shah. 32a
Hos. 14:10
Mak. 10b
1 Sam. 24:13 Scripture says: "The righteous do walk in them; but transgressors do stumble therein." This is how it has to be understood. The Talmud has this to say: " 'As saith the proverb of the ancients: Out of the wicked cometh forth wickedness.' Of whom does the text speak? Of two persons who had slain, one in error and another with intent, there being wit-

nesses in neither case. The Holy One, blessed be He, arranges for them to meet at the same inn; he who had slain with intent sits under the ladder and he who had slain in error comes down the ladder, falls and kills him. Thus, he who had slain with intent is duly slain, while he who had slain in error goes into banishment [for manslaughter]." This refers to the *ẓaddik* who committed some sin in error and who repents of it but who still requires the atonement of temptation, as above. The man who has committed a sin with intent, and has not repented, is brought together with the *ẓaddik* by the Holy One, blessed be He, to the same inn. This means that He brings temptation to the *ẓaddik* in the form of a man who has sinned with intent and has not repented of it. This one is duly slain, for he has slain himself, and this *ẓaddik* goes into banishment, namely his sufferings and pain are considered as if he had been banished. Now the reason why the Holy One, blessed be He, does not punish the guilty at once is in order for the righteous "to walk in them" and in order to blind the eyes of the wicked. The reason why the wicked are eventually punished, as were Nimrod and his associates, is because the punishment is bound to follow automatically, for falsehood has no leg upon which to stand and the wicked commits suicide, except that for as long as the Holy One, blessed be He, can save him by virtue of some merit he possesses, he is spared for the time being. And after all the other tests, the Holy One, blessed be He, tested Abraham our father, on whom be peace, by ordering him to bind his son on the altar in order for his merits to endure and so that the ashes remain heaped up on the altar for the sake of future generations. So, too, all the *ẓaddikim* who have opponents (*Mitnaggedim*) will be justified. These rise against them, speaking falsehoods and determined to quarrel. Yet our eyes see how righteous the *ẓaddikim* are, for their prayers are answered just as the prayers of the righteous were in ancient times. May we be worthy of enjoying the fruits of their deeds and may their merits stand us in good stead.[4]

It is possible that there may be found a great scholar in his generation belonging to the best of families who also quarrels with the ẓaddikim. It may be that this is because that scholar had committed some sin for which he forgot to repent or it may have been the sins of youth for which great remorse is required and great abasement. Who is greater than King David, on whom be peace, and yet he used to pray constantly to be pardoned for the sins of his youth, as

Ps. 25:8

it is said: "Remember not the sins of my youth." What can I do if his conscience obliges him to do these things in order to prove that the ẓaddik is justified as my father, may his light shine, has replied.[5]

I also asked my father, may his light shine, to tell me why they (the Ḥasidim) have changed the version of the prayers. This was his reply. Behold the *Beit Josef* [Rabbi Joseph Karo], the first among the codifiers, refers to these versions. After him came the Rema (Rabbi Moses Isserles), who is also first among all the codifiers, and he investigated all that has to be put right (through prayer) on behalf of all Israel. He saw the great light in this version but since he appreciated that the world is unworthy to use it he arranged for us the Ashkenazi version, which is suitable for all people of our rank. But so far as the ẓaddikim are concerned, those who have washed themselves clean of their filth and who are careful in their conduct to an hairsbreadth, his intention, his memory is for a blessing, was certainly not to prevent them from using this version that is recorded by the *Beit Yosef*. And both these and these are the words of the living God.[6]

If you ask, there are many who do not belong in this rank I have recorded, and yet they dare to use this version, associating themselves with the Ḥasidim of the highest rank and calling themselves Ḥasidim? I shall tell you the reason for it. Behold in connection with the Song at the Sea we

read: "And they believed in the Lord, and in His servant *Ex. 14:31*
Moses." What difference does it make that the people believed in Moses? True, the Holy One, blessed be He, had
promised Moses: "And may also believe thee for ever," but *Ex. 19:9*
what did Moses get out of it? Was it his wish that the people
believe in him? Surely, all Moses wanted was for the people
to believe in God. However, the Torah is telling us an important thing and that they were obliged to believe in
Moses. For the aim of God, when he brought them out of
Egypt, was that they would accept the Torah. For this purpose it was essential that they be thoroughly refined and purified, like fine silver. Therefore, all the events and all the
miracles, such as the parting of the sea, had to take place
and our teacher Moses, on whom be peace, had to sanctify
himself until he reached the degree of prophecy, when he
ascended to heaven to bring down the Torah to Israel. Now
it was obviously beyond the capacity of all the people of Israel to attain to the stage of Moses so as to be able to receive the Torah through the degree of prophecy. But since
they believed in Moses and became attached to him, he
caused the influx of the holy spirit to be theirs. Thus it was
as if they, too, were of this stage so that they were able to receive the Torah through their unification with Moses and
their attachment to him. The moral is plain to see.

But if anyone refuses to accept this, I say unto him as follows. First let him repent for the sins of his youth. Then let
him seclude himself and consider how many times he in-
sulted someone, even a member of his own household, how
many times he has told lies, even if only in jest, and let him
consider all the other moral rules laid down in the moralistic works and let him feel acute remorse and resolve to sin
no more, especially avoiding the sin of pride, worse than
any other.

I once heard this comment on a verse from the mouth of
my master and father, may his light shine. I do not know
whether it was his own idea or whether he said it in the

Ps. 45:12 name of a book he had read. Scripture says: "So shall the king desire thy beauty." In the previous verse it says: "Forget also thine own people, and thy father's house." This is the meaning of these verses: When you will forget your own people, your father's house, your aristocratic birth and your pride in these, then will the King, the King of all the earth, desire your beauty.

He should also be careful to an hairsbreadth to keep all that is stated in the Codes, especially in the *Shulhan Arukh*, *Orah Hayyim*, and in the moralistic works whose authors are now in Paradise. Then he is permitted to use this version recorded by the *Beit Yosef* of blessed memory and he will undoubtedly flavor its good taste so that he will be unable to prevent himself using it and he will take no heed of those who quarrel with him and will be ready to bear everything (rather than give it up).

Thus said my master and father, may his light shine: If you take note of these my words you see that they are right and true. As for one who still has doubts about the servants of the Lord, this is the advice I give him. Let him seclude himself and scrutinize his deeds, as I have explained above, although I have said very little for the page is too small to record it all. I give him further advice to begin to study the Torah for its own sake at every opportunity that presents itself, without any ulterior motive. He should rise regularly at midnight to weep for all the sins he has committed from the days of his youth until that day, with bitterness of soul. When he studies the Torah for its own sake, the Torah will remind him of the sins he has committed and his hair will stand on end. The Torah will teach him how to repent, so that a sin that was formerly no more than a jest to him will now be very serious and his flesh will tremble in dread. Then all his doubts will be resolved and he will be healed and he will appreciate the rank of the *zaddikim* who serve the Lord in truth.

Beloved brother, take no heed of those cold words from

those who are one day here and perish the next. I have seen with my own eyes that, for our sins, many departed this life before their time because of their involvement in such controversies. Wait for but a little time and you will see wondrous things, for falsehood does not have a leg to stand on and the ẓaddik lives by his faith. Only pay heed to my words in order not to belong to that group of the blind, God forbid.

Beloved brother, if I were to record all that my master and father, may his light shine, told me about these ẓaddikim the page would be too small to contain it. For all that you see of the way the ẓaddikim serve the Lord in public is no more than a drop in the ocean compared with their inner life. In brief: they take care not to go outside their homes so as not to have to remain in an unclean place because of their holy thoughts. The writings of the Ari of blessed memory provide them with a key through which the fountains of wisdom are opened to them and great unifications (yiḥudim). Even when they converse with other human beings their thoughts soar aloft towards the exaltedness of God, and they perform various unifications. When they study the holy Gemara, fire actually consumes them so great is their love and holiness. The fountains of wisdom, whether of the revealed or the secret things, are open to them. This is what my father, may his light shine, said in the name of his teacher of blessed memory. He is very surprised at a man who can mention the name of a tanna without that tanna appearing to him. The ẓaddikim never allow midnight to go by in sleep but sleep only a little on some of the shorter nights. All the time they mourn over Israel's exile and pain and that of the Shekhinah for whom they pray at all times in a spirit of utmost self-sacrifice, in truth and sincerity.

Who can record in writing all the other things I heard from my master and father, may his light shine. Ah for this confusion! See with whom they quarrel! Woe to our souls!

Were it not for this, it is certain that no people or tongue could ever have dominion over us because of the power of their prayers with holy thoughts. I advise you run back from whence you came, there to repent sincerely. If the fire has broken out among the cedars what shall the hyssop by the wall do! Let not your thoughts be confused through these things for it is very short-sighted.

Thus said my father, may his light shine. The *yihudim* they carry out before their meals and the repentance they engage in before eating, would that we should do likewise when we offer our prayers. You can imagine with your clear mind the heights they reach. This applies to weekdays. On the Sabbath even simple folk like me can understand something of their sanctity. My master and father, may his light shine, related to me that among them there are *zaddikim* who are unable to sing and yet their voice during their prayers is sweeter and more fragrant than honey. Such a marvelous thing is no simple matter. I wished to tell you many new things I heard from my father, may his light shine, about the *zaddikim*, but I have heard a comment by my father, may his light shine, on a certain verse and because of this I shall keep it to myself.

Ps. 145:4
Yoma 38b

This is my father's comment on the verse: "One generation shall laud Thy works to another." The *Gemara* tells us that before the sun of Eli had set the sun of Samuel had begun to shine. Before the sun of Rabbi had set, etc. For no generation is without its *zaddikim*. It is only that the man who has a holy soul, unsoiled by sin, is alone capable of believing in them. When proof is offered (to the unbelievers) from the *zaddikim* of former times the reply given is: "we believe in the *zaddikim* of former times because they were gifted with the holy spirit but such a thing is not possible

1 Sam. 10:11

nowadays." This has been their argument in every generation, as we find in connection with King Saul, on whom be peace, as is well known. Beloved brother, be sure that in the time of the holy Ari of blessed memory, they also quarreled with him. This is the meaning of the verse: "One generation shall laud Thy works to another," that is to say, the present generation themselves admit that those of previous generations had attained to high stages of the spirit. That is why it says: "Shall laud They works." They laud His works, the great things He gives to the *zaddikim*. But they say that it cannot happen nowadays. This is the meaning of the saying of the *Gemara*: "The *zaddikim* are greater when they are dead than when they were alive." For during their lifetime they met with opposition but now that they are dead all acknowledge that they had attained to the high spiritual degrees we have mentioned.

Ḥul. 7b

This is why I kept myself from telling all. I have written that which I heard from my master and father, may his light shine, and I rely on him for it is certain that he would never utter a false word even if he were given the whole world, and nothing he says is without purpose. My father said to me that every man can reach this stage quite easily provided he is enough of a scholar to be able to study the *Gemara* together with Rashi's commentary, even if he is not such a brilliant casuist but if he is, so much the better. But many who have drunk will drink no more because they separate themselves from the world because of their love of the world. They run after fame and love money more than body and soul. This confuses them so that they have no pure thoughts and it is all to no avail. For it is certain that if the Holy One, blessed be He, wishes a man to be wealthy, wealth will come to him without any effort on his part, and fame too. Even though they pretend to be very meek, it is all for the sake of fame which they pay for bitterly with their very life. It is impossible to record it all in writing but the wise and he whom God wishes to draw near to Himself will understand it of his own accord.

I heard a great man refer to the saying that "the Men of

Yoma 69b

the Great Synagogue slew the evil inclination of idolatry."
This is very puzzling. How could they have slain an angel, a
pure, spiritual entity? It can only mean that they took his
function away from him. In that case, what is his function
nowadays since every angel was created for some special
purpose? The answer is that his function, nowadays, has to
do with wealth. He confuses men by means of money and
wealth, which is akin to idolatry, for our sins. A man must
be free with his wealth, as we find in connection with our
father Jacob, on whom be peace. He was very free with his
Gen. 28:22   money, giving a fifth away, as it is said: "And of all that
Thou shall give me I will surely give the tenth ['*asser a'as-
serennu* = two tenths] unto Thee." And yet for all that he
Hul. 91a   went back for some little jars he had left behind. This required great wisdom. Even though these matters are more
than appears to be the literal meaning, yet the literal meaning is also true. Great assistance is required here and it is a
main principle for those who serve the Lord in truth.[7]

If you wish to know why they (the *zaddikim*) love one another so much, spending their money to visit one another,
longing to meet one another more than they long to meet
their own father, I will tell you, on the basis of a comment
on a certain verse which I heard from my father, may his
light shine, and even though I do not recall it as it was told
I still believe that you will be pleased with it. "Let not the
Isa. 56:3   alien say: 'The Lord hath separated, hath separated me
from His people.' " Why the doubling of "hath separated?"
He explained it by means of a problem he set. Why is it, he
asked, that two *zaddikim* whose holy deeds are of equal
merit love one another and yet two wicked men, whose evil
deeds are of equal blame, hate one another and speak ill of
one another? Why do they not love one another? He
replied that the problem is non-existent so far as the *zaddikim* are concerned. I will tell you a parable. A king has two
servants. For as long as they serve the king sincerely and

honestly and desire always, in love, for the king to be pleased and very happy so as not to be pained by any man, when they see a man making the king happy they love this man greatly and if they could give him the whole world they would do so as a reward for making the king happy. Now it is impossible for a man to love the king properly in this way unless he separates himself entirely from the things of this world and considers himself as nothing, as Moses our teacher said: "And what are we?" Were it not that he occupied such a stage he could not have had such joy in the happiness and delight of the king, for he would be interested, too, in his own delight and joy and whatever he does is partly for himself so that his love for the king is incomplete. But when his stage is that of the one who only loves the king, he then thinks nothing of himself. When he sees someone making the king happy he loves that man more than he loves himself. Since he is nothing in his own eyes, whatever he does for the king seems very little to him as if he had done nothing at all. His friend has the same opinion so that their love for one another is boundless and without limit. But the two wicked men hate one another since no man sins unless the evil inclination burns within him. Every man is tempted to sin and his eyes are blinded by the evil inclination so that he imagines that at times he performs good deeds. But when he sees his fellow committing that very sin which he himself has committed, he despises him, for his eyes have only been blinded so far as he himself is concerned but when his fellow does it he sees how low a thing it is. This is the meaning of the verse: Let not the alien, whose deeds have made him alien to his Father in Heaven, say: I have been separated from His people, both from the ẓaddikim and from the wicked. That is why the word "separated" is repeated. For from the ẓaddik he is undoubtedly separated since he does not experience any joy in the fact that the ẓaddik makes God glad. And he is separated from the wicked, too, and hates him when he sees him commit a sin, for he sees him in his abjectness and committing evil deeds. But let him not say this, since nothing stands in the way of repentance and the Holy One, blessed be He, accepts him.

Perhaps you will say, if the ẓaddikim hate gain so much, why do they accept gifts of money from people, even if they give them all day? Beloved brother, I know of many secret reasons which one cannot record in writing. But it is also simply true that they never place their money in a chest and it does not remain with them for even a single night but they spend it in order to attend to the needs of the poor of Israel and provide dowries for Jewish girls than which there is no greater *mitzvah* nowadays when, for our sins, the notorious decree (against celebration of Jewish marriages) has been issued in our lands. My father, may his light shine, declared that they would never have had the power to issue such a decree were it not for the quarrels with the ẓaddikim, and they have printed ugly letters. Even when they send these letters, O my beloved brother, do not look at them. For my father, may his light shine, said that whoever reads these letters and feels pleased at their contents, he will not be worthy of seeing the consolations of Zion, the joy of the Leviathan and the canopy of the ẓaddikim. Or else they give their money for the cause of redeeming captives and they support those scholars when others neglect, as the *Sefer Hasidim* explains it is right and proper to do. This is the

Prov. 11:21   meaning of the verse: "Hand to hand, he shall not be free of evil." This means: When he takes with one hand and gives away with the other he does a favor to the one from whom he takes. For by taking from him he also takes away the evil the accuser presents for him on high so that evil will not be able to make him free, free in the sense of the saying: So-and-so has been "freed" of his property.[8]

All this I have written very briefly, my ear taking only a

little from my master and father, may his light shine. My mouth cannot declare it all and I certainly cannot put it in writing. If your heart longs and yearns for the words of a wise man that are gracious set your steps hither and hear his sweet talk and the honey of his so fragrant utterances.

The humble Eleazar the son of our master Rabbi Elimelech, may his light shine as brightly as at mid-day.

II

Your holy epistle has arrived. My beloved uncle, you believe that I have been ill as a result of the self-torments to which I subjected myself. The truth is, and Heaven my witness, that it is not so. I have never subjected myself to these kinds of self-mortification, and as for immersion in the *mikveh*, I did it occasionally when the need arose but only when I was in a state of good health. Whenever I experienced any weakness or infirmity I never went to the *mikveh* at all.[1]

My beloved uncle writes that I have been guilty of separating myself from my holy ancestors but I fail to understand. On the contrary, I do walk in the footsteps of the holy Hasidim, men of reknown, marvels of the generation, in whose merit we endure in this bitter and remorseless exile.

Beloved uncle, if I were to explain adequately all the details of their good deeds and their holy conduct the page would be too little to contain it. I shall relate to my beloved uncle just a few of their holy practices in a general way and it is no more than a drop in the ocean.

First and foremost in their thoughts is to do the will of God with a perfect heart and to worship Him in truth without the slightest admixture of self-interest and without any pride and self-congratulation whatsoever. At all times they occupy themselves in the Torah of the Lord studying for its own sake to learn how to conduct themselves. Their further motive in study is to learn how to refine and purify themselves and their thoughts so as to be able to offer their prayers without any extraneous thoughts whatsoever.[2] Thus their prayers ascend on high with great concentration. Their further motive in their studies is in order to purify themselves and their thoughts so that no lustful thought should be able to enter their minds during the day and thus they avoid pollution at night, God forbid. When they study the *Gemara* they wrap themselves round with dread, fear, trembling and tremendous awe of the Lord, blessed be He, and the Torah shines on their faces. When they make mention of a *tanna* or the author of a talmudic saying, they depict to themselves as if that *tanna* were actually present there as a living man together with the source of his light from the Heavenly Chariot, as the Jerusalem Talmud advises, that when one makes mention of the author of a saying one should depict him as if he were actually present. The result is that dread and tremendous awe of the Lord, blessed be He, falls upon them without any limit or confinement and the love of the Torah and her light burns within them unceasingly. When they go from this kind of study, miracles and wonders are performed on their behalf just as in former generations so that they can heal the sick and draw down the influx of divine grace to all Israel. They are called "the eyes of the congregation," those who watch over the needs of the congregation and offer supplication for all their needs, whether of the spirit or the body. In short, they sanctify themselves to such a degree that all physical desire has left them and they have no desire or lust whatsoever for any worldly pleasure.

Speaking of this quality, I shall mention to my beloved uncle a comment on a certain verse: "If ye walk in My statutes . . . then I will give your rains in their season."

Lev. 26:3–4

Rashi of blessed memory explains that "in their season" means on the nights of the Sabbath. This means that a man must so attach himself in his pure thoughts to the worship of God, blessed be He, that he reaches the stage in which all bodily desire is totally absent and he has no lust for worldly pleasures, whether those of food or drink or sex or other things from which human beings derive pleasure such as fame and the like. However, if a man is in this stage, he is incapable of carrying out the marital act which is incumbent upon him by the Torah law. The answer is that God, in His great mercies, has pity on such a man who has reached this stage and when absolutely necessary He endows him, for that time alone, with physical power and desire so that he can fulfill his obligation. Afterwards he reverts to his former state and he remains in the state in which all physical delight and pleasure are totally absent as he has made himself to be through his pure deeds and holy thoughts. Consequently, the meaning of the verse is now obvious. "If ye walk in My statutes." This means, as I have written before, that the *zaddik* walks always with his thoughts on God unceasingly until he attains to this stage in which there is total cessation of all desire, as above. "Then I will give you rains in their season." God promises that He will endow that *zaddik* with renewed physical desire when it is necessary in order for him to carry out his marital duty as the Torah enjoins him to do. Therefore Rashi comments that it is on the nights of the Sabbath, for that is the time when the scholars perform their marital duties. Is anything sweeter to the palate than this comment?

The truth is that I have no real comprehension of how far their holy thoughts reach. But this I know for certain; by the help of God, I have investigated it thoroughly and have never seen them having any pride or vanity or giving utterance to any kind of falsehood or flattery or that they ever desired wealth or that, God forbid, they ever spoke a single word when they derived any bodily pleasure. I have lived among them these many years and yet have never seen them commit any low act. It has never happened that money remained in their chest overnight. All their days they occupy themselves in the study of the Torah, in carrying out the *mitzvot* and in performing good deeds, marrying off orphaned boys and girls, freeing those in prisons, redeeming captives, healing the sick, comforting those who mourn, performing acts of benevolence to every man, entertaining guests, receiving all men with cheerful countenance, having pity upon the needy and grieving constantly over the tribulations of Israel.

They study the Torah day and night and discover new ideas in the Torah. They uncover the secrets of the Torah and the mysteries thereof and all their words are sweeter than honey. Whenever they utter a word of Torah or of the fear of God or of some new idea, there falls upon the man who hears it fear and dread of the awesome Lord, blessed be He. I am incapable of comprehending that which they achieve and the reach of their achievements during the night with their mighty *yihudim* and their worship from midnight onward. But all can see their great sanctity as demonstrated by their holy acts. Water is made ready for them from the beginning. As soon as it is midnight, they arise from their sleep in dread and with great bodily trembling. They wash their hands and cleanse and purify themselves, evacuating their bowels thoroughly as enjoined in the *Shulhan Arukh*, all in dread, awe and fear. Then they sit upon the ground with ashes on their head and they weep with a broken heart torn into twelve shreds over the exile of the *Shekhinah*, the tribulations of Israel, the yoke of exile and the severe decrees of the king. They pray that the compassionate God should speedily have mercy on His holy people and that He should turn the hearts of the king and his counselors to do good unto them, to save them from all trouble and all kinds of sickness and suffering and from all evil hours, and that the holy people should not be in need of one another or of any other people, and that their sustenance be provided amply even before they are in need, and to turn their hearts to the fear and love of God and to remove the heart of stone and give them a heart of flesh, in order that they might all of them acknowledge God's majesty and serve Him with joy.

After this they study the *Gemara* and the *Tosafot* together with the other commentaries to the Talmud and they study the works of the early and later codifiers and the works of Maimonides of blessed memory. Afterwards they study the secret works such as the Zohar and the writings of the Ari of blessed memory. And they also study the four sections of the *Shulḥan Arukh*, a passage from each section daily. And they also study the Bible. Afterwards they begin to seclude themselves; alone with their Creator they prepare themselves for prayer for they see that day is approaching. Then they separate themselves from every thought of temporal vanity and attach themselves, their thoughts, their *nefesh*, *ru'aḥ* and *neshamah* with great love to the exaltedness of God and they reflect on man's lowliness and his later end and without contrivance set in front of their eyes the day of their death.[3] So powerfully do they attach themselves to God that they virtually reach the state in which all corporeality has been stripped away from themselves. It all follows that which is recorded in the *Shulḥan Arukh* on how prayer has to be offered. So brightly does great love burn in their heart that the light appears on their faces so that creatures stand in awe of them and sinners flee before them in terror at their extreme holiness and their fear of Heaven. Believe me, my beloved uncle, these things are true, for in our lands these things are known to hundreds and thousands of people. When they pray obvious miracles occur, and they achieve the same effects by their prayers as were achieved in former generations. Occasionally they achieve things by mere words as if they had offered prayer, on the pattern of that which is said: "Thou shalt also decree a thing, and it shall be established unto thee." If my beloved uncle would come here I would prove it all to him and he would see for himself. As it is, please believe me for I have not yet acquired, God forbid, any reputation as a liar.

Job 22:28

Believe me, there are among them such *zaddikim* as are capable of virtually raising the dead through the power of their prayer. I have seen it with my own eyes, not simply heard it by report, how on many occasions they brought to them invalids for whom there was no hope at all and yet through their pure prayer these were restored to perfect good health as before.

In brief, they are hardly of this world at all but their thoughts are always in the worlds on high. We observe that in their great attachment to God it happens occasionally that they do not hear what people say to them and while their body walks on earth their soul is attached to the worlds on high. As soon as they see an unworthy person they sense immediately what he is and what his state is and sometimes they know exactly the sins he has committed. They restore many to the good life without having the slightest admixture of pride or selfhood, solely by virtue of their love and great fear before the exaltedness of the Creator blessed be He. What shall I write to my uncle! There are among them such *zaddikim* who know beforehand that a certain pain or sickness will come to a man and they give alms on his behalf and pray for him. Sometimes it happens that the man is spared from that pain but at other times the pain comes at the very moment the *zaddik* had declared that it would, not a moment earlier or later, I have experienced this myself and it happened to me personally. There is a certain *zaddik* in our land who knows and senses the sufferings that are to befall me before they actually happen.

He states explicitly: "At such and such a time tomorrow this will happen to you" and he gives alms on my behalf. Generally, his almsgiving and his prayers are successful and I am spared but although the whole of it does not happen some of it generally does so that I might know of his great righteousness and how true it is and this happens even if I am many miles away from him.

Why should I continue to relate their great spiritual worth! Who can tell of it, for it is limitless! At all times they publish abroad their offenses and put themselves to shame in public. Whenever they have an unworthy thought or whenever they have uttered some light word without any sanctity or whenever they have taken a single step without sanctity, they publish it abroad and make it known so as to put themselves to shame.

At once they repent of it and it is, for them, as if, God forbid, they had committed the most serious sin and for them it is no different. At all times they find reasons for blaming themselves but excuses for the conduct of their fellows. Their company is exceedingly pleasant to God and man. Their love for one another is greater than the love of a father for his child or a husband for his wife. Complete unity prevails among them so that they virtually share the same pocket and no distinction is made by them between their own children and those of their friends. One can hardly tell who is the father of whom so great is their love for one another and the complete unity that prevails among them. It all stems from their great longing to do the will of God, blessed be He, with a perfect heart. When two of them engage in conversation, all one hears is of the love and fear of God, of His exaltedness and His holy Torah. They assist one another to serve God in truth. Each one of them is inferior in his own eyes and his friend is superior to him. They teach one another how to serve God and how to keep His holy Torah. They never pride themselves on any good trait they possess but all their days they are engaged in repentance. Hardly a moment passes without them having a thought of repentance. They have a rebuker sitting within their heart. At all times they rebuke one another with open rebuke but with hidden love. And they carry out that which the *Shulḥan Arukh* states at the very beginning that man should always set the Lord before him. They fulfill this quite literally, depicting the Tetragrammaton in front of their eyes in illumined letters. At all times they see it, as it is said:

Ex. 13:21   "And the Lord went before them." If on occasion the Tetragrammaton does not appear, God forbid, or if they see another divine name such as *Elohim* or *Adonai*, they then know for certain that judgment prevails in the upper worlds, God forbid, and they then immediately donate sums of money to charity and engage in prayer and supplication and perform great *yiḥudim* until they see once again the Tetragrammaton and they then know for certain that judgment has been changed to mercy. This is why the *Gemara* states that the *ẓaddikim* cause the quality of judgment to be converted into the quality of mercy.[4]

Consequently, perhaps my beloved uncle will be good enough to write to inform me the meaning of his accusation that I have departed from the ways of my holy ancestors. Would it have been right to separate myself from such *ẓaddikim*. And how were my fathers in truth? For I was brought up by my famous uncle, the Rabbi, the Gaon, the great Ḥasid, the man of God, the teacher of all the generation, he is the head of the court of the holy community of Nikolsburg and the province, may the Lord protect him.[5] I know that all his conduct followed this pattern and I am obliged

BB 110a   to walk in his holy steps, as the *Gemara* states: "Most children take after their mother's brother." Please explain it to me and please read between the lines. Thus speaks his beloved nephew (lit. "son of his brother") who sends his greetings, wishes him only good and desires him to be justified.

The humble Zechariah Mendel

Comments

I

1. The "Hasid of Zelechow" is better known as Rabbi Levi Issac of Berdichev.

2. The remark about the *zaddik* being "almost insane" is no doubt directed to the frequent accusation that hasidic piety was wild and unbridled.

3. Elimelech's interpretation of the passage in tractate *Berakhot* is that "repentant sinners" is not to be taken literally but as referring to the very highest type of *zaddik* who is not only a "complete *zaddik*" but also a "repentant sinner" in that all his days he constantly feels remorse for the slight peccadilloes of which he has been guilty.

4. Elimelech uses the term *Mitnaggedim* for "opponents," the term which came to be used for the rabbinic opponents of the hasidic movement.

5. By the "great scholar" who quarrels with the *zaddikim* Elimelech in all probability, as Dubnow and Wilensky suggest, means the famous Gaon of Vilna, the arch opponent of Hasidism in Lithuania whose opposition spread as far as Galicia.

6. The Hasidim adopted the Lurianic version of the prayer book in the belief that it contained the more authentic kabbalistic "intentions." The *Mitnaggedim* objected to this on the grounds that it was wrong for the Ashkenazim to depart from the Ashkenazi tradition as codified by Rabbi Moses Isserles in the 16th century.

7. The Men of the Great Synagogue are the members of the body of scholars traditionally said to have furthered the teachings of the Torah after the return from the Babylonian exile. In the Talmudic passage quoted, the "evil inclination," the perverse force in man, is personified. The Men of the Great Synagogue are said to have captured the "evil inclination" and to have attempted to slay him. In this they were unsuccessful, but they did succeed in slaying the particular impulse towards idolatry. This is, of course, a mythological way of expressing the idea that whatever the faults of the community in Erez Israel after the re-

turn, idolatry was no longer practiced by any of the people as it was during the period of the First Commonwealth.

8. Eleazar here defends the ḥasidic practice of providing the ẓaddik with gifts of money. Elimelech in his *No'am Elimelekh* similarly devotes a number of passages to a defense of this practice, one severely attacked by the *Mitnaggedim* who accused the *ẓaddikim* of greed and mendacity. The "notorious decree" refers, according to Dubnow, to the decree of Joseph II in 1782 forbidding Jews to marry before the age of 18, but Wilensky points out that as early as the year 1773 the Jews of Galicia were forbidden to marry without the permission of the governmental authorities. The interpretation of the verse in Proverbs is: Because the ẓaddik takes the money from the hand of the giver he renders the evil powers incapable of "freeing" that man of his money. The ẓaddik, therefore, does the man from whom he receives the gifts a great favor.

II

1. It appears from the opening words of this letter that Zechariah Mendel's uncle had accused him of engaging in ascetic exercises to the detriment of his health. Although Ḥasidism generally frowns on undue asceticism, there appears to have been some ambivalence on the question in the school of Elimelech of Lyzhansk.

2. "Extraneous thoughts," *mahashavot zarot*, are thoughts of pride or lust or self, anything other than the prayers themselves. Much of early ḥasidic literature is taken up with the problem of how these thoughts can be avoided or, in some versions, "elevated."

3. "*Nefesh, ru'ah, neshamah*" designate the three parts of the soul.

4. The reference to the "*Gemara*" here is inexact. The correct source is the Midrash *Genesis Rabbah* 33:3.

5. The uncle referred to here is the famed Samuel Shmelke Horowitz of Nikolsburg, a disciple of the Maggid of Mezhirech, the organizer and leader of the ḥasidic movement after the death of the Ba'al Shem Tov.

18

The Mystical Accounts
of Kalonymus Kalman
Epstein of Cracow

∽◦

Introduction

Rabbi Kalonymus Kalman Epstein (d. 1823), a disciple of
Rabbi Elimelech of Lyzhansk, was the leader of a hasidic
group in Cracow where he came under severe criticism for
his hasidic views and especially for his fervent mode of worship. His *Ma'or va-Shemesh* (Breslau, 1842; Tel Aviv, 1965) is
one of the most popular of the hasidic books. The following
extracts from the book all deal with ecstatic experiences
and in them the author appears to be drawing on his own
and his teachers' experiences. Text I is from page 50a; Text
II, from 56b; Text III, from 63a; and Text IV, from 151a.

Text

I

It is exceedingly difficult to possess the trait of humility since man's evil inclination entices him, so that he imagines himself to be one who has reached a high spiritual rank and in his own mind he becomes exalted and magnified. Consequently, much effort is required in order to cast out the evil inclination and this notion from his heart. Once a man attains to humility he becomes automatically stripped of his corporeality to some extent since haughtiness and pride stem from the corporeality and desires of this world. When, however, a man attains to the quality of humility, so that he thinks of himself as naught and nothingness, he is then, to some extent, stripped of his corporeality. In proportion to the extent each man succeeds in humbling himself the more does he become stripped of his corporeality and the more does he remain in his purely spiritual state so that he then attaches himself to the worlds on high and becomes a chariot to that which he draws down into himself, namely humility. This explains the Rabbinic saying: "If this ugly one [the evil inclination] encounters you, draw him into the house of study"; "If he leaves you alone well and good, otherwise recite the *Shema* . . . Recall the day of your death." We can ask, why recall particularly the day of death? This surely can lead only too easily to melancholy, the denigration of which has often been stressed. But according to our remarks the meaning is as follows. He should think of what is eventually to be and consider his end, that separation is bound to come one day, the separation of the hylic soul from the physical body, for this is the end of all men that the soul eventually becomes stripped of corporeality. Since it is so, he should see to it now, while he is still alive, that he at-

Kid. 30b

Ber. 5a

tains to this quality, namely, the stripping away of the corporeality of this world from himself so that only the spiritual remains. Then he will become attached to the worlds on high and will be saved from the evil inclination that makes him sin. This is well known, and I have witnessed it myself, that when the great *zaddikim* attach themselves to the worlds on high and have the garments of the body stripped off from themselves, the *Shekhinah* rests upon them and speaks from out of their throat so that their mouth utters prophesies and tells of future events. These *zaddikim* do not themselves know afterwards what they had said, for they were attached at the time to the worlds on high and the *Shekhinah* spoke out of their throat.

II

Especially in our generation the main way of refining the soul so as to have knowledge of God's divinity and of how to worship Him, blessed be He, is prayer. From the time of the coming of the Ba'al Shem Tov of blessed memory, the light of the essence of holy prayer has shone for every one who wishes to draw near to God's service, blessed be He. But in order for prayer to be refined, much ministering to the sages is required, and much effort, by day and by night, in studying the Torah and carrying out good deeds, so that, as a result, one can truly arrive at the stage when one knows how to pray in fear and with great love, as the discerning know full well.

Now the true *zaddik* proceeds in his prayers through all the upper worlds until he reaches the Supernal Intelligences and from there he proceeds until he reaches *Ein-Sof*, the negation of all comprehension. Once he reaches that stage he draws down from there to the children of Israel the influx of grace and blessing for children, life and unrestricted sustenance as well as health of body and mind and all good things.

This, however, must be appreciated. The following can happen occasionally to those who fear the Lord, striving hard to pray, pouring out their souls to God in proportion to their degree of understanding, in fear, love and burning enthusiasm (*hitlahavut*). It seems to them, occasionally, during their devotions, that they have fallen away from all their attempts to comprehend and they do not know where they are and so are aggrieved. But the truth is rather, and this applies occasionally even to those of a lesser rank than that of the great *ẓaddik* who is capable of proceeding to that place where comprehension is negated to draw down from there the influx of grace, as above, yet even for them a pure happening can take place because, stripping themselves of corporeality, they, too, have reached the place of nothingness where all are equal, as above, that this is why it seems to them that they are incapable of offering their prayers. Consequently, happy is the portion and the lot of those who reach this stage. Let Jacob rejoice and Israel be glad at being worthy of it so that the influx of grace can flow from there to the Community of Israel. This is the main thing in prayer, to pray until a man reaches the negation of his comprehension. Then he will know that he is not permitted to proceed further and, as above, he should rejoice in his lot.

Now I have written earlier that if a man wishes to attain to the state of refined prayer, with a stripping away of corporeality, great effort is required of him. He must study the Torah, carry out good deeds, and offer many supplications that he be worthy of attaining to pure prayer. For there are numerous accusers and antagonists on high who seek to hinder him in his ascent to the heavenly halls. These, as is well known to those who embrace the dust of the *ẓaddikim*, are the letters and words of the prayers. After he has ministered to the sages, studied the Torah and offered many sup-

plications, he will become worthy of offering pure prayer.
Then will illumination come to him from on high so that he
will truly be able to offer pure prayer with a stripping away
of corporeality. He will proceed in his contemplation until
he reaches the place at which comprehension is negated.
Then he will know, as above, that he is in a high place and
then through him will come the influx of grace to the Community of Israel.

III

It is written: "The secret [*sod*] of the Lord is with them that   Ps. 25:14
fear Him." It is necessary to understand the meaning of "the
secrets of the Torah" (*sodot ha-Torah*). All Jews use this term
but what does it mean? It cannot refer to the science of the
Kabbalah and the writings of the Ari of blessed memory and
the holy Zohar, for a "secret" is that which cannot be communicated to others, whereas the Kabbalah, the writings of
the Ari and the Zohar can be imparted to others and explained very thoroughly to them. Consequently, these, having been revealed, are no longer secret. What, then, is the
secret it is impossible to impart? It is "the secret of the
Lord," that is to say, the essence of divinity, that He was, is
and will be and that He is the ground and root of all worlds.
This cannot be imparted to another but each man has his
own degree of comprehension of the divine in proportion to
his degree of understanding and the manner in which it is
assessed in his heart. The more a man refines his character,
the more effort he puts into the attempt to comprehend,
the more will his refined intellect be able to comprehend.

Now that which a man comprehends in his mind of the
divine he cannot possibly communicate to others, to convey from the deep recesses of his own heart that which he
has in heart and mind. To be sure, he is able to converse

with others so as to convince them of the existence of God, blessed be He, and that men should fear Him, blessed be His name. But it is impossible for him to communicate to them all that is hidden in his heart, as is well known to anyone who has begun to worship sincerely. Consequently, this is called "secret." Verily it is a "secret" since a man cannot possibly communicate to others that which is in the very innermost point of his heart and thoughts. Each man can only grasp this in proportion to his efforts and the refinement of his spiritual nature. The more a man comprehends of the divine, in general and in particular, that is to say, the more he attains to profound degrees of comprehension through the refinement of his character, the more difficult does it become for such a one to explain and to communicate to others the secrets of his heart, since he has so much more in his heart and thoughts of that which cannot be conveyed to others. Hence the verse says: "The secret of the Lord is with them that fear Him," that is to say, for them it always remains an incommunicable secret since the more God-fearing a man is the less capable is he of revealing the secrets of his heart, and those inferior to him cannot possibly have any understanding of the mighty degree of comprehension he has attained of God's divinity, blessed be He. But the man who has not as yet attained to any profound comprehension of the being of God, blessed be He, such a man can communicate to others that which is in his heart. For he has in his heart nothing like the profundities of that other superior one, as above, and from him ordinary folk are far more able to receive than from one who has attained to great comprehension, as above. Consequently, if a man great in the fear of the Lord, having attained too profound comprehension of the being of God, blessed be He, wishes to reveal the secrets of his heart to others, that they might understand, he requires an interpreter, that is to say, the services of a man of lesser spiritual rank who can understand that which he is told and who can then communicate it to others. These will then be able to grasp it since it comes to them from a man of inferior rank from whom they are capable of receiving it and understanding it.

IV

The way of the *zaddikim* who walk in the way of the Lord is well known. They occupy themselves mightily in the study of the Torah or in prayer with such great burning enthusiasm (*hitlahavut*), as they experience the fragrance and sweetness of God, blessed be He, that it would take but little for them to become annihilated out of existence in their great longing to become attached to God's divinity, as they ascend from heavenly hall to heavenly hall and from spiritual world to spiritual world. Then they proceed until they come to that high place where comprehension is impossible, except in the way one smells something fragrant, and even this only in a negative way, since that which is there cannot be grasped by thought at all. When they comprehend this, so great is their longing to attach themselves to His divinity, blessed be He, that they have no desire to return to the lowly world of the body. However, since the One on high, who caused the worlds to be emanated from Himself, wishes to have the *zaddik* worship Him in this world, He shows that *zaddik* that the whole earth is full of His glory and that even in this world he can experience some of this sweetness and fragrance. He is then willing to return, desiring to live in this world, since he appreciates now that even in this world he can experience the sweetness of His divinity, blessed be He. The Zohar calls this "one who goes in and comes out again." For one who is unable to return because of his great longing, after the mystery of "the living creatures ran and returned," is called "one who goes in but does not come out again." *Ez. 1:14*

Comments

I

Humility is generally linked in hasidic thought to the idea of *bittul ha-yesh*, "self-annihilation," i.e., self-transcendence through attachment (*devekut*) to the divine. Man's ego is attracted to material or corporeal things, hence self-transcendence is called "stripping away of corporeality." Kalonymus Kalman, no doubt quoting from memory, has combined two different talmudic sayings on the theme of man's conquest of the evil inclination. To be melancholy is to be guilty of a severe defect of character according to the Hasidim. Recalling the day of one's death is, therefore, understood to mean not a morbid dwelling on the decomposition of the body but an anticipation of the state of pure spiritual being. This can be man's, to some extent, even while he is still in the body, provided he learns how to transcend his ego. The *Shekhinah* then rests upon him and he becomes an instrument of the divine. The divine speaks in his unconscious mind and he then utters things of which he himself is unaware.

II

Kalonymus Kalman understands the efficacy of the *ẓaddik's* prayers for his followers that they will be blessed with "children, life and sustenance" to be due to his having reached in his ascent of soul that stage where there is no comprehension at all. There there is no evil, no multiplicity, only the simple unity of *Ein-Sof* so that from that "place" only grace flows. *Hitlahavut* is the state of burning enthusiasm in the worship of God. Kalonymus Kalman here observes that this leads to a state of complete passivity in which man is totally lost to the divine and has gone beyond all experience, even spiritual experience. Hence this stage should not be seen as a "fall" but as an ascent to the highest realm. According to hasidic doctrine the letters and words of the liturgy are the form assumed on earth by spiritual realities on high. The words and letters of the prayers *are* the heavenly halls and by his attachment to them the saint attains the *unio mystica*.

III

On this theme of the "secret" as mystical experience see the remarks in the Introduction to this book. As an experience, the mystical state cannot be communicated to those who have never enjoyed it. The "interpreter" is the man whose spiritual rank is inferior to that of the great *zaddik* but superior to that of ordinary folk. Such a man can act as an intermediary between the saint and the people. He is sufficiently advanced in the mystical way to have some notion of that which the saint wishes to communicate but also sufficiently close to the ordinary people for him to be able to give expression to the experience in a language they can understand.

IV

Were it not for the fact that he can taste the sweetness of attachment to God even here on earth the *zaddik* would expire in longing during his ascent of soul and he would have no desire to return to the body. Hasidic legend tells of Rabbi Elimelech, Kalonymus Kalman's teacher, that he would place his watch in front of him before he began to pray, to serve as a reminder to him that he must return to the world of time and not allow himself to be lost to eternity.

19

The *Tract on Ecstasy* by Rabbi Dov Baer of Lubavich

∽∾

Introduction

Rabbi Dov Baer of Lubavich (1773–1827) succeeded his father as the leader of the Ḥabad group of Ḥasidim. Dov Baer's father, Rabbi Shneur Zalman of Lyady (1745–1813), a disciple of the Maggid of Mezhirech (disciple of the Ba'al Shem Tov), founded the Ḥabad movement as an intellectual movement in Ḥasidism. The word Ḥabad is formed from the initial letters of *Ḥokhmah, Binah, Da'at*—Wisdom, Understanding, Knowledge—referring to the three *Sefirot* of that name (according to some kabbalistic schemes, *Da'at* is also one of the *Sefirot*). The emphasis in the Ḥabad pattern is on severe contemplation during prayer. Ecstasy can and should result from such contemplation if adequately carried out but "the heart should follow the mind," not the other way round, i.e., there should be no emotional whipping up of feeling and religious fervor.

The text translated here is from two sections of the final

part of the *Tract on Ecstasy, Kunteres ha-Hitpa'alut*, first published under the title, *Likkutei Bi'urim*, in Warsaw, 1868. Dov Baer's chief aim in this tract, sent as an epistle to his followers soon after he had succeeded his father as leader of the Ḥabad fraternity, was to guide his followers in the matter of profound contemplation leading to ecstasy. His main contention is that there are sham as well as authentic forms of ecstasy and these have to be distinguished from one another if the worshipper is to avoid the perils of self-delusion. An English translation of the text was published by L. Jacobs in 1963 under the title *Tract on Ecstasy*. The translation is that of the English edition except that the notes have been incorporated into the text in parentheses. Some of the parentheses are, however, Dov Baer's own but these can easily be distinguished. Dov Baer frequently writes *"etc."* and this usage has been preserved. He uses a good deal of Yiddish in order to convey his exact meaning. These Yiddish expressions have been transliterated and an English translation has been supplied. The sections are from pages 141–52 (56a–61b of the Hebrew edition) and 168–76 (65a–67b of the Hebrew edition).

Text

I

After these words of truth concerning the general distinctions to be found, intelligible to anyone who has begun to taste the flavor of the words of the living God, each man can recognize his stage and the place he has attained, according to his mind, knowledge and heart, and according to the extent of his training from youth in the service of the heart, and he can discern in his soul all the detailed errors into which he has fallen. And if there be those whose souls are perfect and hearts truly firm in the Lord let them take good care to know themselves at all times, that they do not fall into self-delusion etc. For it appears that the main confusion, resulting in a diminution of the light of the Torah and the service of the heart even among those who seek and desire the nearness of God, is none other than self-delusion. The cause is weakness of effort in seeking God to the full extent with the whole heart. Man desires to be near but this desire is from afar and his heart is absent. Concerning this it is said: "To buy wisdom where the heart is absent." For the important thing is to pay the fullest attention to the proper understanding of the truth concerning the subject of the words of the living God. To this man should devote soul and heart all the days of his life of vanity. Why should he allow falsehood and vanity to enter the soul that it all becomes remote and not near, God forfend? (Yiddish: *mi soll sich nit narren*—"One should not fool oneself"). It is well known and widely admitted that the main admixture of good and evil is to be found in one who fools himself etc.

Prov. 17:16

However, all this concerns those who seek the Lord, who search for and desire in truth the nearness of God. But this is not to be found among the majority of our fraternity. It is therefore necessary to rebuke openly, out of hidden and unconcealed love, to uncover and make known to each his malady. Even though his soul weeps in secret and he is truly aggrieved, pride and the ties of self-love cover everything, to the extent that he sees no fault at all in himself and in his own eyes the way of every man is pure. For this there is no hope etc.

Now, actually, self-delusion in ignorance is not the main cause of error. It is rather brought about by a general faintheartedness in will and concern for the words of the living God. For most people are fully absorbed in business matters with their whole *nefesh, ru'ah, neshamah, hayyah* and *yehidah*

of the natural soul. Even if there is a periodic revival of the
spirit, or at the time of prayer, man still cannot bear the
yoke of effort in his mind, to delve profoundly into the subject of "filling" and "surrounding" (that God "surrounds all
worlds" and "fills all worlds," i.e., is both transcendent and
immanent), even in a general way and certainly not in the
detailed manner that would result in the above-mentioned
category of the "goodly thought." It is never more than the
category of "cold thought," where the subject is of no personal concern whatsoever, as is well known to those who
admit the truth without wishing to delude themselves, God
forbid. The resolve which stems from this is with great cold-
ness. It has no more than a temporary effect, that is to say,
he is encouraged to study a little Scripture for a moment or
two after prayer. In an hour or two even this resolve evaporates and it is as if it had never been. In the category of
yeḥidah of the natural soul he engages in business concerns
(i.e., even the highest degree of soul is absorbed in business)
or attends to his other bodily needs as if it were a matter
that actually concerned the apple of his eye, as in the category mentioned above of "all my bones shall say" in the ser-   *Ps. 35:10*
vice of the Lord (i.e., the state of utter absorption, which
should be reserved for God's service, is applied to worldly
matters). Even when he hears or sees the words of the living
God he does so only from a great distance. And even if the
words are properly appreciated he merely acknowledges
them etc. "And wilt thou set thine eyes upon it and it is   *Prov. 23:5*
gone," forgetting it all completely so that it is as if it had
never been etc. This is in no way a "hearing ear." But, in
truth, there does remain, nevertheless, the category of essential Jewish nature, the category of the *nefesh* of the divine soul in turning from evil and doing good, clothed in a
resolve, in the category of "residue" at least (i.e., there is
still some impression of the divine light, however faint).

But even here there is great laxity. Excuses are soon invented for the hindrances caused by the body's materialism, absorption in business matters and the attraction of the soul's essence by this world, until they sink to the category of inanimate things. This is known as "stoppage of the brain," where there is hearing only from afar and in which there is no capacity whatsoever for understanding or acceptance by the intellect. This is well known to those who admit the truth so that the question "What benefit?" (i.e., of what use is contemplation) does not arise, for there is no "hearing" at all (i.e., those who "hear" may question the value of contemplation but for one who does not "hear" in any event the question does not arise).

However, even among these two groups there is to be found much that is good and praiseworthy from an entirely different point of view. When a man notices that he does not "hear" or attain any ecstasy, neither in the mind with acknowledgment and even less in the heart, he is moved to the category of simple repentance in the heart, to the category of bitterness and lowliness in his own eyes because of the body's gross materialism and so forth. And he recalls the sins of his youth and so forth and cries out with a sudden great cry, without reflection on the divine but only in a general way. After the manner of that which is said, "Their heart cried out to the Lord," in particular, in repentance out of the heart's depths in great bitterness and with extreme humility.

Lam. 2:18

Observe, the following emerges from all the distinctions mentioned above etc. The Lord sees into the heart of those who repent by crying aloud, whether or not the cry is authentic, even if it is without any reflection. For the cry comes from the awakening of the divine soul. As we have explained above, it is possible for a sinner to repent in the category of the *yehidah* of the divine soul to the extent that the soul expires. At least, there is the category of *ru'ah* or *neshamah* (i.e., even if his repentance is not in the highest category of soul—*yehidah*—it is at least in those categories higher than *nefesh*, the lowest of all) which rouses him to repentance. This produces the cry in prayer. As it is written, "They cried out to the Lord in their troubles." It is further written: "Their heart cried out" etc. This ecstasy is included in the divine ecstasy of the divine soul but is attained as a result of opposition (i.e., the cry is produced by a deep awareness of the strength of opposition to the divine in man's soul). Since the divine soul is in nearness and attachment she is moved with a sudden cry in the fleshly heart. As it is written: "My flesh and my heart sing to the living God," as mentioned above. It amounts to the same thing, only here it derives from opposition etc. (i.e., it is not direct joy in the Lord but the longing for Him which comes as a result of the opposition to the divine).

Ps. 107:6

Lam. 2:18

Ps. 84:3

In this matter many are confused. They deride this crying out in prayer but in truth are too blind to see that this is actually referred to in the *Likkutei Amarim* (the work *Tanya*, by his father, chapter 35) as "weeping fixed in my heart from this side and joy from the other side" etc. For the joy is the divine delight in the mind which comes into the heart with sensation etc. It is the portion of nearness of the divine soul. And yet, in that very stage itself, the divine soul is bitter and she weeps at her remoteness from the One etc. This is the meaning of "weeping from this side" etc., and yet, at that very moment, there should be "joy from the other side" etc. However, among the above-mentioned two groups there is only to be found "weeping from this side," the second aspect mentioned (i.e., but there is no "joy from this side"). This is the category of the divine soul in its most inward category for which the Lord seeks and searches exceedingly. As it is written: "The Lord is near to the brokenhearted," to the heart broken by its sense of unworthiness and remoteness from God, as is well known. And this is sufficient for him who understands.

Ps. 34:19

The third group is of those men who have attained ecstasy in thought (known as: *der hoert tief be-maḥashavah* =
"well-heard [= comprehended] in thought"), as mentioned
above. The result of this is a desire with great longing for
the divine to be revealed in the doing of good etc., even if it
is not, as yet, sensed in the heart, as mentioned above.

Here there is a great and powerful rebuke. We clearly observe among the majority of men, even among those who
are well-trained and well-versed and who desire in truth the
words of the living God, that although they do possess this
talent for "hearing," known as the "hearing ear," yet it is really turned actually to dross, the very opposite! For such a
person is moved to ecstasy when he hears and absorbs thoroughly in thought the details of a divine matter, and he ex-
Isa. 44:16 claims: "Ha! I am warm, I have seen the light." But here the
matter ends. Even if he practices it two or three times etc.,
it is no more than the category of a flash or a glance in mind
and heart. It all remains hidden and greatly concealed in his
soul, until it actually ceases to be. For he immediately reverts to the interests of his body and does not tend it assidu-
ously and constantly, so as to fix it firmly in the soul with
every kind of length, breadth and depth, and revive therewith his poor soul; for this is very life, and yet he removes it
from himself. He feels that in studying the matter and understanding it to the extent that he is moved to ecstasy, he
has carried out his duty and is entitled to be called a Ḥasid,
and that now he is permitted to attend to his business concerns with proper care in all that they require. Added to
this is his holiness in his own sight so that eventually he becomes completely confused and deludes himself greatly.
When the time of prayer arrives it all remains in the category of concealment and "surrounding" (i.e., the divine
light is not "clothed" by the soul but remains outside the
soul, as it were) and even if he exhausts himself until he attains ecstasy of the mind, he can recognize neither its na-

ture nor its good fruits, as is well known to all who are perplexed in this matter.

All this is due solely to the malady of the natural soul.
For she has become accustomed in the fullest extent to the
materialism of the body; how, then, can she bear to receive
the true sensation of the words of the living God in the
above-mentioned "hearing?" This is also due to laxity and
absence of effort, except in a superficial manner, simply
in order to carry out one's duty, as one hears a song or
a melody etc. For there are many stages in the above-
mentioned talent for "hearing." Some "hear" with great
profundity. Others "hear" and are moved to ecstasy but
only quickly and superficially (*fun oben zehr*, "very much on
the surface"). That is to say, even their ecstasy of mind is
only an external one and not at all inward. All this is well
known to those who admit the truth and have no wish to
delude themselves. Consequently, when one falls he descends completely, in but a little time and as the result of
but a few hindrances, such as his business concerns, from
the stage he has attained. He falls into egotistical lust, becoming very gross and so forth, until his talent for "hearing"
ceases entirely, as is well known to the experienced.

And this is sufficient for he who understands.

However, after proper and subtle reflection on the cause
of this malady, which afflicts most people, it seems that it
has a different cause. This is that they do not possess a truly
broken heart (Yiddish: *zu brochenkeit*, "brokenness") in
their very nature. For they have not received the first words
of the living God from their youth by means of true repentance from the heart's depths, but only in a superficial, temporary manner. Even the category of "residue" has long
departed from this so that he is in his own eyes a perfect
man (Yiddish: *ganz zehr bei sich beli shum zu brochenkeit*,
"very perfect in his own sight, without any 'brokenness'").
Consequently, the words of the living God concerning this

perfection are not at all properly appreciated and inwardly grasped with heart and mind, but only in a superficial manner as one hears or sees some external thing. Even if he delights in the subject and is actually moved to ecstasy for the time being, it becomes hidden immediately and is as if it had never been etc.

Whoever possesses a broken heart in his very nature has the divine soul to thank, for she is melancholy in her prison of the body's materialism. This appears to be part of human nature because of the garments of the natural soul, and is called "natural melancholy." But, in reality, it is not at all due to the natural soul, for the nature of this soul is to be melancholy only because of physical lack and deprivation and not because of deprivation of the divine light etc. (For this reason the Rabbis said of those who receive the secrets of the Torah that their heart must be constantly anxious within them [Ḥagigah 13a]. This refers to the state of natural essential melancholy from the essence of the divine soul, without which the light that comes from the secrets of the Torah cannot illumine the soul and can in no way endure; on the contrary, without it he enters into darkness. The result is only pride and irresponsibility, as is well known from actual experience.)

This I have heard from my master and father, of blessed memory, who heard it in these very words from the Rabbi, the Maggid (of Mezhirech, his father's teacher) of blessed memory. A man cannot possibly receive the true secrets of the Torah and the deepest comprehension of the light of *Ein-Sof*, to the extent that these become fixed firmly and truly in the soul, unless he possesses a natural, essential melancholy, implanted within him from his youth in particular; and only if this is in the category of general essence (*atzentzia* = "essence") and only if it is truly profound. (This refers to true *zu brochenkeit* in nature, to the extent that he actually loathes his life, constantly, hour by hour.) Then there will dwell within him the Source of all life, the Source of all, to revive the spirit of the contrite. As it is written: "With whom do I reside," with the contrite and humble of spirit" etc. Then, in all that he does in contemplating on the secrets of the Torah, these are delivered into his heart with true revelation, if his heart is humble within him. (If not, they are not delivered into his heart at all, even though he does know and comprehend their superficial meaning etc.) So, too, with regard to all the ways of divine worship, the Lord will accept him. And then his sighing and natural melancholy will be turned into joy and delight, only because of the divine which actually rests upon his soul. But without this (and, especially, if, on the contrary, his nature is sanguine, with natural hilarity) even if he is a vessel ready to receive every secret etc., it will not endure in his soul and he will walk all his ways in darkness, and self-delusion. For the Lord is in no way with him etc. Thus far is the gist of his (the Maggid's) words.

Isa. 66:2

From this one can learn a lesson for the "average men," too, according to their rank, that this is the main cause of the above-mentioned malady of soul, if only they will open their eyes in pity for their soul and not destroy themselves in self-love by refusing to notice their faults etc. And this is sufficient for him who understands. How much more so in our generation, when new ones have recently arisen who have not even begun to cultivate the above-mentioned broken heart from their youth, but have opened their eye immediately in the divine science to comprehend and understand everything at once like one of the great, as is well known. They are perfect in all their being, children in whom there is no blemish, and they recognize nothing evil in themselves. They are very lenient to themselves, for they rejoice, in their self-love mainly, at their comprehension and great knowledge. Even the little they do possess of the broken heart is of small consequence to them. It belongs, so they imagine, to the most inferior of stages, which they call "natural *frumkeit*" (natural, simple piety). For this they have been told by the preachers who lord it over them, saying: "I have a secret" etc. But this is a most extreme error. Upon my soul, into this error fall the majority of the great ones among the newcomers, except for a few of the maturer ones who know the truth. They, too, have departed from this way because they have fallen into worldly interests etc. Even though they have heard in preachments (by Dov Baer) on this subject many words in the light of the true doctrine of our master and father, our teacher and instructor of blessed memory, they claim that it is only for the uninitiated, such as penitent sinners and so forth. But, upon my soul, the great ones need it more than the Small. This is the main cause of their downfall, little by little, without their recognizing it in themselves at all, as is obvious and well known. And this is sufficient for he who understands.

There is a further main reason for the above-mentioned severe malady. This is their small amount of effort and labor in the words of the living God, to bring them into the soul *in practice*, in particular. For though there are many who work hard, and with great effort, at understanding and at practicing the subject many times until they are thoroughly familiar with it and their tongues are fluent when they reply to those who ask etc., it is not this at all that is called divine worship and service. This is no more than the category of mere external study, outwardly from the lips, without the heart and soul being committed. For they have not engaged in the divine service of fixing the matter firmly in the soul with a strong and powerful attachment, actually to live by it (known as *lebedigkeit*, "liveliness," in the soul, and the contrary is called *totigkeit*, "deadliness"). To those who seek them, the words of the living God are actually life. As it is *Deut. 4:4* written: "And ye that cleave" etc. "are alive all of you etc.," and the contrary is considered as dead. Even in worldly affairs there is a great difference between one for whom all the details of a subject are imbued with great vitality (*der inyan is lebedig lebt zehr*, "the subject is a lively one, very lively") and one for whom the subject lacks life (*der inyan is tot zehr*, "the subject is very much a dead one") etc. It is well known that the category of the soul's vitality in the words of the living God follows only as a result of labor in divine service and great effort in prayer, and of study of the subject in the doctrinal teachings (of Hasidism), the holy Zohar and the holy books (of the Kabbalah), to delve deeply into them and to bind both soul and heart sincerely to them (Yiddish: *ein stark klep be-emes fun nefesh*, "a strong attachment in truth from the very soul"), until the soul revives with real, fresh vitality. This must be constant and with great industry until it becomes fixed firmly in the soul so that it lives for ever, never to slip, its light never to be extinguished. Then, when a man seeks the words of the living God, they will be fixed firmly in his soul for ever. His light will break through as the dawn, to sate his soul with tangible satisfaction, to increase the divine light with great expansiveness and with an everlasting root and foundation. Then shall he be as a tree planted by the waters etc. with all the evil winds in the world unable to move him etc. And this is sufficient for him who understands. . . .

II

The fifth group is of those in whose soul the category of *yehidah* (the highest stage of soul) shines. This is the category of simple, essential will and delight, higher than concentration and reason of the mind etc., as mentioned above in connection with the fifth stage of the natural soul. In this is clothed the essential ecstasy of the *yehidah* of the divine soul. As Rabbi Simeon ben Yohai said: "To Him attached" etc. Concerning this it is said: "And ye that cleave" etc. involuntarily, as mentioned above at length. *Deut. 4:4*

Now although this stage is not found in one man in a

city etc. it is, nonetheless, possible for the hidden illumination of *yehidah* in the spark of every Israelite, as mentioned
above, to come periodically, even in slight unconcealment
(i.e., it is not completely hidden in the unconscious), when
man is moved to ecstasy by the above-mentioned divine delight (known as a great *kvell*, "delight," in the mind). He
can then attain the stage of simple, essential delight, higher
entirely than reason. But it remains firmly fixed in the soul
for only a moment and, in the absence of a container, immediately evaporates. This is because of the materialism of
the body etc.

Many delude themselves in this matter, imagining that
they have attained, only too easily, this simple delight etc.
Of this it is unnecessary to speak for it is an utterly vain
delusion which stems from over-heated blood and essential
imperfections in the instruments of the mind (i.e., there is
an element of madness in such delusion; it is pathological),
known as "essential falsehood" (Yiddish: *ein genarter mensh*,
"a deluded person," by nature, in particular) for which
there is never any remedy. Such falsehood and vain delusion stem from this, that he imagines that his soul is about
to leave him (known as *ausgehen*, "expiring" [i.e., in ec-
stasy]) and that he cannot remain in the body etc., and he
sees frightening and terrifying visions (i.e., he is subject
to hallucinations) etc. Of such lunatics it is unnecessary to
speak.

However, something of this kind happens even among
those who understand knowledge (i.e., adepts in hasidic
doctrine), and they take note of it if they do not wish to delude themselves. This is because of the admixture of heart
ecstasy. When a man is moved to ecstasy in the very point
of his heart, even higher than reason, there is an admixture
of this with the category of delight of *yehidah*, which, as
mentioned above, illumines to some extent. It then seems
to him to be this authentic, simple ecstasy of delight etc.

and he thinks that it is this that is sensed in the fleshly heart. He imagines this to be the state mentioned in the verse: "My flesh and my heart faileth." However, there is here an admixture of very severe error. For if this fleshly heart contains an admixture of good and evil, in the category of *Nogah* (the kabbalistic term for the "shell" or "husk," *kelippah*, which contains both good and evil and is not, like the other *kelippot*, entirely evil), how then can it be a container for the essential divine delight, unless it has been purged thoroughly of its materialism? And this is hardly ever found. Consequently, it is certain that this is not truly authentic but that there is here an admixture of error (known as *genart*, "deluded") etc.

Ps. 73:26

However, from one point of view, it is possible for this experience to be completely and truly authentic. For it is well known that there exists a state of ecstasy, even in the fleshly heart, which comes from the point of the heart, known as the category of the "beast." Although this is lower than knowledge its root is higher than knowledge (i.e., this instinctive desire for God comes from a very lofty source) etc. As it is written: "I was a beast before Thee" etc. (i.e., even though it is the category of the "beast" yet it is "before Thee"). Even though those who understand knowledge reject this state, their eyes are too blind to see that there is here a root of the above-mentioned essential delight, without any admixture whatsoever. This is because it stems from the category of true simplicity of heart, as is written: "Be perfect" (the Hebrew can mean "be simple"). This simplicity is the category of *yehidah* which illumines the heart to its innermost point. The test of authenticity and its main condition is as follows. Ecstasy of the fleshly heart is also induced in the category of simplicity alone, without any self-awareness whatsoever (i.e., the experience is in no way artificial or self-induced but a completely spontaneous reaction of the soul).

Ps. 73:22

Gen. 17:1

For instance, when a man is severely tortured, his heart cries out with a sudden cry in the fleshly heart from the very point of his soul and heart and reaching to the very soul etc. (i.e., he does not say to himself that this is the proper reaction to torture and then behaves accordingly but cries out in pain because he feels the pain). It is certain that there is nothing here of admixture whatsoever but only the authentic as it is in actual essence etc. This is true, conversely, of an exceedingly marvelous delight, for instance, where a man actually sentenced to death receives the news that his life has been spared and so forth. His heart of flesh will then actually revive from its essential source. As it is written:

Gen. 45:27 "And the spirit of Jacob their father revived" when he received the tidings concerning Joseph whom he loved as himself and so forth. And this is also possible with regard to a truly penitent sinner who cries out in excessive bitterness of soul, from out of his actual fleshly heart, until this

Av. Zar. 17a reaches to the category of *yeḥidah* etc. just as the soul of Rabbi Eleazar ben Dordia expired in weeping. Conversely, when he finds delight in the Lord with an exceedingly great delight, then the vitality of this fleshly delight reaches to the category of the essential delight of *yeḥidah* etc. This is ecstasy of the fleshly heart, lower than knowledge, as it is written: "But I am a beast" etc. But, as mentioned above, this only applies when it is in the category of simplicity, for then it is without any self-awareness whatsoever (for where there is self-awareness the experience is inauthentic). Then the materialism of the body will not darken the light for him, as is clearly well known concerning the truly simple, faithful in heart and soul, to the extent that they expire (in longing) without their knowing of it or sensing anything of it in themselves etc.

This type is more frequently found among the unsophisticated rather than among the sophisticates and the sages, but there is a division into many different stages of the truth of the matter. He who is wise in this matter will find it all as clear as the sun etc. And this is sufficient for he who understands.

After all these words of truth concerning all the different stages to be found among our fraternity, each one can recognize his own place and stage. He should keep watch over himself not to delude himself in striving after that which is too great for him. As it is written, "Who shall ascend" etc., *Ps. 24:3* the implication being that if he cannot ascend he should descend etc. No man should reflect on the evils of his neighbor nor should he be envious of his neighbor's superiority and goodness, for each has his own special place, and envy only creates a severe admixture in all one's ways etc. But each should behave as he is in essence (*naturelich nit nach gemacht*, "naturally and not aping others").

When we have the opportunity, there is much to be said in open rebuke about the bad and harsh customs frequently found among our fraternity and which stem from error over the years. But all the people sin unwittingly; may the Lord pardon the remnant that is left which still seeks the nearness of God etc. There is further much to be said concerning the main duty of Torah study for its own sake in its many aspects, for this is hidden even from the majority of those who understand knowledge and certainly from the youths and the newcomers etc., and concerning the nature of the precepts in all their details and of charity and the general principles of benevolence. I want to deal, too, with the dispensation (they have given themselves) of engaging in the earning of a livelihood with the depths of the heart so that all man's days are wasted in vanity. For this is the main cause of downfall among the majority of our fraternity, great and small, old and new, until the Lord will pour out His spirit upon them from on high etc. and they awake from their sleep etc. This is the chief meaning of "exile," which is compared to sleep, as it is written: "When the Lord is re- *Ps. 126:1*

stored . . . we were as them that dream." And this is sufficient for he who understands.

But O, my beloved brethren, all whose soul is attached
to mine, who seek the words of the living God and hear
them in truth and faithfulness, and in whose heart there is
no root that beareth gall and wormwood to gaze with an
evil eye, God forbid, especially since you know me and recognize me from my youth. You will believe me when I say
that all these words of mine are spoken from the whole
point of my heart, as they are in my heart and soul in my essential nature and being, as I have been trained in them
from my youth at the command of my master and father, my
teacher and instructor of blessed memory, day by day. They
should not say, God forbid, that there are mysteries here
only to be revealed to initiates etc. or that many things
recorded here are only on the surface etc. to provide an opportunity for those who have not, as yet, been trained in the
truth of the matter. For such are the pretexts of those who
desire to be swollen with pride and to acquire fame for
themselves by saying: "I have a secret" etc., unknown to
others etc., and all this they attribute to me. But, truly and
faithfully, I swear, by my life, that there is not even half a
word of all the matters I have explained to you which has
not come from the point of my heart, and they are all to be
discovered and understood by anyone who has tasted the
flavor of engaging in the words of the living God from his
youth. For all these words of mine are built on my experience from my youth, for these twenty years and more, in the
holy temple of our master and father, our teacher and instructor of blessed memory. From him I know all the details
of the sufferings (the spiritual pangs) of our fraternity and I
have myself examined the heart of each and the error of
each as far as my comprehension permits. Therefore let him
obey who is willing. I await your reply by the hand of our
distinguished friend, the Rabbi's messenger, who will produce this letter, if all these words, always for your good, are

truly acceptable. And this will restore my soul etc. The words of their friend who seeks the true goodness of their souls with heart and soul all the days of my life of vanity, Dov Baer.

Comments

In Ḥabad thought, man has two souls: the "natural soul" (the vital force which sustains the body) and the "divine soul," conceived of as a divine spark deep in the recesses of the human psyche. When the "divine soul" is moved to ecstasy it is the attraction of like to like, the divine in the soul meeting its Source. The "natural soul," however, derives from the "shell" or "husk" (*kelippah*) of *Nogah* in which there is an admixture of good and evil. Consequently any emotion experienced in the "fleshly heart" is bound to contain an element of self-seeking. There are five categories of soul in ascending order: *nefesh*, *ru'ah*, *neshamah*, *hayyah* and *yehidah*. These find their expression both in the "natural soul" and in the "divine soul." There are thus ten categories in all and each can find its expression in one or other of the varied forms of ecstasy. The *Tract on Ecstasy* is an analysis of these ten states of soul. In the two selections from the *Tract*, Dov Baer's method is evident. Here he summarizes the arguments he has presented earlier in the *Tract* and rebukes his followers for deluding themselves and for not taking adequate pains in their worship. The "words of the living God" referred to here are the Ḥabad doctrines as expounded by the teachers of the movement. These deal with such topics as how God becomes manifest in the universe and how the divine light is all pervading. It should be noted that the majority of the members of Ḥabad were small traders and businessmen who had somehow to spare time for lengthy periods of prayer and contemplation, hence the warnings in the *Tract* about worldly distractions. The term for contemplation is "hearing," resulting in ecstasy. When the "hearing" is "near" it is powerful and authentic, where it is "from afar" it is far more remote and "hits home" to a far lesser degree.

20

The Secret Diary of
Rabbi Isaac Eizik
of Komarno

∽∾

Introduction

Rabbi Isaac Judah Jehiel Safrin (1806–1874), known as
Rabbi Isaac Eizik of Komarno, was a ḥasidic master, son and
successor of Rabbi Alexander Sender, founder of the Komarno dynasty, and nephew of the famous kabbalist Rabbi
Zevi Hirsch Eichenstein of Zhidachov. Rabbi Isaac Eizik was
in many ways an independent ḥasidic thinker. For instance,
although the latter ḥasidic master tended to reject the older
ḥasidic doctrine of the sublimation of "strange thoughts" or,
at least, to limit the process to the great saints, Rabbi Isaac
Eizik is insistent that it is heretical to reject the doctrine.
The "strange thoughts" are sent to man so that he might elevate them to their source in God. To deny that the
"strange thoughts" were sent for a purpose is, in fact, to
deny that God has control over all and that He has sent
them that they might be elevated.

Rabbi Isaac Eizik's secret diary, *Megillat Setarim*, circu-

lated among a few chosen Ḥasidim of the Komarno dynasty.
N. Ben-Menahem published the diary on the basis of two
manuscripts (1944). He records in the name of Professor G.
Scholem that a lithograph edition of the diary appeared in
Warsaw in 1924 but no copies of this edition have been pre-
served. The following selections from the diary, in transla-
tion, deal with the author's peak religious experiences.
Selection I is from pages 13–14; Selection II, from page 10;
Selection III, from page 22; and Selection IV from pages
25–26.

Text

I

At the age of sixteen I married my true partner. She belonged to the *ru'ah* ("spirit") aspect of my soul but since I
myself had not attained as yet to the *ru'ah* aspect there were
many obstacles to the match. However, thanks to the power
of my repentance and industry in studying the Torah, no
stranger passed between us. After this I attained to many
lofty stages of the holy spirit, the result of my industry in
Torah study and in divine worship. The truth be told, I did
not appreciate at the time that it was not the result of my
own efforts since I was still remote from true worship. But
after reflecting on the matter I separated myself entirely
from the world. It happened in the year 5583 (= 1823) at the
beginning of winter. My special room was so cold that it had
not been heated even once during the whole of the winter.
It was my habit to sleep only two hours a day, spending the
rest of the time studying the Torah, the Talmud, the Codes,
the Zohar, the writings of our Master (Isaac Luria) and the
works of Rabbi Moses Cordovero. But I fell away from all

these stages and for three months was in a state of immense smallness of soul. Many harsh and demonic forces (*kelippot*) rose against me to dissuade me from studying the Torah. Worse than all was the state of melancholy into which I was hurled. Yet my heart was as firm as a rock. During this time the only pleasure I allowed myself was to drink a little water and eat a morsel of bread daily. I had no delight whatever in the Torah I studied or the prayers I recited. The cold was very severe and the demonic forces extremely powerful so that I actually stood equally balanced between two paths, depending on how I would choose. Much bitterness passed over my head as a result of these blandishments, really more bitter than a thousand times death. But once I had overcome these blandishments, suddenly, in the midst of the day, as I was studying tractate *Yevamot* in the name of the eternal God, in order to adorn the *Shekhinah* with all my might, a great light fell upon me. The whole house became filled with light, a marvelous light, the *Shekhinah* resting there. This was the first time in my life that I had some little taste of His light, may He be blessed. It was authentic without error or confusion, a wondrous delight and a most pleasant illumination beyond all comprehension. From that time onward I began to serve the Creator of all with a marvelous, unvarying illumination. The blandishments had power over me no longer. Afterwards I fell once again for a time so I came to realize that I must journey to the saints who would draw down His light, blessed be He, upon me since I already had a refined vessel wherewith to receive the light.

II

5606 (= 1845). The twentieth day of the *Omer*. I was in the town of Dukla. I arrived there in the middle of the night and there was no one to offer me hospitality until a certain tanner invited me to his home. I wanted to recite the night prayers and count the *Omer* but was unable to do so in the home of the tanner so I went to the *bet ha-midrash* of the town to pray there. I came to realize the meaning of the descent of the *Shekhinah* and Her anguish as She stood in the street of the tanners. I wept sorely in the presence of the Lord of all because of the anguish of the *Shekhinah*. In my distress I fainted and slept for a while. I saw a vision of light, a powerful radiance in the form of a virgin all adorned from whose person there came a dazzling light but I was not worthy to see the face. No more of this can be recorded in writing. Her light was brighter than the sun at noonday.

III

The year 5607 (= 1846). On the night of the Sabbath, the twenty-fourth of the month Ḥeshvan. In my dream I saw my friend the Ḥasid Joshua of Brody. I forget whether he was still alive in this world or was already in the world on high. I asked him with great anticipation: "Tell me, dear brother, whence come you?" "From the world on high," he replied. I asked him further with great anticipation: "Tell me, brother, how do I fare in the world on high?" "You fare well," he replied, "and are of much worth there." I then put a further question to him. The previous week I had been very angry with my wife because she had caused me great suffering and the result was that there departed from me the illuminations, souls and angels who are wont to accompany me. Did this cause me any harm on high? He did not reply to the question so I embraced him and kissed him saying: "Do not imagine that I ask these things of you because of my ambition to become a rabbi or a ḥasidic master. It is only that I long for my portion to be with the Lord God of

Israel among the people of Israel." He replied: "All is well" and I awoke.

The year 5607 (= 1847). On the holy Sabbath, the eighteenth day of the month of Adar I saw many souls who criticized my book *Oẓar ha-Ḥayyim* on the 613 precepts and they ordered me to desist from writing any more and from revealing such secrets. They showed me my book, complaining about many of the ideas contained therein. I said to them: "Thank God I have expounded many of the precepts up to the portion *Be-Har* (Leviticus 25) and the book contains true and wondrous reasons for the precepts." They admitted that the teachings found in the book were true, yet, for all that, they came to the conclusion that I should not write any more. But I replied that if the Lord will keep me in life I shall certainly continue to write since we are commanded to know the reasons for the precepts. Afterwards I had the merit of seeing a spark of Elijah of blessed memory. I entreated him: "Master! Greet me I pray you!" he did greet me and I was filled with joy. I met many souls to whom I said: "I have been worthy of being greeted by Elijah." Then I awoke. After the Sabbath I saw a splendid but terrifying lion. This was a symbol of sovereignty, that my prayers had been accepted through the lion on high.

IV

5610 (= 1850). The night after the Sabbath, the nineteenth day of the month of Adar. I saw that they brought me a robe belonging to our Master the Ba'al Shem Tov, may his merits be a shield for us, and they related a miracle wrought by our Master at the time he wore this robe but I have forgotten what it was. I took the robe, rejoicing over it as much as over all the treasure in the world. The interpretation is that when I expounded the Torah at the third meal on the Sabbath, illuminations, souls and angels were there with me, among them a soul belonging to the sparks of the souls of our Master's disciples. On the night of the third day, the twenty-first day of the month of Adar, I saw my teacher our Master Rabbi Naphtali of Ropshits, may his merits be a shield for us. I conversed with him about many things and I then asked him why I have the merit of seeing souls even in my waking state. He replied that it was a reward for the Sabbath and its illuminations, for we celebrated a Sabbath illumined with a wondrous light.

5610 (= 1850). The second of Nisan, the night of the sixth day (= Thursday night). It was the night of immersion (of my wife). I studied the Torah until midnight and completed the laws of Passover in the *Tur*. When I fell asleep I dreamed in a vision of the night that I saw our Master Elimelech of Lyzhansk who gave expression to the great warmth he felt for me. They said to me that the place of our Master the divine Ba'al Shem Tov is not far from that of the above-named Master. Longing greatly to see the face of our holy master I ran to his abode and stood in the outer room. They told me that he was reciting his prayers in the inner sanctum but he opened the door and I had the merit of seeing the radiant form of our Master the Ba'al Shem Tov, may his merits be a shield for us. I was in such a state of joy and dread that I could not move but he came up to me, greeting me with a smile on his face. I delighted greatly in this and his form is engraved on my mind so that I can recall it. It is possible that I became worthy of this because I had given alms on that day in a fit and proper manner.

Comments

I

The reference to *ru'aḥ* is to the kabbalistic doctrine of the three parts of the soul—*nefesh*, *ru'aḥ* and *neshamah*. In a proper marriage, the souls of husband and wife are in complete accord because they share the same category of soul. The "smallness of soul" is the mystical "dark night of the soul" as opposed to "greatness of soul" (see the general Introduction to this book). The demonic forces are known in the Kabbalah as *kelippot* ("shells" or "husks"). The *Shekhinah* is the Divine Presence which in the Kabbalah is a kind of female element in the Godhead, identified with the *Sefirah Malkhut*. The reference to the "saints" (*zaddikim*) is to the hasidic masters, Hasidism believing that a man can only make real progress in the spiritual life if he associates with the Guru-like masters.

II

The counting of the *Omer* is the counting of the 49 days from Passover to Shavuot (Leviticus 23:15). Dukla is a town in southeast Poland. Ben-Menahem observes that he has been unable to discover the source of the legend about the *Shekhinah* in the street of the tanners. The vision of the *Shekhinah* as a virgin resplendent in light is extraordinary.

III

The identity of Joshua of Brody is uncertain. The lion is king of the beasts, hence the lion is the symbol of sovereignty, probably here meaning that R. Isaac Eizik would "reign" as a hasidic master. The "lion of high" probably refers to the lion's face of the holy living creatures seen in Ezekiel's vision; see chapter 1 of this book.

IV

The Ba'al Shem Tov is the founder of the hasidic movement. It was the practice of the hasidic masters to deliver discourses on the Torah on the Sabbath during the third meal. R. Naphtali Zevi of Ropshits (Ropczyce) (1760–1827) was a hasidic master and teacher of Rabbi Isaac Eizik. The *Tur* is the code of the Jewish law compiled by Jacob ben Asher (d. 1340). Elimelech of Lyzhansk (1717–1787) was an early hasidic master. The reference to alms giving is based on the kabbalistic teaching that the giving of alms on the day one has marital relations is an aid to having male children.

21

Aaron Roth's
Essay, "Agitation of the Soul"

かん

Introduction

Rabbi Aaron Roth (1894–1944) was born in Ungvar. He studied under Rabbis Isaiah Silverstein and Moses Forhand in Hungary and came under the influence of various ḥasidic masters, especially Rabbi Issachar Dov of Belz and, his main teacher, Rabbi Zevi Elimelech of Blazowa, who urged Roth to become a ḥasidic master himself. A group of Ḥasidim gathered around Roth in the town of Beregszasz (Beregovo) and towards the end of his life a similar group was formed in Jerusalem. Roth's emphasis was on simple faith and on ecstatic prayer. The essay translated here was first published by Roth in the year 1934. Later, the essay, entitled, *"Hitraggeshut ha-Nefesh"* ("Agitation of the Soul"), was published as the first part of *Kunteres Ahavat ha-Bore* ("Tract on the Love of God") in volume 2 of Roth's collected writings, *Shomer Emunim* (1964), 372a–76a.

Text

I thought to myself that it was right and proper to add here an essay on ḥasidic thought among my writings which the Creator in His great mercy gave me the grace to compose. For the topics treated here provide encouragement in setting hearts on fire to worship our Father in Heaven. For this reason I have called the essay: "Agitation of the Soul."

It is written in the book of Psalms (119:129–32): "Thy testimonies are wonderful; Therefore doth my soul keep them. The opening of Thy words giveth light; It giveth understanding to the simple. I opened wide my mouth, and panted; For I longed for Thy commandments. Turn Thou towards me, and be gracious unto me, As is Thy wont to do unto those that love Thy name." At first glance it is hard to see the connection between these verses; see Rashi's commentary. Furthermore, why does the verse not say: "Thy statutes are wonderful" or "Thy Torah"? Again, why does the verse say: "Therefore doth my *nefesh* keep them" and not "*my ru'aḥ*" or simply: "Therefore do I keep them"?

The following appears to be a possible explanation, as my poor intellect sees it with the help of the Creator, blessed be He. The holy Torah is sometimes called *ḥok* ("statute") and sometimes *mishpat* ("judgment"). For there are rational precepts, where reason acknowledges that the law should be as stated, and there are also statutes. These latter have no reason but are a decree of our King, blessed be He and blessed be His name. But occasionally the holy Torah is called "testimony" (*edut*), for it testifies on our behalf. Each precept in itself testifies on our behalf: "So-and-so performed me in this manner and So-and-so in that manner." As the Talmud puts it: "Rabbi Joshua ben Levi said: 'All the good deeds which Israel does in this world will testify on their behalf in the world to come, as it is said: "Let them bring their witnesses that they may be justified"—this

Av. Zar. 2a

refers to Israel. 'And let them hear and say: It is truth'—this   Isa. 43:9
refers to the nations of the world.' "

Now the Holy One, blessed be He, the Torah and Israel
are one. For the light of His Holy Name, blessed be He, resides in the letters (of the Torah) and when a man moves
his lips in holiness and adheres with all the power of his
thought and inwardness of heart to the innermost light of
the holy letters, he then becomes a veritable palace and
sanctuary for the holy *Shekhinah*, provided he has this in
mind. . . .

Now it is well known from the books of wisdom (the
kabbalistic works) that just as man has three categories of
soul—*nefesh*, *ru'ah* and *neshamah*—so, too, our holy Torah
has these three categories. When a man studies the Torah
or carries out the precepts in a plain manner, his own *nefesh*
adheres to the *nefesh* of the holy Torah and the influence
then extends to the World of Action. When a man studies
the Torah or worships the Lord in a spirit of greater inwardness, there rests upon him that degree of holiness which derives from the category of *ru'ah*, of greater inwardness. If he
worships the Lord in fear and with refined thoughts, there
then rests upon him the degree of holiness of the *neshamah*
with the result that he achieves holiness of thought. Thus
nefesh becomes bound to *nefesh*, *ru'ah* to *ru'ah*, and *neshamah* to *neshamah*, reaching back to *Ein-Sof*, blessed be
He and blessed be His name.

Know, too, that there are times when a man burns in
rapture and as with flaming torches even where there has
been no preparation for it. There are many categories here.

I shall record only one detail. Know, my brother, that
there are times when, by the mercy of God, an illumination
of the soul shines upon man (i.e., from the category of *neshamah*) even though he belongs in no way to this stage (of
neshamah). It is only that in God's great mercy He has compassion on the people near to Him so that He reminds man

(of his destiny) and awakens and bestirs him from heavy sleep. Or it may be because a man has performed a certain good deed, by its power an illumination comes to him from Heaven, since the force of the good deed's ascent brought about a certain unification in Heaven. For Heaven is beyond time so that a good deed or Torah study or prayer can ascend long after the actual performance. Or it may be because a man has become worthy to have clothed within him some spark of the soul of a saint or a repentant sinner as a result of his carrying out a good deed in a spirit of self-sacrifice.

In order to clarify this topic I must quote the holy language of the book *Pardes* (*Sha'ar ha-Neshamah*, chapter 3): "Behold, it follows that in proportion to the degree of engagement by man in this world so is the flow of divine grace to his *neshamah* or his *ru'ah* or his *nefesh*. It all depends on the amount of worship and the manner of its flaws, even if these had taken place not necessarily in his body etc. Occasionally it happens that there is an influx to the soul when a man carries out a good deed or studies some Torah. Then providence ordains that there be an influx of soul in order for it to become whole." The meaning of this is obviously that a man receives an influx of divine grace from the root

Deut. 32:9 of his soul in Heaven above, in the category of: "Jacob is the lot of His inheritance." But so long as a man fails to bind his innermost thoughts and heart to the worship of God, blessed be He, that man is like one who embraces the King while wearing many garments. The Torah is not then united with him and he can only draw down to himself an illumination that is in the [inferior] category of *nefesh*.

Thus it is possible to explain the verse as follows: "Thy testimonies are *pela'ot*." *Pela'ot* (does not mean "wonderful"

Num. 6:2 but) means "separation," as in the verse: "shall separate [*yafli*] himself to utter a vow." That is to say, the Torah is still in the stage of *pela'ot*, separate from man and not

united with him. And the verse speaks of "testimonies" because the holy Torah ascends on high to testify. Now when
a man engages in the study of the Torah with intelligence
and with inwardness of heart the holy Torah causes an influx of holiness to endow him with the intelligence he
needs. But when "Thy testimonies are *pela'ot*," namely,
when the holy Torah is still remote from man and is not
united with him, then: "Therefore doth my *nefesh* keep
them," that is to say, I only have then the merit of the illumination that derives from the *nefesh* category.

Now the fool who walks in darkness desires only a plain
approach. He wants to study the Torah in its plain meaning
and offer his prayers in their plain meaning. He does not believe that in every generation the Holy One, blessed be He,
affords illuminations to the holy people of Israel when they
yearn longingly for Him. "For I the Lord change not." For   *Mal. 3:6*
there is no change in Him, blessed be He, for all the precepts of the holy Torah are eternal. And it is written: "and   *Deut. 11:23*
to cleave to Him" and Scripture speaks of loving God and
fearing Him and we recite daily: "And thou shalt love the   *Deut. 6:5*
Lord thy God." Shall we say that this only applied to former
generations? Obviously not since the holy Torah is eternal.

This is the purpose for which we have come into the
world, to become bound to Him, blessed be He, even if it be
only for a moment, if one is sometimes worthy. It is possible
for each person to make available to himself some aspect of
these precepts. For this is the purpose of all the Torah and
the precepts, as the holy work *Toledot*, section *Ḥayyei Sarah*,
writes in the name of a commentary to Maimonides, that
the purpose of the whole Torah is for man to achieve the
positive precept of cleaving to God. The author quotes this
frequently in his work. He explains on these lines the talmudic saying that good is done to everyone who performs   *Kid. 39b*
even a single precept. This means, he says, that good is
done to whoever carries out a precept with the express in-

Mak. 24a
tention of fulfilling the precept "and to cleave to Him."
This is the meaning of another talmudic saying, "Habakkuk
Hab. 2:4
based all the precepts on one principle: 'The righteous shall
live by his faith.'" The meaning of this is that the precept of
faith is the purpose of the whole Torah. It is the aim of
Torah study, prayer and the performance of all good deeds
that a man, while carrying these out, should have in mind
to attain to faith in God and adhesion to Him by means of
the Torah and the precepts. My brother, remember this
principle, for it is a basic rule in God's service.

And when, out of great darkness of soul and blockage
and distress, the Holy One, blessed be He, brings illumination to man, he then begins to long for God, blessed be He.
This longing depends on the period and time and is in proportion to the degree that the soul finds favor in His sight,
blessed be He, and in proportion to the ascent of the Torah
he has studied and the good deeds he has performed at that
time. Then whoever is intelligent seizes hold and grasps
Song 3:4
firmly at this point, fulfilling the verse: "I held him, and
would not let him go, until I had brought him into my
mother's house." For there is then an indication that the
soul has proved acceptable or a subject of special grace to
her Maker.

I shall explain the matter to you by means of a parable,
all having to do with the idea of love. A man is in prison
where he has sat so long in darkness that he is unaware that
there is any such thing as light. Adjacent to his prison is a
room in which there shines a brilliant light. Suddenly a
small aperture is opened and he sees the light. Or the illustration can be given of a man who is locked up in a low and
dark dungeon. Near the dungeon is a huge precipice and on
the precipice a high wall. Beyond this wall are further walls
and beyond these a great and awesome palace containing
many residences. Beyond all these residences is a house in
which there shines a great and wonderful light, immeasur-

able and incomprehensible. This house is surrounded by many walls and that hidden light can only shine through the crevices and spaces. The light shines more brightly the nearer one is to the house, and near the outer wall the light is not at all bright. Yet even this light is most powerful when compared with the darkness of the dungeon. There are doors and windows through which the light beams directly and other windows through which it beams indirectly. It can happen that a certain door or window is opened in such a way as to beam the light directly onto the man who dwells in darkness and he then experiences great joy. He then longs to escape from the dark dungeon in order to climb the precipice. At times of great rejoicing and celebration a tiny aperture is opened (in the house) which beams the light directly. Even though the light which comes through this aperture is as nothing compared to the light which shines through the open doors, yet since it shines directly on the recipients a great and holy illumination is theirs. When a man is worthy of seeing this light his soul longs and is set on fire without limit until he feels that he is about to expire (in ecstasy). In his great longing he risks his life to break open the door of his dungeon and springs energetically to enjoy the light. But as soon as he emerges (from the dungeon) the light is concealed and there he stands at the foot of the precipice which he is unable to climb because his limbs ache and the precipice is so steep and high. A man at the top of the precipice then lowers a ladder down to him. But it is very difficult to ascend by means of this ladder for agility is needed and willingness to risk one's neck by missing the step. He tries to ascend on the ladder but no sooner does he manage to climb a short way up, then he falls back again. This occurs again and again until the lord of the manor has pity on him and he reaches down to grasp his right hand so that he can pull him up. The application of this parable is very profound and it is impossible to explain it in full, but those in need of it will understand. See the holy work *Sha'arei Gan Eden* (*Derekh Emet*, I:7) and the prayer book of Rabbi Koppel at the beginning of the Intentions for the Sabbath and you will understand. This is the meaning

Song 5:2–6 of "Open to me, my sister" etc. "My beloved put in his hand" etc. "But my beloved had turned away" etc., and the whole of that chapter. If you have understood the parable you will grasp the meaning of all these verses. This is the idea behind attachment to the ẓaddikim (the ḥasidic masters). It resembles the parable quoted in *The Duties of the Heart* (*Sha'ar ha-Beḥinah*, chapter 6) of the child born in the king's dungeon. See there his holy and sweet words and they will revive your soul.

Now, when the fool sees that the light was revealed to him at a certain time but was later concealed, he imagines that once it has been concealed it will never be revealed again. Furthermore, he then experiences the darkness even more acutely than before. But the intelligent man thinks to himself, why did such a thing happen to me, that such a light be revealed to me? It probably means that the Lord of the manor is hinting to me that if I try hard enough it is within my power and my capacity to attain to the holiness of that light.

We have by tradition from our masters that two types of counsel are available for whoever wishes to speed his escape from the deep and dark dungeon. The first is that he should cry out constantly, shouting aloud and in tears, that pity be shown to him to bring him out of this darkness, until the Lord of the manor takes pity on him and beams a light onto him so that he can see the way to escape. This is the way of pity. But the more ready way is to yearn constantly for the light and to engage in contemplation on the greatness and wonder of the precipice and the great and awesome palace and the marvelous light within it. Now this light is a spiritual one and the thoughts and yearning are also of a spiritual nature. It is well known that spirit calls to spirit so that when a man's soul yearns to serve her Creator and when the Lord of the manor observes how powerful is his longing, then, even though that man is not really worthy of it, He elevates him to reach a category of that light in proportion to his understanding of holiness.

The holy Rabbi Ze'ev of Zbarazh expounds the verse: "And the angel of the Lord appeared unto him in a flame of fire out of the midst of a bush . . . but the bush was not consumed." Even though the bush is not consumed and is still full of evil character traits, yet the Lord appears there if there is "a flame of fire," namely, yearning and longing. My brother, if you will reflect on these words you will discover in this parable counsels and paths and encouragement for the worship of God.

Ex. 3:2

All this only applies when man digs deep into the recesses of his heart in order to recognize Him at whose word the world came into being. But if he makes not the slightest effort to search for it, then: "The fool walketh in darkness" and "A fool hath no delight in *understanding*," that is to say, in repentance from the depths of his heart. And he then knows nothing of how remote he is from the Lord. He imagines he is near and that he knows all.

Eccles. 2:14
Prov. 18:2

As I have seen it recorded in the holy book *Zemaḥ ha-Shem li-Zevi* (section Ḥukkat) on the verse: "How great are Thy works, O Lord etc." He explains that the main purpose is to know that one does not know. This can only be attained by much effort in the worship of God. After that a man knows that he knows nothing. But if a man does not even begin to contemplate on the greatness of the Creator, blessed be He, then he does not know that he does not know. Thus he explains the verse: "How great are Thy works, O Lord! Thy thoughts are very deep." That is to say, who can grasp Thy greatness and Thy splendor. "A man is brutish and knoweth not," that is to say, even one who is in

Ps. 92:6–7

the category of a "man," which denotes a lofty spiritual degree, is also "brutish and knoweth not," for, as above, this is
the aim of all knowledge. The verse continues: "But the
fool does not understand this." He does not know that he
does not know for he imagines that he knows.

The punishment is that God hides His face, as it were.
The meaning is that a man descends to such a low degree
that he forgets his great worth, until, in the course of time,
the heart's yearning has departed, the desire and longing
for the service of God, sweeter than honey and the honey-
comb. All your desires cannot equal it and can in no way be
compared to it. The punishment is remoteness from the
BK 46a   light of the countenance of the Living King. For "whoever
has an ache goes to consult the physician" and he cries out
in weeping that they should take pity on him and provide
him with a cure. But if the malady is so severe that the sufferer no longer feels any acute pain, then he is, indeed,
greatly to be pitied because the holy soul sleeps deep in her
exile in heavy slumber.

I have seen among the writings of the holy Rabbi Shalom
Duber of Lubavich, the memory of the righteous is for a
blessing, that there are many categories of sleep. There is a
sleep that is no more than a light nodding, when the sleeper
is half-awake. There is the category of real sleep. There is
the category of deep slumber. And there is the category of
fainting, far worse, God forbid, where it is necessary to mas-
sage the sleeper, to strike him and to revive him with every
kind of medicine in order to restore his soul. . . . And there
is a category of still deeper unconsciousness that is known
as a coma where, God forbid, only a tiny degree of life still
remains in deep concealment so that even shouting at the
sleeper and striking him fail to revive him. In this age we
are in this deepest state of unconsciousness. To be sure,
there are still to be found holy men in Israel who are still
alert. And even the ordinary holy Israelite is in the category

of: "I sleep, but my heart waketh." But there are some   *Song 5:2*
whom nothing can succeed in awakening, as, God forbid, in
the last of the stages we have mentioned. Only if God has
pity on him to some extent can such a one be restored to his
former vigor, as the discerning will understand. So there are
those whom neither suffering nor anything else can avail,
God forbid. They have descended to the lowest degree. But
efforts at revival can be effective for those who are in the
category of a faint and *a fortiori* for those only in the category of sleep. And there are those who are only half asleep
and who wake up as soon as they are called by name, even
though they fall asleep again.

Now when a man becomes aware that he is falling asleep
and begins to nod and he is afraid that a strong, heavy sleep
may overcome him, the best advice for him is for him to request his friend to wake him from time to time or that he
should go among people who are awake and where a light
shines brightly. But when he is on his own who can wake
him? My meaning is that he should obtain a mentor, a
friend who will converse with him from time to time on
matters having to do with the fear of God. These words are
in the category of a seed, the holy words they speak being
sown in the heart. Even though he is not aware of it at the
time, yet later on he will become conscious of it. This is
marvelous counsel. See the holy work *Derekh Emet*. This
was the way of the disciples of the holy Ba'al Shem Tov, that
each encouraged the others and that is why they attained to
such lofty spiritual stages.

However, two conditions must be fulfilled. The first is
that the friend who is to awaken him should be at least
more wide awake than he is. For if the friend is also half
asleep, there can be no guarantee that he will wake him,
even though it is more reliable than when he is on his own,
for then no one is there at all. But the main thing is for the
friend to be more alert than he is, that is to say, the friend

should be more intelligent in the service of God and more burning with fire for the service of the King. Then he can be sure that the friend will wake him up in due course. But where it is not possible, he should see to it that he has at least a loyal, God-fearing friend so that the loss caused by their association should not outweigh any gain there is in it.

The second condition is that the friend should know something of the great loss sleep brings about and how necessary it is to awaken the sleeper so that he can be about his business. But if the friend fails to appreciate this he may not try so hard to wake him up. Thus he must know how great is the loss caused by sleep and indolence in the worship of our King, blessed be He, than which no loss in the whole world is greater. And he must know, therefore, how essential it is for one to wake up the other, namely by means of the words they speak to one another, and these should be for the sake of Heaven, to encourage one another to serve God. If, however, his sole intention is to demonstrate how learned he is in ḥasidic doctrine and that he is able to converse at length on ḥasidic topics and that he is thoroughly familiar with the ḥasidic books, as people generally do, then it will have no effect whatsoever. For no self-seeking and egoistic motive can have any effect even on a man's own heart, to say nothing of the heart of his neighbor. His intention should be to converse with his friend on ḥasidic themes and so offer encouragement for the service of God. Then the *Shekhinah* will rest on their association and the Holy One, blessed be He, will hearken to all the words they utter regarding the fear of Heaven and their longing for the service of our King. Occasionally they can succeed by their conversation in anulling a harsh decree, God forbid, as we shall explain presently. For in them is the verse fulfilled: *Mal. 3:16* "Then they that feared the Lord spoke one with another; And the Lord hearkened, and heard, And a book of remembrance was written before Him, For them that feared the Lord, and that thought on His name."

This verse requires study. Why does it say: "And the Lord hearkened, and heard"? Does the Holy One, blessed be He, need to hearken and hear? Is He not: "He that fashioneth the hearts of them all"? Furthermore, what is this book of remembrance that is before Him? Are not all thoughts revealed to Him?

Ps. 33:15

Now it is well known that the Kingdom on High resembles the kingdom of earth. It is the practice of a mortal king to have a book of remembrance in which all historical events are recorded and the names of all his friends who risked their lives for their king or who performed some service for him or for his people and land. These matters are recorded in the book of remembrance. When the king is sad they bring this book of remembrance to him and when he sees how his friends risked their lives for him joy enters his heart and his sadness departs. This is what happened in the case of Ahasuerus, as it is written: "On that night the king could not sleep; and he commanded to bring the book of the records of the chronicles." It is well known that Ahasuerus was in a state of distress because the angel had frightened him in a dream. He then saw that therein was recorded the account of how Mordecai had saved his life.

Esth. 6:1

Now it is written: "The companions hearken for thy voice: 'Cause me to hear it.'" Rashi explains that the angels come to the synagogue to hear the voice of Israel's prayers and then "Cause me to hear it"—they cause their words to be heard above in association with Israel's prayers. Similarly, when holy Israelites meet together for the purpose of encouraging one another, the Holy One, blessed be he, gets there first, as it were, in order to hearken to the holy words they speak. It is possible to explain the verse to mean that the Holy One, blessed be He, makes these words to be heard by the Court on High and He is proud of them. Furthermore, va-yishma (translated as "And He hearkens") can mean, as is well known, "He gathers," that is to say, God gathers together all their words and records them in the

Song 8:13

book of remembrance. And when there is an accusation (against Israel), God forbid, the Holy One, blessed be He, is Isa. 63:9 sad, as it were, for: "In all their affliction He was afflicted"; Judg. 10:16 "And His soul was grieved for the misery of Israel," as it Prov. 29:4 were; and "The King by justice establisheth the land." Then the Holy One, blessed be He, takes the book of remembrance and sees there those of His lovers who yearn for the holiness of His name, blessed be He, and He is filled with joy, as it were. When the King rejoices all sorrows and tribulations are automatically set at naught. Observe, then what can be achieved by those who speak of the fear of Heaven and whose intention is for the sake of Heaven.

It is possible to explain further: "For them that feared the Lord, and that thought on His name." For the holy book *Porat Yosef* states that if a man grieves and yearns constantly to adhere to God, grieving because he cannot attain it, that man's portion in the world to come will be with the saints who adhere to God. Thus one can explain the verse: "And He wrote down . . . For them that feared the Lord . . ." On the face of it this verse is difficult, however it is understood. For if the man is of those who think on His name, that man's name will obviously be recorded, so why state it? Furthermore, just because they converse with one another, is it a sufficient reason for considering them to be of those who think on His name? But the true meaning is that it refers to those who are remote from the rank of those who fear the Lord and who think on His name, which is a very lofty rank. But even though they themselves do not belong here, yet since they grieve over their failure and since they speak about those who fear the Lord and who think on His name and since they meet together with servants of the Lord and relate the deeds of the saints—how these worshipped the great and awesome Name in great dread and fear and with heart all aflame and in wondrous longing—and they grieve that they themselves are so remote and have been made remote by virtue of their sins, then, they, too, are recorded among those who fear the Lord and who think on His name.

It is written at the end of the book of Daniel: "And at that time shall Michael stand up, the great prince who standeth for the children of thy people; and there shall be a time of trouble, such as never was since there was a nation even to that same time; and at that time thy people shall be delivered, every one that shall be found written in the book." The reference here is to the birth-pangs of the Messiah, to be saved from which great mercy is required. At first glance why does it say: "thy people shall be delivered, every one that shall be found written in the book"? Which book is it? One can surmise that the reference is to the book of remembrance of those who fear the Lord and think on His name. In the holy book *Or ha-Me'ir* (section *Be-Shallah*) it is said that companions who sit together at the third (Sabbath) meal will be saved from the birth-pangs of the Messiah. Consult that work.

Dan. 12:1

Observe, my brother, that which I have explained briefly regarding the significance of friends gathering together in love to speak of the topics of the fear of Heaven. But their intention must be for the sake of Heaven. This was virtually the main principle of the disciples of the Ba'al Shem Tov, I mean the plain approach, though they adopted inner ways as well. I have seen that one of the great *zaddikim* writes that the main thrust and strategy of the wicked Amalek, before the coming of the Messiah, is to prevent meetings of this nature, and when they do take place he sees to it that there is there an admixture of folly, nonsense and slanderous talk, God forbid.

We must now return to the topic we treated earlier, namely, to show the connection between the verse: "The opening of Thy words giveth light. It giveth understanding to the simple" and the other verses. Rashi explains the verse

Ps. 119:130

as follows: "The opening of Thy words illumined for Israel that it is Thou who giveth understanding to the simple when Thou didst say: 'I am the Lord thy God.' " If you have understood the parable quoted earlier you will see that it is hinted at in Rashi's holy words, that the Holy One, blessed be He, Himself taught Israel and delivered to them the two precepts of faith. These are the positive precept: "I am the Lord thy God" and the negative precept: "Thou shalt have no other gods"; so that it might be possible to adhere to belief in God even during every kind of spiritual descent and *Lev. 26:44* fall (from grace). "And yet for all that, when they are in the land of their enemies, I will not reject them, neither will I abhor them, to destroy them utterly," God forbid. This is the power of faith, shining in our hearts until the end of time. Therefore, the verse states that by means of these opening words (of the Decalogue) understanding has been given to the simple. For with regard to faith everyone is a simpleton, as is stated in the book *Tanya* (chapter 18). On *Ps. 73:22* the basis of this idea he explains the verse: "But I am brutish, and ignorant; I was as a beast before Thee," namely, because of this (that I was stupid as an ignorant beast) I am always with Thee.

One can further explain the verse: "The opening of Thy words giveth light" that it means, at the beginning of man's worship, God sends down to him an illumination for the purpose of providing the simple with understanding. That is to say, the illumination should have the effect of making him realize that he is remote from God and a simpleton so far as faith and comprehension are concerned, whereas up till now he did not appreciate this. "The fool does not understand," as we have noted.

The next verse says: "I opened wide my mouth, and panted; For I longed for Thy commandments." That is to say, as a result of the agitation (in my soul) brought about by my belief in God I open wide my mouth in words of prayer and longing in order to pant as I draw Thy love into me, as in the parable quoted above. The verse continues: "For I long for *mitzvotekha*" (translated as "Thy commandments"). This word means "joining" (*zavta*) and adhesion, namely, "I long to be joined to Thee, O Blessed One."

In the following verse it is written: "Turn Thou towards me, and be gracious unto me. As is Thy wont to do unto those that love Thy name." The meaning, as I have said previously, is that as a result of the yearning on the part of a son of Israel, the Holy One, blessed be He, turns aside, as it were, from all His occupations to hearken to the longings of a son of Israel. Therefore, the verse says: "Turn Thou unto *me*, and be gracious unto *me*, As is Thy wont to do unto those who love Thy name." At first glance this seems difficult whichever way we look at it. For if he is truly one of those who loves God's name why should it even be thought that he should be treated worse than others? But the reference is to one who has not reached the degree of loving God's name, yet he entreats God: "Since I have these longings turn Thou to me as is Thy wont to do to those who really love Thy name, that I should be counted among them." This is the same idea as that expressed in the prayer: "Let me be numbered among the saints." All this have I expounded only as a possible interpretation, as it seemed fit in the poverty of my mind. May God lead us in the way of truth for His name's sake. May His great name be sanctified through us. And may we constantly yearn to love and to fear His great and holy name that is called over us, from now and for evermore. Amen.

Comments

The maxim: "The Holy One, blessed be He, the Torah and Israel are one" is frequently quoted as if it were a maxim of the

Zohar. It is not, in fact, found in this form in the Zohar and appears to have been used first in this way much later.

The book *Pardes* is the famous kabbalistic classic, *Pardes Rimmonim* by Moses Cordovero (1522–1570). "The holy book *Toledot*" is *Toledot Ya'akov Yosef* by the disciple of the Ba'al Shem Tov R. Jacob Joseph of Polonnoye. The "holy work *Sha'arei Gan Eden*" and the "prayer book of R. Koppel" are both by the pre-hasidic kabbalist Jacob Koppel ben Moses Lifshitz of Mezhirech (d.c. 1740). "Duties of the Heart" (*Hovot ha-Levavot*) is a famous medieval moralistic work by Bahya Ibn Paqudah. "The holy Rabbi Ze'ev of Zbarazh" (d. 1800) was an early hasidic master, son of Jehiel Michael (Michal) the Maggid of Zloczow. "The holy book *Zemah ha-Shem li-Zevi*" is by the 18th-century teacher Zevi Hirsch of Nadworna. "The holy Rabbi Shalom Duber (Dov Baer) of Lubavich" (1866–1920) was the leader of the Habad group in Hasidism and a great-grandson of R. Dov Baer of Lubavich, whose treatise is the subject of chapter 19 of this book. "The holy book *Derekh Emet*" is by Meshullam Phoebus of Zbarazh, a disciple of the Maggid of Zloczow. *Porat Yosef* is *Ben Porat Yosef*, another work by Jacob Joseph of Polonnoye. "The holy book *Or ha-Me'ir*" is by the hasidic master Ze'ev Wolf of Zhitomer (d. 1800). The work *Tanya* is by R. Shneur Zalman of Lyady, father of Dov Baer of Lubavich and founder of the Habad movement.

Bibliography

∾

1. Ezekiel's Vision of the Heavenly Throne

M. Buttenwieser, "The Character and Date of Ezekiel's Prophecies," in *Hebrew Union College Annual*, 7 (1930), 1–18.

O. Eissfeldt, *The Old Testament: An Introduction* (1965), 365–82. "Ezekiel," in F. C. Grant and H. H. Rowley (eds.), *Hastings' Dictionary of the Bible* (1963²), 283–5.

S. Fisch (ed.), *Ezekiel*, The Soncino Books of the Bible (1950).

R. G. Horwitz, "Throne of God," in *Encyclopaedia Judaica*, vol. 15, 1125–27.

Y. Kaufmann, *The Religion of Israel* (1960), 436–8.

J. Muilenburg, "Ezekiel," in M. Black and H. H. Rowley (eds.), *Peake's Commentary on the Bible* (1962), 568–71.

The New English Bible, The Old Testament (1970), 1175–6.

R. Otto, *The Idea of the Holy* (1950²), 77.

H. H. Rowley (ed.), *The Old Testament and Modern Study* (1951), 153–61.

G. Scholem, "Merkabah Mysticism," in *Encyclopaedia Judaica*, vol. 11, 1386–89.

E. E. Urbach, "The Traditions about Merkavah Mysticism in
    the Tannaitic Period," in *Studies in Mysticism and
    Religion Presented to G. Scholem* (1967), 1–28 (Heb.
    section).

2. The Four Who Entered the King's Orchard

B. M. Lewin (ed.), *Oẓar ha-Ge'onim* (1931), 4, Ḥagigah 13–15.

A. Neher, "Le voyage mystique des quartre," in *Révue de
    l'Histoire des Réligions*, 140 (1951), 59–82.

R. Otto, *The Idea of the Holy* (1950^2), 77.

G. Scholem, *Jewish Gnosticism, Merkabah Mysticism, and
    Talmudic Tradition* (1960), 14–19.

E. E. Urbach, "The Traditions about Merkavah Mysticism in
    the Tannaitic Period," in *Studies in Mysticism and
    Religion Presented to G. Scholem* (1967), 1–28 (Heb.
    section).

3. The Riders of the Chariot

H. Odeberg, *III Enoch or the Hebrew Book of Enoch* (1973).

G. Scholem, *Major Trends in Jewish Mysticism* (1955^3), 40–79.

————, *Jewish Gnosticism, Merkabah Mysticism, and Talmudic
    Tradition* (1960).

M. Smith, "Observations on *Hekhalot Rabbati*," in A. Altmann
    (ed.) *Biblical and Other Studies* (1963), 142–60.

S. Wertheimer, *Battei Midrashot*, 1 (1950), 2 (1953), (especially for
    this text, 2, 127–34).

4. Maimonides on Being with God

A. J. Heschel, *"Ha-he'emin ha-Rambam she-Zakhah li-Nevuah?"*
    in *Louis Ginzberg Jubilee Volume* (1945), 159–88 (Heb.
    section).

5. The Mystical Piety of Rabbi Eleazar of Worms

J. Dan, "Eleazar ben Judah of Worms," in *Encyclopaedia Judaica*,
    vol. 6, 592–4.

G. Scholem, *Major Trends in Jewish Mysticism* (1955^3), 80–118.

6. The Prophetic Mysticism of Abraham Abulafia

A. Berger, "The Messianic Self-Consciousness of Abraham
    Abulafia: A Tentative Evaluation," in *Essays on Jewish
    Life and Thought Presented to Salo Wittmayer Baron*
    (1959), 55–61.

A. Jellinek, "*Sefer ha-Ot*, Apokalypse des Pseudo-Propheten
    und Pseudo-Messias Abraham Abulafia," in *Graetz-
    Jubelschrift* (1887), 65–88.

G. Scholem, *Major Trends in Jewish Mysticism* (1955³), 4, 199–255.

7. Responsa from Heaven

H. J. D. Azulai, *Shem ha-Gedolim* (1921), s.v. *Rabbenu Ya'akov he-
    Ḥasid*.

8. The Zohar on the High Priest's Ecstasy

G. Scholem, *Major Trends in Jewish Mysticism* (1955³), 123, and
    378, note 9.

I. Tishby, *Mishnat ha-Zohar* (1961), 2, 229–30.

9. The Visions and Mystical Meditations of Abraham of Granada

G. Scholem, "Abraham ben Isaac of Granada," in *Encyclopaedia
    Judaica*, vol. 2, 145–6.

10. The Communications of the Heavenly Mentor to Rabbi Joseph Karo

S. Schechter, "Safed in the Sixteenth Century—A City of
    Legalists and Mystics," in *Studies in Judaism*, 2nd series
    (1908), 202–306.

R. J. Z. Werblowsky, *Joseph Karo—Lawyer and Mystic* (1962).

11. The Visions of Rabbi Ḥayyim Vital

A. Z. Aescoly (ed.), *Sefer ha-Ḥezyonot* (1954).

G. Scholem, "Vital, Ḥayyim ben Joseph," in *Encyclopaedia
    Judaica*, vol. 16, 171–6.

12. The *Maggid* of Rabbi Moses Ḥayyim Luzzatto

J. Dan, "Luzzatto, Moses Ḥayyim," in *Encyclopaedia Judaica*, vol. 11, 599–604.

S. Ginzburg, *Rabbi Moshe Ḥayyim Luzzatto u-Venei Doro* (1937).

13. The Mystical Epistle of the Ba'al Shem Tov

D. Ben-Amos and J. R. Mintz, *In Praise of the Ba'al Shem Tov* (1970), 322, tale 60, note 1.

S. Dubnow, *Toledot ha-Ḥasidut* (1967), 60–63.

G. Scholem, *The Messianic Idea in Judaism* (1971), 182–4 and notes.

14. The Mystical Meditations of Shalom Sharabi

A. Bension, *The Zohar in Moslem and Christian Spain* (1932), ch. 15, 242–6.

M. Y. Yeinstock, *Siddur ha-Geonim ve-ha-Mekubbalim*, vol. I (1970), 24–39; vol. 3 (1971), 668; vol. 7 (1973), 37.

15. The Mystical Experiences of the Gaon of Vilna

R. J. Z. Werblowsky, *Joseph Karo—Lawyer and Mystic* (1962), Appendix F: "The Mystic Life of the Gaon Elijah of Vilna," 307–12.

16. The Prayer Meditations of Alexander Susskind

J. Klausner, "Alexander Susskind ben Moses of Grodno," in *Encyclopaedia Judaica*, vol. 2, 586–7.

17. Two Epistles in Praise of the Ḥasidic *Ẓaddikim*

S. Dubnow, *Toledot ha-Ḥasidut* (1967), 186–7.

B. Landau, *Ha-Rebbe Reb Elimelekh mi-Lyzhansk* (1963).

M. Wilensky, *Hasidim u-Mitnaggedim* (1970), vol. 1, 168–176.

18. The Mystical Accounts of Kalonymus Kalman Epstein

B. Landau, *Ha-Rebbe Reb Elimelekh mi-Lyzhansk* (1963), 261–2.

R. Schatz-Uffenheimer, *Ha-Hasidut ke-Mistka* (1968), 118–9.

20. The Secret Diary of Rabbi Isaac Eizik

H. J. Berl, *Yizhak Eizik mi-Komarno* (1965).

E. Liebes (Zweig), "Safrin, Isaac Judah Jehiel," in *Encyclopaedia Judaica*, vol. 14, 635–6.

21. Aaron Roth's Essay, "Agitation of the Soul"

A. Roth, *Shomer Enumim* (2 vols., 1964).

———, *Shulḥan ha-Tahor* (1966^2).

———, *Iggerot Shomerei Emunim* (letters, 1942).

E. Kohen Steinberger (ed.), *Uvda de-Aharon* (1948).

H. Weiner, $9^1/2$ *Mystics* (1969), ch. 9, 206–15.

Abbreviations

Biblical and Rabbinic Sources

Av. Zar.	*Avodah Zarah* (talmudic tractate)	I (or II) Kings	Kings, Book I or II
BB	*Bava Batra* (talmudic tractate)	Lam.	Lamentations
Ber.	*Berakhot* (talmudic tractate)	Lev.	Leviticus
BK	*Bava Kamma* (talmudic tractate)	Mak.	*Makkot* (talmudic tractate)
I (or II) Chron.	Chronicles, Book I or II	Mal.	Malachi
Dan.	Daniel	Meg.	*Megillah* (talmudic tractate)
Deut.	Deuteronomy	Micah	Micah
Eccles.	Ecclesiastes	Nah.	Nahum
Esth.	Esther	Neh.	Nehemiah
Ex.	Exodus	Num.	Numbers
Ez.	Ezekiel	Obad.	Obadiah
Ezra	Ezra	Prov.	Proverbs
Gen.	Genesis	Ps.	Psalms
Hab.	Habakkuk	Ruth	Ruth
Hos.	Hosea	I (or II) Sam.	Samuel, Book I or II
Hul.	*Hullin* (talmudic tractate)	Shab.	*Shabbat* (talmudic tractate)
Isa.	Isaiah	Song	Song of Songs
Jer.	Jeremiah	Suk.	*Sukkah* (talmudic tractate)
Job	Job	Ta'an.	*Ta'anit* (talmudic tractate)
Josh.	Joshua	Yal.	*Yalkut Shimoni* (Midrash)
Judg.	Judges	Yoma	Yoma (talmudic tractate)
Kid.	*Kiddushin* (talmudic tractate)	Zech.	Zechariah
		Zeph.	Zephaniah

Glossary

∽

**Amplified explanations are found in the
Comments that appear after each text.**

Adar, twelfth month of the Jewish religious year, sixth of the
civil, approximating to February-March.

Bar, "son of . . ."; frequently appearing in personal names.

Ben, "son of . . ."; frequently appearing in personal names.

Devekut, "devotion"; attachment or adhesion to God; communion with God.

Galut, "exile"; the condition of the Jewish people in dispersion.

Gaon (pl. **geonim**), head of academy in post-talmudic period,
especially in Babylonia; title of honor for scholarly rabbi.

Gemara, traditions, discussions, and rulings commenting on
and supplementing the Mishnah, and forming part of the
Babylonian and Palestinian Talmuds (see Talmud).

Genizah, depository for sacred books. The best known was discovered in the synagogue of Fostat (old Cairo).

Golem, automaton, especially in human form, created by magical means and endowed with life.

323

Habad, initials of *hokhmah, binah, da'at:* "wisdom, understanding, knowledge"; hasidic movement founded in White Russia by Shneour Zalman of Lyady.

Halakhah (pl. **halakhot**), an accepted decision in rabbinic law. Also refers to those parts of the Talmud concerned with legal matters.

Hanukkah, eight-day celebration commemorating the victory of Judah Maccabee over the Syrian king Antiochus Epiphanes and the subsequent rededication of the Temple.

Hasidei Ashkenaz, medieval pietist movement among the Jews of Germany.

Hasid, adherent of Hasidism; or very pious person.

Hasidism (1) religious revivalist movement of popular mysticism among Jews of Western Germany in the Middle Ages; (2) religious movement founded by Israel Ba'al Shem Tov in the first half of the 18th century.

Heikhalot, "palaces"; tradition in Jewish mysticism centering on mystical journeys through the heavenly spheres and palaces to the Divine Chariot (see Merkabah).

Hevra kaddisha, title applied to charitable confraternity now generally limited to associations for burial of the dead.

Hol ha-Moed, intermediate days of festivals.

Kaddish, liturgical doxology.

Kasher, ritually permissible.

Kavvanah, "intention"; term denoting the spiritual concentration accompanying prayer and the performance of ritual or of a commandment.

Kedushah, addition to the third blessing in the reader's repetition of the *Amidah* in which the public responds to the precentor's introduction and connecting text with verses praising God.

Kelippah (pl. **kelippot**), "husk(s)"; mystical term denoting force(s) of evil.

Lulav, palm branch; one of the "four species" used on Sukkot together with the *etrog, hadas,* and *aravah.*

Maggid, popular preacher; also, divine spirit speaking to Kabbalist.

Malkhuyyot, part of *Musaf* prayer for *Rosh ha-Shanah.*

Marheshvan, popularly called Heshvan; second month of

the Jewish religious year, eighth of the civil, approximating to October-November.

Menorah, candelabrum; seven-branched oil lamp used in the Tabernacle and Temple.

Merkabah, *merkavah,* "chariot"; mystical discipline associated with Ezekiel's vision of the Divine Throne-Chariot (Ezek. 1).

Megillah, Scroll of Esther.

Midrash, method of interpreting Scripture to elucidate legal points (*Midrash Halakhah*) or to bring out lessons by stories or homiletics (*Midrash Aggadah*). Also the name for a collection of such rabbinic interpretations.

Mikveh, ritual bath.

Minḥah, afternoon prayer; originally meal offering in Temple.

Mishnah, earliest codification of Jewish Oral Law.

Mitzvah, biblical or rabbinic injunction; applied also to good or charitable deeds.

Musaf, additional service on Sabbath and festivals; originally the additional sacrifice offered in the Temple.

Nefesh, Ruaḥ, Neshamah, three parts of soul according to Kabbalah.

Notarikon, method of abbreviating Hebrew words or phrases by writing single letters.

Responsum (pl. **responsa**), written opinion (*teshuvah*) given to question (*she'elah*) on aspects of Jewish law by qualified authorities; pl. collection of such queries and opinions in book form.

Rosh Ha-Shanah, two-day holiday (one day in biblical and early mishnaic times) at the beginning of the month of Tishri (September-October), traditionally the New Year.

Samael, angel of evil, chief force of evil.

Sanhedrin, the assembly of ordained scholars which functioned both as a supreme court and as a legislature before 70 C.E.

Shabbatean, adherent of the pseudo-messiah Shabbetai Zevi (17th century); beliefs held by this sect.

Shaddai, name of God found frequently in the Bible and commonly translated "Almighty."

Shavuot, Pentecost; festival of Weeks; second of the three annual pilgrim festivals commemorating the receiving of the Torah at Mt. Sinai.

Shekhinah, Divine Presence.

Shema (*Yisrael*; "hear . . . (O Israel)," Deut. 6:4), Judaism's confession of faith, proclaiming the absolute unity of God.

Shofar, horn of the ram (or any other ritually clean animal excepting the cow) sounded for the memorial blowing on Rosh Ha-Shanah, and other occasions.

Sivan, third month of the Jewish religious year, ninth of the civil, approximating to June-July.

Sukkah, booth or tabernacle erected for Sukkot when, for seven days, religious Jews "dwell" or at least eat in the *sukkah* (Lev. 23:42).

Sukkot, festival of Tabernacles; last of the three pilgrim festivals, beginning on the 15th of Tishri.

Tallit (gadol), four-cornered prayer shawl with fringes (*zizit*) at each corner.

Tallit katan, garment with fringes (*zizit*) appended worn during the day by observant male Jews under their outer garments.

Talmud, "teaching"; compendium of discussions on the Mishnah by generations of scholars and jurists in many academies over a period of several centuries. The Jerusalem (or Palestinian) Talmud mainly contained the discussion of the Palestinian sages. The Babylonian Talmud incorporates the parallel discussion in the Babylonian academies.

Tammuz, fourth month of the Jewish religious year, tenth of the civil, approximating to June-July.

Tanna (pl. **tannaim**), rabbinic teacher of mishnaic period.

Targum, Aramaic translation of the Bible.

Tefillin, phylacteries, small leather cases containing passages from Scripture and affixed on the forehead and arm by male Jews during the recital of morning prayers.

Terefah, food that is not *kasher*, owing to a defect in the animal.

Tetragrammaton, YHVH, the Holy Name of God.

Tikkun ("restitution," "reintegration"). (1) order of service for certain occasions, mostly recited at night; (2) mystical term denoting restoration of the right order and true unity after the spiritual "catastrophe" which occurred in the cosmos.

Tishah be-Av, Ninth of Av, fast day commemorating the destruction of the First and Second Temples.

Tosafist, talmudic glossator, mainly French (12th–14th centuries), bringing additions to the commentary by Rashi.

Tosafot, glosses supplied by tosafist.

Yihud, "union"; mystical term for intention which causes the union of God with the *Shekhinah*.

Yozer, hymn inserted in the first benediction (*Yozer Or*) of the morning *Shema*.

Zaddik, person outstanding for his faith and piety; especially a hasidic rabbi or leader.

Zizit, fringes attached to the *tallit* and *tallit katan*.

Acknowledgments

∽∾

Most of the translations are my own, but my thanks are due to Professor S. Pines and the Chicago University Press for the translation from Maimonides' *Guide*; to Professor G. Scholem and Schocken Books for the translations from Abraham Abulafia and his pupil as well as for other quotations from the classic *Major Trends in Jewish Mysticism*; to Professor R. J. Z. Werblowsky and the Clarendon Press for the translation of Ḥayyim of Volozhyn's account of the experiences of the Vilna Gaon; and to Messrs Routledge for the quotation from Ariel Bension's *The Zohar in Moslem and Christian Spain*. Dr. Geoffrey Wigoder suggested that I compile this anthology. For this and for much help I am deeply grateful to him. With his profound insight into Jewish mysticism Jonathan Omer-Man (Derek Orlans) has skillfully edited the manuscript. I am indebted to him for his many valuable suggestions, his constant help and encouragement and his care in seeing the book through the press.